DOWN
WITH THE
OLD CANOE

ALSO BY STEVEN BIEL

Independent Intellectuals in the United States, 1910–1945

Down with the Old Canoe

"An effective commentary on our relentless need to find a higher meaning in disaster and, on occasion, to elevate it into myth." —*Washington Post*

"Biel's skepticism and detachment make him a perfect guide, in his refreshing new book *Down with the Old Canoe,* through the *Titanic's* overlapping cultural meanings. Biel rummages through not only previous accounts of the disaster, but also through decades of folk songs, popular novels, Broadway plays, and television drama to compile a book that's as subversive as it is fascinating." —Dwight Garner, *Salon*

"Dredges the national psyche and comes up with some authentic treasures." —Suzanne Ruta, *Entertainment Weekly*

"As Steven Biel's new book ably demonstrates, the 1912 *Titanic* disaster can apparently be turned by historians, ideologues, and novelists into a symbol of just about anything." —Michiko Kakutani, *New York Times*

"Steven Biel examines the myths that the disaster inspired, and he combines scholarly research with an ear for the telling phrase to show how those myths have been exploited." —Milton Garrison, *New York Times Book Review*

"Writing with both historical authority and a sense of humor, Steven Biel shows how the ship has become part of the culture: the boat bobs to the surface in everything from Delta blues songs to Broadway musicals to all those political speeches in which some poor fool is accused of rearranging deck chairs on the *Titanic.*"

—Editors' favorites, Amazon.com Books

"Scholarly and entertaining. The best book we've read on the subject."

—Carolyn Nizzi Warmbold, *Atlanta Constitution*

"Insightful, scholarly, exhaustive."

—J. Ford Huffman, *USA Today*

DOWN WITH THE OLD CANOE

A CULTURAL HISTORY
OF THE *TITANIC* DISASTER

STEVEN BIEL

W. W. NORTON & COMPANY
NEW YORK LONDON

For Jean, Jake,
and his grandparents,
Claire and Morton Biel

"Desolation Row" by Bob Dylan. Copyright ©1965 by Warner Bros. Music.
Copyright renewed by Special Rider Music. All rights reserved. International
copyright secured. Reprinted by permission.

"Interview: Robert Ballard." Reprinted by permission of *Omni*, ©1986, Omni
Publications International, Ltd.

"The Man with Titanic Vision" by Frederic Golden ©1987 *Discover*
Magazine.

Jacket illustration from *A Night to Remember* by Walter Lord. Copyright
©1955 by Walter Lord. As appeared on the cover of *Publishers Weekly*, August
27, 1955. Reprinted by permission of Henry Holt and Co., Inc.

"The Titanic." Words and music by Huddie Ledbetter. Collected and adapted
by John A. Lomax and Alan Lomax. TRO -©- Copyright 1936 (Renewed)
Folkways Music Publishers, Inc., New York, New York. Used by permission.

Material from the *Titanic Commutator* is used by permission of the Titanic
Historical Society, P.O. Box 51053, Indian Orchard, MA 01151-0053.

The text of this book is composed in Granjon with display set in Trio Light.
Composition by Justine Burkat Trubey using Adobe PageMaker 6.0.
Manufacturing by Courier Companies, Inc.
Book design by Chris Welch

Library of Congress Cataloging-in-Publication Date
Biel, Steven, 1960–
Down with the old canoe: a cultural history of the Titanic disaster/Steven Biel.
p. cm.
Includes bibliographical references and index.
ISBN 0-393-03965-X
1. Titanic (Steamship) 2. Shipwrecks—North Atlantic Ocean.
I. Title
G530.T6B585 1996
910' .91631—dc20
96-5543 CIP
ISBN 0-393-31676-9 pbk.
W. W. Norton & Company, Inc., 500 Fifth Avenue, New York, N.Y. 10110
http://web.wwnorton.com

W. W. Norton & Company Ltd., 10 Coptic Street, London WC1A 1PU

2 3 4 5 6 7 8 9 0

Contents

PART I   MEANINGS

Foreword   NATURE JEERS AT OUR FOLLY   3

Chapter 1   APRIL 1912   9

Chapter 2   THE RULE OF THE SEA AND LAND   23

Chapter 3   MAMMON   59

Interword   A NOBLE STRUCTURE OF ENDURING STONE   85

Chapter 4   UNKNOWN AND UNSUNG   97

PART II   MEMORIES

Chapter 5   A NIGHT TO REMEMBER   143

Chapter 6   ENTHUSIASTS   174

Chapter 7   MISSION TO DESTINY   203

Afterword   REARRANGING DECK CHAIRS   226

List of Abbreviations   235

Notes   239

Acknowledgments   281

Index   283

Hello, hello! I see the Titanic's sunk again.

> —British comedian Peter Cook,
> imagining a 1950s suburbanite's
> response to the headline
> of his morning paper

PART I

MEANINGS

NATURE JEERS AT OUR FOLLY

SEVENTY-FOUR YEARS old in 1912, Henry Adams felt as much enthusiasm for crossing to Europe on the *Titanic* as an old man who believed that the world was collapsing could muster. The *Titanic* would leave New York on April 20, after its maiden voyage from England. "I think I shall take rooms on it, by way of venture," Adams wrote his confidante Elizabeth Cameron. With the rivalry between William Howard Taft and Theodore Roosevelt splitting the Republican party, Adams was convinced now more than ever that society had "become incapable of managing its own affairs." A trip to Paris, he hoped, would take his mind off the dismal state of politics and society. In March a British coal strike threatened to delay his escape, and April 20 seemed too far off as it was. "I hope that it can't last beyond April 1, and that the Titanic will sail on time. If not, I shall be in a mess." The purpose of the strike, he imagined, was to prove the power of international organized labor, which one day soon would call a general strike and "give the coup-de-grace to our society." Still, he hoped that the bothersome workers would save their coup de grace for later and that he would sail as planned. When he learned that the *Titanic* had set out on April 10, he felt certain that "unless she drops me somewhere else," he would be in France "in a fortnight." [1]

Adams received the news of the *Titanic* disaster with shock and an agonized kind of satisfaction. "The Titanic is wrecked," he proclaimed, and then connected it to Roosevelt's victory in the Pennsylvania primary; "so is Taft; so is the Republican party; all in one brief hour. . . . We all foundered and disappeared." As a man who had predicted and reveled in catastrophe and decay for years, and who had constructed an image of himself as a holdover from the eighteenth century in a chaotic modern world, Adams could not help deriving an anguished thrill from the disasters that had befallen the ship and the beloved party that his father had helped create. His letters almost quiver with the "delightful shudder" he felt. "By my blessed Virgin, it is awful! This Titanic blow shatters one's nerves. We can't grapple it. Taft, Titanic! Titanic—Taft!" [2]

The metaphorical possibilities of the disaster proved irresistible. The *Titanic*, Taft (both immense, both sunk), the Republican party, Henry Adams, society, the predictable and secure world of the nineteenth century—all had crashed and foundered. "The republican party is at the bottom of the deep sea, and the corpses are still howling on the surface. Whatever happens, our old party is done. Our society has politically run on an iceberg, and the confusion and darkness are fatal." Adams, the self-described anachronism, regretted his narrow evasion of an exquisitely appropriate death on the *Titanic*; he had missed the boat again. But he also basked with wicked delight in continuing to have lived too long. He booked passage on the *Olympic*, the *Titanic*'s sister ship, and dramatically announced to his friends his hope that it too would sink. A noble nineteenth-century death, at any rate, would be better than the ignominious twentieth-century death that he was bound to suffer and that he summed up in a racist joke: "It will be a good job anyway if it saves one from being mangled by a nigger in an auto-taxi."³

Most tormenting of all was that he could not gloat. The disaster had upset his friends so much that he was denied his "sole compensation"; he couldn't "even tell them:—I told you so!" And Adams *had* told them so, seven years earlier, in his *Education*, where—challenging the sacred American belief in progress—he predicted that humanity in the twentieth century would fall prey to technologies it lacked the wisdom to control: "Every day Nature violently revolted, causing so-called accidents with enormous destruction of property and life, while plainly laughing at man, who helplessly groaned and shrieked and shuddered, but never for a single instant could stop." The *Titanic* had vindicated his pessimism, but it was a lusterless vindication that he could share with only a few of his friends. "The sum and triumph of our civilization, guaranteed to be safe and perfect, our greatest achievement," he now observed, "sinks at a touch, and drowns us, while nature jeers at our folly."⁴

A writer of historical fiction, with the freedom to choose characters and create situations, could not do better than to give Henry Adams a ticket for the *Titanic*. The only possible improvement might be to put him on board and let him go down with the ship, but then, unless the writer allowed him an interior monologue in his final moments, we would be denied his ruminations on the disaster. Adams, America's most eloquent critic of technology and progress, booked reservations for the never-to-be return voyage of the unsinkable triumph of modern shipbuilding. It is poetic.

Nine days after the *Titanic* sank, Adams suffered a stroke. In his delirium he thought that his mother had gone down with the ship, and he tried to communicate with her. Fearing that he was losing his mind, he attempted suicide.[5] The convalescent Adams wasn't aboard the *Olympic*, which didn't sink in any event. He recovered and lived for another six years.

Walter Lord, author of the 1955 bestseller *A Night to Remember*, recently remarked, without much exaggeration, that a new book about the *Titanic* disaster is published every week. The appearance late in 1992 of Don Lynch and Ken Marschall's *Titanic: An Illustrated History* prompted a reviewer to ask whether "we need another" *Titanic* book, to which he answered, "Resoundingly, yes." This is, of course, an obligatory question for historians when confronted with a new book about a familiar subject. When the subject is the *Titanic*, however, the more appropriate question is "Why not?" Given the seemingly insatiable demand and limitless supply, it is no wonder that *Titanic* historians tend to engage in self-fulfilling prophecies about the market for their productions. "Patently destructible in life," wrote the marine historian John Maxtone-Graham, "the Titanic has proved indestructible in memory."[6]

People who write about the disaster are, for the most part, remarkably immune to jealousy or territoriality. Lord says that the "story has something for everyone," and there seems to be a kind of open invitation to join in the fun. Even so, I have to admit to some trepidation. Lord's inclusiveness aside, the disaster belongs almost entirely to those whom he describes as "nautical enthusiasts" and "trivia lovers."[7] I can never hope to compete with *Titanic* buffs in mastery of detail. My experience and love of ships are minimal. No matter how many books I read, I can't keep track of who was where when, stateroom and lifeboat numbers, menus and china patterns, speed and displacement. I have no strong feelings one way or another about the famous *Californian* controversy—whether that vessel was in any position to come to the rescue of the *Titanic*. I'm not interested in finding fault with either the American or British inquiries into the disaster.

The *Titanic* is the stuff of what academically trained historians sometimes condescendingly refer to as "popular history," in which complex processes are ignored in favor of antiquarianism—amassing facts without significant interpretation—or reduced to single dramatic moments. Professional historians are uncomfortable with unselfconscious narrative, with arguments that seem insignificant, and with arguments that seem too bold. A statement like Lord's, that "the *Titanic* more than any other single event marks the end of the old days, and the beginning of a new, uneasy era," makes academics like me squirm. In my opinion the disaster changed nothing except shipping regulations. It did not, as Wyn Craig Wade has written, produce a "loss of innocence" and replace "certainty" with "doubt." It was not "the birth cry of a growing animosity" between Great Britain and Germany; the *Titanic* wireless operator's snub of his counterpart on the *Frankfurt* had nothing to do, despite Charles Pellegrino's suggestion, with the coming of the First World War. (When the *Frankfurt*'s operator tried to interrupt an exchange between the *Titanic* and the *Olympic*, the *Titanic*'s operator tapped out, "You fool, stand by and keep out." According to Pellegrino, this somehow set off a "chain reaction" leading to war.)[8] Any search for the social or political effects of the disaster is bound to yield facile generalizations and tenuous connections.

But the importance of an event doesn't necessarily reside in its effects; we need not treat the *Titanic* disaster as the "end of an epoch" or a transformative moment to recognize its cultural significance. It was, as Lord and others have noted but professional historians have not, an event of deep and wide resonance in Edwardian England and Progressive Era America. To say that it had resonance is to say that it was meaningful, and in the American context, which will be my focus, its meanings were neither simple nor universal. Beyond shock and grief, the disaster produced a contest over meaning that connected the sinking of an ocean liner in a remote part of the North Atlantic with some of the most important and troubling problems, tensions, and conflicts of the time. To my landlubber's consciousness, the reverberations onshore rival in their intensity the drama at sea that remains the subject of endless retellings. Henry Adams never made it onto the *Titanic*, but he and many other Americans even farther removed from the actual disaster reflected on it in complex and powerful ways.

Lord, Wade, Pellegrino, and others are on to something when they discuss the *Titanic* in terms of the emergence of the modern world. The disaster was neither catalyst nor cause, but it did expose and come to represent anxieties about modernity—about deeper changes that were occurring regardless of whether an ocean liner struck an iceberg and sank in the spring of 1912. If not a transformative event, it was nonetheless a highly dramatic moment—a kind of "social drama" in which conflicts were played out and American culture in effect thought out loud about itself.[9] Americans understood the disaster according to concerns they already felt, hopes they already harbored, beliefs and ideas they already held and were struggling to preserve. What it meant to them and what it has meant to others since 1912 are the subject of this book. I too hope to make sense of the disaster by exploring how and why it took shape as one of the great mythic events of the twentieth century.

CHAPTER I

APRIL 1912

ᴏᴏ One way to begin to think about the *Titanic* disaster is to look at other events that occurred at the same time. Synchronicity, of course, may or may not imply deeper connections, but for now let's simply juxtapose them, as if they were snapshots taken at the same time but from different vantage points. Stephen Kern has pointed out how the *Titanic* disaster dramatized changing perceptions of time and space. Through wireless telegraphy people experienced the distant catastrophe almost as it was happening.[1] The wireless, to which the *Titanic*'s survivors owed their lives, helped create a modern sense of simultaneity by revolutionizing the reporting of news. Newspapers covered more and more distant events with increasing speed and immediacy. It is only fitting, then, to start with simultaneity—with concurrent glimpses of the United States in April 1912.

These glimpses remind us that the *Titanic* disaster did not occur in an Edenic pre–World War America of unity, stability, and peace. April 1912 was a time of conflict and violence, instability and uncertainty, of intense concern about the "race problem," the "woman problem," the "labor problem," and the "immigration problem." The *Titanic* went down at a cultural moment rather than in a vacuum—not an isolated moment but one full of resonances, implications, relations, and associations. It would have been impossible for Americans *not* to think and feel about the disaster in the vital terms of their culture. Unlike the actual ship, which collided with the iceberg on a calm night, the symbolic *Titanic* plunged into some very rough seas.

By the count of the National Association for the Advancement of Colored People (NAACP), sixty-four Americans were lynched in 1912, sixty-one of them African Americans, ten of these sixty-one in April and May.[2] On April 14, the night the *Titanic* struck the iceberg, Samuel Arline, an alleged murderer, was lynched in Barstow, Florida. Mobs killed Henry Etheridge near Jackson, Georgia, and an "unnamed negro" in Delhi, Louisiana, nine days later, as the *Mackay-Bennett*, known as the "Titanic Funeral Ship," steamed its way to Halifax after recovering John Jacob Astor's body. On May 3, in Yellow Pine, Louisiana, Ernest Allums was lynched for "insulting white women." Two men were killed in Mississippi on May 7—one, also unnamed, for "attempted rape," the other, G. W. Edd, for murder. Daniel Davis of Tyler, Texas, and Jacob Samuels of Robertson County, Tennessee, both accused of rape, were murdered on May 25 and May 27.

Arline had shot a white man, C. M. McIntosh, after McIntosh interceded in a domestic dispute and complained about "quarrelsome niggers." Sheriff John Logan formed a posse and, with two bloodhounds, tracked Arline to a swamp. Surrounded, he tried to make a dash for it. Logan "brought the negro down with a bullet through his body." He died in jail the next morning, before the agitated citizens of Barstow could take more action.

Etheridge's body was found in the Towaliga River riddled with bullets, his arms and legs bound, a rifle tied to his coat. The mob appeared at his home on Wednesday night, April 24, demanded that he come outside, and, when he did, opened fire. His offense was trying to recruit other blacks for a colony in Africa.

That same night some men were playing a slot machine in Delhi, a town crowded with refugees from the flooding Mississippi River. When a white officer broke in and put a penny into the machine, one of the players protested. The officer gave the protester "a good beating," but this apparently did not silence him. A crowd, incensed by his alleged threats of violence against whites, returned later, found him, and lynched him. The next morning Captain Philip Gayle led Company D of the Louisiana National Guard into Delhi to control what the *Atlanta Constitution* called the "surliness and impudence" of the "negro flood refugees." The refugees had complained about being forced to work, for long hours and without pay, cleaning up the flood's debris.

Two thousand people watched Daniel Davis burned at the stake in the town of Tyler. While one report said that the "work of the lynchers was done quickly and quietly," the NAACP described it differently. Already tied to the stake, Davis had "confessed" to attacking Carrie Johnson. "It was really only ten minutes after the fire was started that smoking shoe soles and twitching of the Negro's feet indicated that his lower extremities were burning, but the time seemed much longer. The spectators had waited so long to see him tortured that they begrudged the ten minutes before his suffering really began." The lynchers denied Davis's request to have his throat cut, and he remained conscious for twenty minutes after the fire was started and he had shouted his last words, "Lord, have mercy on my soul." The flames had burned the flesh from his legs up to his knees when it occurred to his torturers that there was not enough wood to finish the lynching. At first, not wanting to miss the spectacle, nobody volunteered to replenish the supply. Finally some men from the edge of the crowd gathered up more dry goods boxes and were rewarded for their "public service" with places closer to the fire. As Davis burned, the crowd jeered, sang, and danced.

In this climate of racial violence the NAACP held its fourth annual conference. A thousand people crowded into the opening meeting at Chicago's Sinai Temple on April 28 to hear how the young organization "differed from the party of silence and compromise"—the accommodationist followers of Booker T. Washington—by demanding full political and legal equality. "We meet to protest," declared NAACP publicity director W. E. B. Du Bois, "but not simply to protest." The conference's purpose was to acknowledge "deeds done" and to make plans for continuing the attack on the color line, for dismantling the racism of which lynching was the most extreme but hardly the only manifestation. The fight, said one participant, had to be carried up to sheriffs, police, and governors, into courtrooms, labor unions, and corporations. Locating the conference in the long history of African American resistance, Du Bois recalled the words of the abolitionist Wendell Phillips: "The proper time to maintain one's rights is when they are denied; the proper persons to maintain them are those to whom they are denied."

Fifteen thousand women crowded John Jacob Astor's funeral off the front page of the *New York Times*. Astor's burial on May 4 coincided with the biggest suffrage parade in American history.[3] At five o'clock that afternoon, in Manhattan's Washington Square, Josephine Beiderhase "mounted her fine bay horse, fixed herself firmly in the saddle and sounded her bugle," signaling the women's cavalry to begin its march up Fifth Avenue. Behind the cavalry Harriot Stanton Blatch led the Executive Board of the Women's Political Union, the parade's organizers. Blatch had insisted that no automobiles be allowed: "Every woman taking part must march on her own feet [or a horse's] and thus demonstrate how much she care[s] for her cause." She had also insisted on careful choreography to keep "the beat of the feet ... in time and tune with the beat of the heart." Opponents of woman suffrage would thus witness their self-discipline and singularity of purpose; most of the marchers wore white, though Marie Stewart, impersonating Joan of Arc, wore armor.

To signify their demands for inclusion in public space, the women marched according to occupation. First came teachers and students, followed by doctors, lawyers, nurses, writers, artists, musicians, actresses, librarians, social workers, factory laborers, clothing makers, milliners, domestic workers, business women, secretaries, bookkeepers, stenographers, telephone operators, and department store saleswomen. "At the close of that parade," a participant concluded hopefully, "it would have been impossible for an intelligent onlooker to contend that woman's place is in the home." Then came the suffrage pioneers, including (in a "lilac-bedecked carriage") eighty-six-year-old Antoinette Brown Blackwell, a veteran of the movement's beginnings in 1848 and the first American woman to be ordained as a minister. She rode with her niece, the writer and activist Alice Stone Blackwell, daughter of another pioneer, Lucy Stone. Observers remarked on the continuity between generations—on "this great sisterhood that asked for better things for all." The international delegations— Swedish, Norwegian, Finnish, Chinese, Australian, Greek— preceded the state delegations, first from the six states where women were already enfranchised, then from the other states. A thousand men also marched, among them Rabbi Stephen

Wise and Columbia University philosopher John Dewey. On the corners a suffragist Brigade of Street Speakers set up its green soapboxes to draw in pockets of listeners after the parade had gone by.

So huge was the crowd lining the avenue that five hundred policemen could not hold it back from the parade route. The barricades collapsed at Union Square, and the marchers, carrying banners celebrating Susan B. Anthony, Elizabeth Cady Stanton, Lucretia Mott, and other movement heroes, had to proceed by twos instead of fours. Some of the five hundred thousand onlookers had come out on the sunny, breezy Saturday afternoon for the spectacle alone. Others stood on the sidewalks or pressed into the street to cheer or heckle the paraders. Clapping competed with "gibes and cat-calls and hisses." A small boy, "uttering shrill cries of derision," made sure he was heard by every line of marchers.

The parade poured into Carnegie Hall and overflowed onto Fifty-seventh Street and Seventh Avenue, where the marchers improvised meetings and speeches. Inside, Anna Howard Shaw, head of the National American Woman Suffrage Association, praised women for letting fall "like a garment the conservatism that has for so many years prevented their best service to the world." Anna Garlin Spencer, another veteran suffragist, announced: "We must now prepare to make over and socialize the State." After the speeches, punctuated with standing ovations, the audience sang "America" and the meeting adjourned. That night, from seven-thirty to eleven, six cars full of suffragists toured Manhattan and the Bronx, making Broadway "an open right of way for the woman suffrage cause" as crowds gathered in anticipation of their arrival and swelled to hear their words. In the euphoria it was easy to underestimate the difficulty that lay ahead. One suffrage leader called May 4, 1912, a "memorable day in the history of the battle for human freedom" and then, transforming the wish into fact, proclaimed it "the last stage of woman's struggle for liberty."

San Diego, its fuse lit the previous winter, exploded in the spring of 1912.[4] Members of the Industrial Workers of the World—Wobblies—had arrived in the city bolstered by recent victories in free speech fights in Spokane and Fresno. Those fights seemed to vindicate the tactic of passive resistance; Wobblies had crowded the courtrooms and jails to defend their constitutional rights against local bans on free speech and assembly. Eventually, by draining the cities' resources and staining their reputations, they had forced the politicians to relent.

In December 1911 the San Diego City Council had passed a law banning meetings on the stretch of E Street between Fifth and Sixth avenues, a popular gathering spot for every kind of dissenter from anarchists to evangelists. Despite their differences, the dissenters banded together to form a Free Speech League and defy the ordinance. Police broke up the league's rallies; by the middle of February the city and county jails were full. Spokane and Fresno seemed to be repeating themselves. "Come on the cushions," urged a Wobbly poet,

> *Ride up on top*
> *Stick to the brakebeams*
> *Let nothing stop.*
> *Come in great numbers*
> *This we beseech*
> *Help San Diego to win* Free Speech!

But San Diego was different. The IWW drew most of its recruits from among the most marginal laborers—migrant farmhands, miners, lumber workers—who were not much of a presence in San Diego. Conservatives, on the other hand, took the Wobblies very seriously. "It is not San Diego society

alone that is being threatened," wrote a California state senator, "but organized society everywhere." Led by the antilabor
San Diego Union and *Los Angeles Times*, business and civic organizations called for a full-scale defense of their city against
these traitors who insisted that the Bill of Rights applied to
them. Even though the police had arrested more than two
hundred Wobblies by March (and sprayed a crowd of five thousand supporters with fire hoses), the forces of law and order
demanded a quicker and more efficient solution.

To help ease the problem of overcrowding in the jails, the
police chief handed the Wobbly prisoners over to vigilantes—
mainly respected businessmen and professionals—who hauled
them out into the desert and told them never to come back.
Vigilantes also greeted undesirable visitors who tried to ride
the rails into the city. On April 5, 400 citizens of San Diego
met a train carrying 140 Wobblies, one of whom described the
encounter:

> The moon was shining dimly through the clouds and I could
> see pick handles, ax handles, wagon spokes and every kind
> of club imaginable swinging from the wrists of all of them
> while they also had their rifles leveled at us. . . . [T]he only
> sign of civilization was a cattle corral. . . . We were ordered
> to unload and we refused. Then they closed in around the
> flat car which we were on and began clubbing and knocking
> and pulling men off by their heels, so inside of a half hour
> they had us all off the train and then bruised and bleeding
> we were lined up and marched into the cattle corral, where
> they made us hold our hands up and march around in the
> crowd for more than an hour. . . . They marched us several
> times, now and then picking out a man they thought was a
> leader and giving him an extra beating. Several men were
> carried out unconscious. . . . [A]fterwards there was a lot of
> our men unaccounted for and never have been heard from
> since. . . . In the morning they took us out four or five at a

time and marched us up the track to the county line . . .
where we were forced to kiss the flag and then run a
gauntlet of 106 men, every one of which was striking at us
as hard as they could with their pick axe handles. They
broke one man's leg, and everyone else was beaten black
and blue, and was bleeding from a dozen wounds.

The governor of California, after protests by labor leaders and
progressive reformers, compared San Diego to tsarist Russia,
but many San Diegans agreed with the journalist who praised
the lesson in "patriotism and reverence for the law."

The fight dragged on, through all the news about the *Titanic* disaster, into May, when on the seventh, IWW member
Joseph Mikolasek tried to speak from a downtown platform.
Attacked by police, he escaped first to Socialist party headquarters and then home, where he was followed and attacked
again. Mikolasek grabbed an ax to defend himself but was
gunned down before he could use it. When news of the murder reached the well-known anarchist and feminist Emma
Goldman in Los Angeles, she was on a lecture tour. Goldman
organized a soup kitchen for the Wobblies who had been
driven out of San Diego and then participated in a public funeral for Mikolasek, who was cremated in Los Angeles since
the San Diego authorities refused to let him be buried in their
city. On May 14 Goldman and her companion Ben Reitman
arrived in San Diego for her scheduled lecture. After narrowly
escaping a crowd that spotted "that anarchist murderer" on a
bus, she and Reitman tried to check into a hotel, but the manager told them that they could stay only if they agreed to be
locked in their rooms. Soon the mayor and chief of police arrived at the hotel. Leaving Reitman in his room, Goldman
went downstairs to meet with them. They warned her to leave
town—they could not protect her from the vigilantes—and
she advised them in turn to use the same powers to disperse

the mobs as they were using against the free speech movement. When she returned to find Reitman, he was gone. Un-
able to get any news of him, after pacing for hours, she "dozed
off from sheer fatigue. I dreamed of Ben, bound and gagged,
his hands groping for me. I struggled to reach him and woke
up with a scream, bathed in sweat." A knock on the door
brought the news that Reitman was safe; he had been run out
of town by the vigilantes. Goldman decided to return to Los
Angeles to meet him. The vigilantes chased her to the train
and fought with the crew in an unsuccessful attempt to pur-
sue her onto it.

Reitman had been kidnapped from the hotel, thrown into
an automobile, and driven twenty miles out of town. The vigilantes formed a ring around him, stripped off his clothes, beat
him, branded the letters *IWW* on his buttocks with a lit cigar,
poured tar over his head and, having forgotten to bring feath-
ers, used sagebrush instead, tried to rape him with a cane,
twisted his testicles, forced him to kiss the flag and sing "The
Star-Spangled Banner," and made him run a gauntlet. The
only reason they didn't kill him, they said, was that they had
promised the police chief they wouldn't.

For a while the Reitman incident emboldened the cause.
The Free Speech League continued its protests, but the authorities made their arrests, and the vigilantes kept up their
violence. By fall the streets of San Diego were quiet.

While one of its subcommittees investigated the *Titanic* disaster, the whole Senate was considering an immigration bill.[5] In
1911, 878,587 immigrants entered the United States—a modest number compared with the 1,285,349 who had come in
1907 and aroused Congress into appointing a commission to
look into the "problem." The commission, named after its
chairman, Senator William P. Dillingham of Vermont, produced forty-two volumes of information in its two-year study.

Its recommendations took the form of the bill now pending before the Senate.

Dillingham explained that the proposed legislation grew out of the commission's finding that there was something even more disturbing about the character of the recent arrivals than their alarming numbers. The problem, he told the Senate, could be summed up in the distinction between the "old" and "new" immigrants. The "old" immigrants—those who arrived before 1882—had come from northern and western Europe, from England, Ireland, Scotland, Wales, Scandinavia, Germany, France, and Holland. The "new" immigrants were coming from southern and eastern Europe: Italy, Russia, Poland, Hungary, the Balkans, Greece. This difference was crucial because the origins of aliens determined how well they would fit into American society. Dillingham conceded that even immigrants of the recent "type and character" were the cream of their respective nations' crop: "While many of the later immigrants are unskilled laborers, we have to say for them that they are the best of the class from which they come. It is the peasant class, but . . . those coming are the individuals who have thrift and courage and enterprise enough to assume the risk incident to such a change and the making of homes in the New World."

Still, no matter how they compared with their less enterprising cousins, these "new" immigrants weren't melting in the pot; they weren't assimilating. Flooding into cities and taking up unskilled manufacturing jobs, they were keeping to themselves while competing with "American" workers and depressing wages. Many of them, the commission discovered, were single males who lived in communities where "they do not come in touch with American life; they live in colonies, where they speak only their own language. . . . The result is that they lead an isolated life, and come less in touch with American life than any other class of American immigrants

whom we have ever received." How then could Congress best
act to keep out "those whom we look upon as being the least
desirable type"? The bill provided the answer: a literacy test.
By making sure that immigrants could read or write, the law
would discriminate on the basis of ignorance rather than
"race." It just so happened that the percentages of illiteracy
were much higher for southern and eastern Europeans than
for northern and western Europeans; the same test applied
"equally" to all.

Even though the accepted distinction between "old" and
"new" implied better and worse, the senators carefully avoided
direct claims of inferiority. "I have no racial objection to these
people . . ." declared the Mississippi senator who tried unsuc-
cessfully to amend the bill to exclude immigrants of African
descent, "but the ignorant man, whatever his race, coming to
a country where he is not governed but becomes a part of the
governing force, is dangerous." Senator (and ex-Secretary of
State) Elihu Root of New York went out of his way to deny
"any assertion of our superiority to the peoples of southeast-
ern Europe," but then, in language that suggested the innate
incapacity of the new immigrants for American democracy,
predicted that the test would bar those who were "the least
intelligent, the least capable of being manufactured into good
American citizens, the most dangerous as a new and
unassimilated element in our body politic."

Responding to colleagues like Root and Senator William
E. Borah of Idaho, who proclaimed himself "in favor of closing down the gates with every possible stringency against those
who have neither the loyalty nor the intellectual capacity to
meet the obligations of citizenship," Senator James A.
O'Gorman of New York pointed out that these were the same
arguments that had once been used against the "old" immigrants. But the rhetoric behind the "impartial" literacy test
proved irresistible to most senators, who felt the weight of

public opinion behind immigration restriction. The Senate passed the bill on April 19, the day on which newspapers printed the first interviews with the newly returned *Titanic* survivors and the subcommittee launched its investigation into the disaster at New York's Waldorf-Astoria Hotel. The House approved the measure soon after. Only President Taft's veto, overridden by the Senate but sustained in the House, stopped it from becoming law.

At 11:40 P.M. on April 14 the Royal Mail Steamer *Titanic*, bound from Southampton, England, to New York, hit an iceberg on its starboard side in the North Atlantic four hundred miles from the coast of Newfoundland.[6] Water began rushing into the enormous ship, thought by many to be unsinkable. Twenty-five minutes later the crew was told to prepare the lifeboats and alert the passengers. The first boat was launched at 12:45; the last, at 2:05. There was only enough capacity in the boats for half the people on board, and some of the boats were not fully loaded. At 2:20 the *Titanic*'s stern disappeared into the sea. The *Carpathia* came upon the first boat and began taking in survivors at 4:10. The last boat was unloaded at 8:30. The *Carpathia* rescued 705 people; 1,503 died.

CHAPTER 2

THE RULE OF THE SEA
AND LAND

A CONVENTIONAL NARRATIVE of the *Titanic* disaster began to take shape before any survivor had been interviewed.[1] Until the *Carpathia* arrived in New York with the survivors the night of April 18, communication had been restricted almost exclusively to lists of the dead and the saved. Information that women and children had survived in much greater numbers than men suggested that the legendary rule of the sea—women and children first—had prevailed. These statistics inspired reporters, editorial writers, politicians, and corporate officials to fashion, without any eyewitness testimony, a tale of first-cabin male heroism in which the men did not merely obey orders or blindly follow established codes of behavior but willingly engaged in chivalric self-sacrifice. Newspapers quoted the vice-president of the White Star Line, who insisted that "[t]here is no rule of the sea . . . which requires such a sacrifice" but that "[i]t is a matter of courtesy extended by the stronger to the weaker, on land as well as the sea." Others attached a visual image to this assumption of chivalry. "To all appearances," said a wire service report on April 17, "the men who were left stayed behind deliberately, calmly, stepping aside to let the weaker ones take their way to safety." The only evidence for such deliberateness and calm was the *Titanic*'s last wireless message: "Sinking by the head. Have cleared boats and filled them with women and children."[2]

Editorialists quickly formed a chorus of praise for those who "bore their fate, we hope and believe, like brave men and courteous gentlemen, whose business it had become to die that the women and children might live." Shock and sadness were tempered by the "one splendid feature of the disaster which is eloquent of superb courtesy and heroic manhood—the women and children were saved." The information that all the lifeboats were accounted for and that none "was swamped or overfilled" meant "that men stood back and chose to die." Declarations that the "world is better" for such heroism instantly furnished the story with redemptive meaning and provided a bulwark against senselessness.[3]

What emerged in the days after the disaster was a myth—not because it was false necessarily but because it located a disturbing event within routine structures of understanding. "Myth," as Richard Slotkin has written, "is invoked as a means of deriving usable values from history, and of putting those values beyond the reach of critical demystification. Its primary appeal is to ritualized emotions, established beliefs, habitual associations, memory, nostalgia."[4] In the case of the *Titanic* the myth of first-cabin male heroism appealed to conventional understandings and sentimental notions of gender roles that involved a series of oppositions: strength versus weakness; independence versus dependence; intellect versus emotion; public versus private.

By the time the survivors reached shore, the myth was firmly in place and their testimony could only confirm what the press and the public already knew. It is highly unlikely, of course, that the first-cabin women whose stories were told in the newspapers would have challenged the myth; their personal grief made the search for redemptive meaning all the more compelling and poignant. General accounts of gallantry were soon accompanied by anecdotes about the *Titanic*'s most famous victims: the financiers, merchants, and industrialists John Jacob Astor, Benjamin Guggenheim, Charles M. Hays, Isidor Straus, John B. Thayer, and George Widener; President Taft's military aide Archibald Butt; the British journalist W. T. Stead; the theatrical producer Henry B. Harris. Out of the conflicting stories and disparate details came confirmation that the disaster had not disrupted the normal relations between the sexes. "[I]n the midst of harrowing recitals," summed up one editorial, "shines the heroism of American manhood, which protected the weak and helpless."[5]

While the myth served to make sense and give comfort, it also functioned as an object lesson. Champ Clark, presidential candidate and Speaker of the House, joined in celebrating the "chivalric behavior of the men on the ill-fated ship" and prophesied that the "memory of their heroism will live forever." The poet Charles Hanson Towne made a similar claim in verse:

> *But dream not, mighty Ocean, they are yours!*
> *We have them still, those high and valiant men*
> *Who died that others might reach ports of peace.*
> *Not in your jealous depths their spirits roam,*
> *But through the world to-day, and up to heaven!*[6]

That chivalry prevailed in such circumstances validated the male role as protector and provider and implied that women should be grateful that this role was fulfilled so admirably. "Does not the heart of every true American woman go out in tender loyalty to those brave men of the Titanic who yielded their valuable lives that the weak and helpless might live?" asked a letter writer called Soror in the *New York Times*. "We know that no country in the world produces men more truly kind and tender of the women committed to their care, none more surely to be relied on in time of stress and danger."[7]

If men under stress and in danger accepted death as "a holy sacrament, sanctified by bravery, self-denial and unequalled consideration for weaker ones than themselves," was it not evident that gender roles were natural and eternal? That nothing could or should alter them? Thus the *New York Times* described the rule of the sea as a law in a "higher and sterner" sense than statutory. It was one of sociologist William Graham Sumner's folkways—"a law founded on the nature of things and of human beings, and resting on the very deepest of physiological and psychological foundations." Other commentators also found the word "law" inadequate to describe codes of behavior that transcended time and inhered in human nature. "They are not laws; they are rules of ideality, of *noblesse*, rules of general consent, which lay down what the high-minded man thinks ought to be done in case of disaster at sea. They are rules of that Christian knightliness which seeks not its own, but the good of others; the captain for his passenger and crew for whom he cares, the men for the women and children of whom they are the natural guardians."[8]

The idea that "heroism is an unconscious race quality"— part of certain groups' cultural or biological inheritance—may have contradicted the claim that the first-cabin men freely chose to die, but it served the more important purpose of reinforcing conventional gender relations. The rule of the sea, observed a *Collier's* editorial, derived from "something deeper" than "the difference in strength" between men and women. It was "the principle that those who control should consider others before themselves"—the sense of obligation at the core of paternalism. "Power and trust carry with them, in emergencies, the privilege to be self-forgetful and to die." Chivalric fantasies, as E. Anthony Rotundo has noted, allowed men to reconcile "feminine" morality—kindness, tenderness, self-forgetfulness—with "masculine" aggressiveness—bravery, physical strength, agency. The role of ruler and protector carried with it the duty of manly self-sacrifice.[9]

Men who refused such obligations and challenged the eternal verities were guilty of nothing less than perversion. This was the moral of the repeatedly told story of the man who dressed as a woman and escaped in a lifeboat. Later identified as a steerage passenger named Daniel Buckley, he and a few other men had found space in a boat but were ordered to leave by officers. While the men were climbing out, a woman, who Buckley believed was Madeleine Astor, tossed him a shawl in which he concealed himself. Most versions, however, were considerably more elaborate. In one of the first books about the disaster, under the heading "THE COWARD," he was described as "a cur in human shape, to-day the most despicable human being in all the world," "still living by the inexplicable grace of God," "born and saved to set for men a new standard by which to measure infamy and shame." "What did he do? He scuttled to the stateroom deck, put on a woman's skirt, a woman's hat and a woman's veil, and picking his crafty way back among the brave and chivalrous men who guarded the rail of the doomed ship, he filched a seat in one of the lifeboats and saved his skin."

Here was the logical result of tampering with gender roles—moral decay, crimes against the natural order, lost manhood. When a reporter asked another male survivor if he had escaped by dressing as a woman, the man punched him.[10]

The rigid rules of gender placed all male survivors—even if they did not face such direct accusations of cowardice—in a difficult position. In the Senate hearings, which began on April

19, the subcommittee chairman, William Alden Smith of Michigan, asked nearly every male officer, crew member, and passenger among the witnesses to describe the circumstances of his escape. The descriptions took two forms, both of which absolved the survivor of possible crimes against nature. In the first scenario the man entered the lifeboat either because there were no women waiting on deck or because he was ordered to do so by an officer. Usually he proved his mettle first by helping the women and children into the boats before taking his place and then by rowing or steering the boat to safety. The second scenario was more dramatic. After assisting in loading the boats, the man either jumped or was swept into the sea. Archibald Gracie, who recounted the experience in articles and a book, felt himself "whirled around" and feared that he would be boiled alive by scalding water surging up from below. Swimming with "unusual strength" and endurance, he pulled himself to the surface and climbed aboard a capsized boat. "Colonel Gracie lived," went a particularly concise apology, "but in nowise dishonored or brought into question as a man and an officer." The author of an early fictional account of the disaster, seizing on Gracie's escape as the model for male survival, rescued his pseudonymous narrator, Oscar, by having him swim alongside the colonel. The physical ordeal, combined with the previous display of paternalistic self-sacrifice, vindicated the survivor's masculinity.[11]

(In *A History of the World in 10 1/2 Chapters* the British novelist Julian Barnes includes an anecdote about Lawrence Beesley, an English schoolteacher and second-cabin passenger who escaped the *Titanic* in a lifeboat. Houghton Mifflin immediately signed him up to write an account of his experiences, *The Loss of the S.S. Titanic*, which he finished in six weeks. Like other male survivors, Beesley was burdened by rumors that he had cross-dressed his way to safety. In the late 1950s he was hired as a consultant for the movie version of *A Night to Remember*.

In an attempt "to undergo in fiction an alternative version of history," Beesley sneaked onto the set as an extra and tried this time to go down with the ship. But he was found out at the last minute by the director, who refused to let a non-Equity actor appear in the scene. "And so," writes Barnes, "for the second time in his life, Lawrence Beesley found himself leaving the *Titanic* just before it was due to go down.")[12]

Yet if paternalism was in the nature of things, the United States in 1912 was experiencing a growing number of unnatural acts. Suffrage agitation, the emergence of feminism, rising divorce rates, changing patterns of work and leisure all threatened to disrupt traditional roles.[13] The appeal to nature—the insistence that these roles were immune to historical change—betrayed an uneasiness with important aspects of modernity. Traditionalists found in the disaster proof against women's claims to equality (which, in their view, would bring women down from their elevated status); they also derived reassurance that men, facing a crisis, would not give in easily. "Possibly the time may come when women are to be regarded as no better than men," gloated the *New Orleans Times-Picayune*, "but it will be long after the old-fashioned fellows are out of the way." An advice columnist neatly summarized the traditionalists' belief that the disaster demonstrated the permanence of gender roles. "In a world jangling today over the parasitism of women, and the triangular love affairs of men, feminism and universal suffrage," the *Titanic* had brought home the lesson "that man is eternally the protector of woman" and that "woman accepts man's protection and obeys man instinctively." Defined against the eternal and the instinctual, changes in gender roles became aberrations. By representing the disaster as a catastrophic return to nature, the conventional narrative made paternalism appear commonsensical and universal.[14]

Acceptance of the *Titanic* gender myth did not preclude a prosuffrage stance, but many antisuffragists were more than willing to use the *Titanic* for polemical purposes. In editorials, letters to the editor, and sermons, antisuffragists ("antis" for short) drew from the disaster the lesson that women were best served by male chivalry rather than by the vote. "Let the suffragists remember this," a letter to the *Baltimore Sun* declared. "When the Lord created woman and placed her under the protection of man he had her well provided for. The Titanic disaster proves it very plainly." The editors of the same paper agreed. "The action of the men on the Titanic was not exceptional," they observed. "But it must be recognized as an act of supreme heroism, and as showing that women can appeal to a higher law than that of the ballot for justice, consideration, and protection." While the men on the *Titanic* adhered to this higher law, suffragists under similar pressure would have readily surrendered their ill-conceived political demands. "Would the suffragette have stood on that deck for women's rights or for women's privileges?" was the rhetorical question posed by a writer identified as Mere Man. The staff poet for the *St. Louis Post-Dispatch* similarly suggested that suffrage agitation would fizzle out once suffragists realized the implications of their position:

> *"Votes for women!"*
> *Was the cry,*
> *Reaching upward*
> *To the sky.*
> *Crashing glass,*
> *And flashing eye—*
> *"Votes for women!"*
> *Was the cry.*
>
> *"Boats for women!"*
> *Was the cry,*
> *When the brave*
> *Were come to die.*

When the end
Was drawing nigh—
"Boats for women!"
Was the cry.

Life has many
Little jests
Insignificant
As tests.
Doubt and bitterness
Assail
But "Boats for women!"
Tells the tale.[15]

(The *Titanic*, incidentally, inspired a vast quantity of poetry, which prompted the *New York Times* to advise amateurs "that to write about the Titanic a poem worth printing requires that the author should have something more than paper, pencil, and a strong feeling that the disaster was a terrible one." Most of the poems it had received were "worthless" and "intolerably bad," and the worst of all were those written on lined paper. *Current Literature* was kinder: "We do not remember any other event in our history that has called forth such a rush of song in the columns of the daily press." While some of it was "unutterably" horrible and none was quite "magically inspired," a surprising amount of *Titanic* verse was "very creditable.")[16]

Other antis sounded a note of warning. "The women who are demanding political rights may well take care, lest they lose what is infinitely dearer," said the Reverend W. S. Plumer Bryan of Chicago's Church of the Covenant. "If men and women are to be rivals, can she [*sic*] expect such chivalrous protection as the women of the Titanic received?" The Reverend Dr. Leighton Parks of New York's St. Bartholomew's Church contrasted the good women of the *Titanic* with the misguided suffragists: "The women [on the *Titanic*] did not ask for the sacrifice, but it was made. Those women who go shrieking about for their 'rights' want something very different. Put the world on a basis merely of 'rights' and you put it on an inclined plane where it will never stop until it has gone to the lowest level of barbarism and bestiality." Women, even those whom the *Tampa Tribune* ridiculed as the "short-haired" kind, would live to regret it if they "forfeited the sweet courtesy, the undisputed precedence which has been the time honored right of the eternal feminine." After the "superb unselfishness and heroism of the men on the Titanic," an anti complained, the plan to go ahead with the New York suffrage parade was abhorrent.[17]

But the *Titanic* gave antis the assurance that regardless of what women wanted, men would never acquiesce in such degradation. "[T]he feeling that the weak, whether they vote or not, should be those first protected is deeply implanted by nature," commented the *New York Herald*. "The suffragettes, by placing a plank in their platform abolishing the rule: 'Women and children first,' will probably make no headway so long as manhood shall endure." To the National Association Opposed to Woman Suffrage, it was clear that manhood would endure, because both men and women had learned from the *Titanic* that sexual difference was natural and permanent:

> In the story that came up from the sea there are many lessons. One of these lessons is that when the final crash came men and women alike were unanimous in making the sex distinction. It was not a question of "Voters first," but the cry all over the ship was "Women first!" In acquiescing to that cry the women admitted that they were not fitted for men's tasks. They did not think of the boasted "equality" in all things. This is not an implication that the women were inferior, it just shows an inequality or a difference.

Much has been spoken and written by thinkers on this phase of the disaster and its influence on the eternal cry of some women to be allowed to take up the activities and responsibilities that belong to man just as woman's responsibilities belong to woman. The disaster tends in its terribly grim way to point out the everlasting "difference" of the sexes.

A St. Louis man was even more blunt about the lessons and uses of the disaster: "I suggest, henceforth, when a woman talks woman's rights, she be answered with the word Titanic, nothing more—just Titanic."[18]

Suffrage was not the only threat to conventional gender relations about which the *Titanic* provided an object lesson. At the heart of the antisuffragist argument, as Aileen Kraditor has shown, was the belief that the "welfare of the human race depended upon women's staying home, having children, and keeping out of politics." Any alteration in gender roles threatened the social order by destroying its primary institution—the home. Of particular concern was the rising rate of divorce. In the polemical literature of moral conservatives, divorce represented the breakdown of the family and thus the beginning of social decay.[19] For some of these conservatives, the women who had "resolutely refused" to get into lifeboats, "preferring to meet death hand in hand with the husbands who could not accompany them and share life with them more," provided inspirational examples of the sanctity of marriage. The most moving and often told story was that of Ida Straus, wife of the Macy's executive, who chose to remain by her husband's side as the ship sank. "In this day of frequent and scandalous divorces," said one editorial, "when the marriage tie once held so sacred is all too lightly regarded, the wifely devotion and love of Mrs. Straus for her partner of a lifetime stands [*sic*] out in noble contrast. The world needed a reminder that married

love and devotion cannot be cast off like a worn garment."
J. H. McKenzie, a poet from Guthrie, Oklahoma, urged "all
girls" who read his tribute to "Emulate the deed of such a
wife, / As went down in the blue." An emblem of "the pri-
mal sweetness, soundness, and goodness of human nature,"
she stood out against "the complex, distracting, and often
demoralizing tendencies of modern civilization"—in this
case, women's demands for more liberal divorce laws.[20]

Religious leaders were particularly eager to invoke the
Strauses as moral exemplars in resisting "that home-destroy-
ing evil of our modern times—divorce." In a sermon on "Marriage," Rabbi William S. Friedman of Temple Emanuel in
Denver praised Mrs. Straus and "brought out the alarming
proportions to which divorce has grown in the past few years."
Adolf Guttmacher of the Madison Avenue Temple in Baltimore combined moral exhortation with ethnic pride. Jews, he
said with reference to the Strauses, have "at all times cherished and cultivated zealously the sense of family life. . . . When
the institution of marriage is losing its divine consecration, it
is well to call attention to the fine examples of conjugal attachment and devotion as exemplified by some of those who
were face to face with grim death on the ill-fated Titanic."
Another Baltimore man urged women to build a monument
to Mrs. Straus as a permanent warning against divorce: "In
the time when critics say that the marriage relations in America
are looked upon too lightly it would be fitting that all good
women of the country join in setting a stamp of approval on
Mrs. Straus and her ideals of fidelity." Though it appeared
infrequently, the corollary to this lesson was to excoriate the
married women who survived. "Perhaps, some day, these widows will explain how it happened that they allowed themselves to be torn away from their husbands instead of going
down with them," wrote a woman columnist. "[W]hile men
are men, and women are women; while there are ideals to be

raised and followed; while there is dependence and courage; while the species continue[s] to be everything and the individual nothing in the scheme of nature, we shall have great, and strong and good men go down to sea in ships, after life boats have drifted away with weak and vain and frivolous, worthless and hapless women and little children."[21]

It was women who launched the movement to etch the *Titanic's* gender lessons in stone. Within two weeks of the disaster, prominent women organized the Women's Titanic Memorial Fund to build a monument as "the tribute of woman to heroic manhood." The fund's secretary, Natalie F. Hammond, a veteran of the National Civic Federation, enlisted the wives or widows of John Hay, William Howard Taft, Champ Clark, Grover Cleveland, E. H. Harriman, Samuel Gompers, Andrew Carnegie, Theodore Roosevelt, Woodrow Wilson, William Jennings Bryan, William Randolph Hearst, and other notables in a national effort to raise five hundred thousand dollars. Helen H. Taft, who symbolically donated the first dollar, announced that she was "glad to do this in gratitude to the chivalry of American manhood." Women's clubs coordinated the fund drive at the local level and appealed to regional pride in their requests for donations. Because Hammond was from the South and because "the South furnished her share of men among the heroic dead whom the arch will commemorate," southern women were urged to give generously. The fund's Georgia representative cast her plea in regional, national, and racial terms. "Our women," she declared, "can not but appreciate that the memorial is one of, not only national significance, but it will stand for one of the greatest expressions of Anglo-Saxon heroism the world has known."[22]

Fund raising efforts were diverse. Charles Dana Gibson contributed a poster that depicted "a young, deep-chested woman" standing in front of the monument's pedestal and "clasping in her hands the mallet and chisel of the builder."

Above her head was the inscription "To the men who gave
their lives that the women and children might be saved."
Gibson's poster was published in newspapers along with requests for contributions. Mrs. Leonard Wood, wife the army
chief of staff, took on the task of soliciting the support of other
army wives for the memorial. Hammond held a well-publicized "lawn-fete," with the Tafts as the guests of honor, at her
Gloucester, Massachusetts, estate. Aware that such an event
might appear snobbish and exclusive, Hammond insisted that
the proposed memorial appealed "to the general public" rather
than "only to certain classes of women." A theatrical benefit
in New York featured twenty of the season's debutantes selling souvenir programs and raised ten thousand dollars. Billie
Burke and George M. Cohan performed a skit, which provided comic relief from a pageant entitled "The Flowers and
the Sea." The pageant concluded with "a procession of weep-
ing Fisherwomen" and an epilogue delivered by the "Spirit of
Woman, beautifully personified by Edith Wynne Matthison."
"We are here to help rear a monument to the nobility of American manhood and American womanhood," said one actor.
"When our children look on that monument they will say,
'Thank God I belong to that race which in the hour of sorest
trial said "Ladies first." ' " Natalie Hammond claimed that
this would be the first American monument "erected to an
ideal" and thus as useful and uplifting an act of philanthropy
as building hospitals.[23]

Hammond and the other organizers of the fund took pride
in the fact that women were entirely responsible for adminis-
tering and supporting their project. But the feminist implications ended there. The monument's didactic purpose was to
reinforce the doctrine of separate spheres and, despite the independence shown by the organizers, to confirm women's position of dependence. The winning design, submitted by
Gertrude Vanderbilt Whitney, featured a white marble "fig-

ure of Heroism, a man of noble proportions, fifteen feet high, the face, arms, and whole posture of the body exemplifying a willing sacrifice, a smiling welcome to death." An editorial described it as "a monument by women to men—by women in the aggregate to men in the aggregate, from the weaker to the stronger, from the grateful to the gallant, from the saved to the saver of life. . . . The women who build this monument are building for themselves—walling their womanhood safe within the chivalry of men."[24] For wealthy women, this image of women constructing their own fortress and celebrating their confinement may even have demonstrated a kind of power— a demand that men live up to their roles as providers and protectors, an insistence that paternalism meant obligations as well as privileges. But it was power limited by class position and severe restrictions on women's range of roles and activities. As the gift and homage of "women in the aggregate," the monument rigidly reinforced the bounds of true womanhood.

The need to reassert the authority of conventional gender relations took on additional urgency from an ambiguity that inevitably crept into accounts of the disaster. Because the *Titanic* was supposedly unsinkable, because the impact of the collision with the iceberg was so slight, and, most important, because the chances of survival in lifeboats in the freezing North Atlantic were uncertain at best, it was by no means self-evident that the men had taken the stronger and braver course.

The attitude of the first-cabin male passengers might just as well have been complacency as heroic calm. "Everyone seemed to realize so slowly that there was imminent danger," recalled a survivor. There was "an almost complete absence of any positive knowledge on any point." Like many others, the *New York Times* said of E. I. Taylor, "he spoke of the lack of comprehension among the passengers, after the accident, that there was the least danger. . . . It appeared from what Mr. Taylor said that at the time he left the Titanic there was difficulty in filling all the boats, as the danger had not yet been fully realized by the passengers." D. H. Bishop described the common response as apathetic. "The confidence that the ship was unsinkable was so great that most felt sure of its safety until the last minute," he remembered. Madeleine Astor told reporters that it was hard to tell how grave the situation was until only two boats were left: "The men for some reason, which, as she recalled last night, she could not and does not now understand, did not seem at all anxious to leave the ship. Almost every one seemed dazed."[25] The myth of first-cabin male heroism attempted to resolve the ambiguity.

Statistics told a far less ambiguous story about class. Though the exact numbers were not immediately available, estimates as early as April 19 established enormous differences in survival rates. These tabulations, which were not significantly different from the final figures, indicated that 94 percent of the first-cabin women and children were saved, compared with 81 percent in the second cabin and 47 percent in the steerage. Of the first-cabin men, 31 percent survived, compared with 10 percent in second class and 14 percent in steerage. In all, 60 percent of the first-cabin passengers lived, compared with 44 percent of the second-cabin passengers and only 25 percent of the steerage passengers.[26]

To compensate for such skewed percentages, the conventional narrative offered a variation on the theme of sacrifice in which the first-cabin men specifically surrendered their places in the boats (and their more valuable lives) so that women and children from the steerage could live. The *San Francisco Examiner* imagined the scene:

> The picture that invariably presents itself, in view of what is known, is of men like John Jacob Astor, master of scores of millions; Benjamin Guggenheim of the famous family

of bankers; Isidor Straus, a merchant prince; William T. Stead, veteran journalist; Major Archibald W. Butt, soldier; Washington Roebling, noted engineer—of any or all of these men stepping aside, bravely, gallantly remaining to die that the place he otherwise might have filled could perhaps be taken by some sabot-shod, shawl-enshrouded, illiterate and penniless peasant woman of Europe.

The same image, presented in virtually identical language, appeared in newspapers across the country and conveyed the message that wealthy and powerful British and American men had died not only for their own women but for less deserving poor and foreign women as well. "While the lowly immigrants and their offspring were being borne to safety," the *Washington Post* reported, "Americans and Englishmen of fame and wealth—Archibald Butt, William T. Stead, Clarence Moore, John Jacob Astor, F. D. Millet, George D. and Harry Widener among them—from the deck of the Titanic watched the last lifeboat disappear, and went to heroes' graves marked by the depthless sea."[27]

With its interest in celebrity, the commercial press tended to represent the disaster exclusively as the story of the first cabin. Newspapers routinely described the bravery of a short list of "notables" in stories with headlines such as NOTED MEN ON THE LOST TITANIC; UNTOLD RICHES REPRESENTED ON THE TITANIC; COL. ASTOR, MAJ. BUTT AND OTHER NOTABLES PROBABLY DROWNED; MEN FAMOUS IN FINANCIAL WORLD GO TO DEATH; KINGS OF FINANCE, CAPTAINS OF INDUSTRY, WORLD-FAMED MEN WHO WENT DOWN IN TITANIC; and WHO'S WHO ON TITANIC. This, of course, was "society," its exploits the regular fare of the daily papers. But the *Titanic* was hardly a regular occurrence, and the fact that heroism immediately came to be associated with a few recurrent names made chivalric self-sacrifice synonymous with wealth and social position. "The Strauses, Stead, Astor, Butt, Harris, Thayer,

Widener, Guggenheim, Hays—," wrote the business "philosopher" Elbert Hubbard in his syndicated column, "I thought I
knew you because I had seen you, realized somewhat of your
able qualities, looked into your eyes and pressed your hands,
but I did not guess your greatness." "There were millionaires
from New York," went a popular song,

> And some from London Town,
> They were all brave, there were women and children to save
> When the great Titanic went down.

Another placed "Astor, Widners [sic], Thayer and Butt among
that noble band / Who went down with the Titanic off the
banks of Newfoundland." Even the *Philadelphia North American*, known for its prolabor editorial stance, offered the standard *Titanic* honor roll:

> John Jacob Astor, true to his record of patriotism and
> gallantry in 1898, smiling and waving farewell to the young
> wife soon to be a mother; Archie Butt, that lovable, debonair
> gentleman of the South, well called by Admiral Dewey
> "nature's nobleman," calmly controlling with perfect
> courtesy the well-nigh frenzied women, and placing them
> in safety; George Widener, kissing his wife good-by and
> with reassuring word falling back into the line, busied with
> the work of rescue, and beside him his son, as true a man as
> his brave father; John B. Thayer, surrendering a place of
> safety in favor of Mrs. Thayer's serving-maid; Ryerson,
> Dulles, Williams, Sutton, and Brewe—all these, with
> hundreds of others, are on a roll of nobility that history will
> preserve.[28]

The "hundreds of others" remained nameless and classless,
while those on the honor roll received nearly inexhaustible
attention. "What need can there be of recounting the heroic

deeds performed by those men who remained on the Titanic?" asked Helen Candee, a first-cabin survivor who wrote her own account of the disaster. "To dwell upon them only sickens the heart, with the realization of how they perished." Yet Candee herself celebrated Astor, Butt, and Isidor Straus, and such a ritualized call not to dwell upon them only added to the mystique. Glimpses of final moments and recollections of last words functioned similarly. Benjamin Guggenheim, newspaper readers learned, instructed a first-cabin steward to tell his wife, "We're dressed up in our best and are prepared to go down like gentlemen. I am willing to remain and play the man's game if there are not enough boats for more than the women and children. I won't die here like a beast. I'll meet my end as a man."[29]

There were many versions of John Jacob Astor's end, but as one paper put it, "they all agree as to the wonderful fortitude and bravery of the New York millionaire." According to one version, related by a survivor who had to admit that "I did not see it myself," Astor placed his wife in a boat, "stood erect and, with a military salute, turned back to take his place on the sinking Titanic." Another depicted a conference among Astor, Butt, Guggenheim, Widener, and Thayer that culminated in Astor's declaring, "Not a man until every woman and child is safe in the boats." Describing him as "a millionaire, / Scholarly and profound," an Oklahoma poet showed Astor refusing his wife's pleas and a seaman's permission to leave the ship.

> *This man a soldier once has been*
> *Of military art,*
> *Proved himself competent then*
> *To do his noble part.*

A song entitled "A Hero Went Down with the Monarch of the Sea" called Astor "a handsome prince of wealth, / Who was noble, generous and brave," and featured his parting words to his wife: "Good-bye, my darling, don't you grieve for me, / I would give my life for ladies to flee." Owen Lynch's lyrics to "The Titanic Is Doomed and Sinking" were even more direct.

> *There was John Jacob Astor,*
> *What a brave man was he*
> *When he tried to save all female sex,*
> *The young and all, great and small,*
> *Then got drowned in the sea.*

Such anecdotes served to conflate wealth and self-sacrifice, power and moral grandeur, social status and character. "Now when the name of Astor is mentioned, it will be the John Jacob who went down with the Titanic that will first come to mind; not the Astor who made the great fortune, not the Astor who added to its greatness, but John Jacob Astor, the hero."[30] Occurring at a time when rich and overly pampered men were regarded as potentially effete and parasitical, the disaster simultaneously fortified their masculinity and their class position. Astor's life of leisure hinted at effeminacy; his heroic death revealed his ultimate social value as a man of wealth.

The lesson concerned the efficacy of noblesse oblige and the necessity of gratitude on the part of the lower classes and immigrants toward their social betters. One account suggested that the phrase itself occurred to grateful passengers in the midst of the disaster (though it is hard to imagine who would have been in a position to think of such things at the time): "The regal motto, 'Noblesse Oblige,' arose in more than one mind as some man of wealth and proud social standing gallantly stepped aside and gave his place to some unknown and poor unfortunate with a grace that could not be excelled in a ballroom." A New York minister made clear that there was absolutely no scientific or economic justification for this kind of heroism, which, like all noble acts, was a gift from the deserving to the undeserving.

> Certainly, it was not a case of the survival of the fittest. There were men lost that the city and the country needed, and there are widows surviving who speak no language that you or I can understand, and who will inevitably become public charges.
>
> They did not ask why, nor if any helpless, poor creature were worth saving. The maxims of commerce were forgotten. There was no question of buying cheap and selling dear. They sold themselves for naught; they gave their lives away. Such a sacrifice can not be justified on any economic ground.

In a Denver columnist's scenario, the "disease-bitten child, whose life at best is less than worthless, goes to safety with the rest of the steerage riff-raff, while the handler of great affairs, the men who direct the destinies of hundreds of thousands of workers, the learned men whose talents are dedicated to the cure of physical afflictions, writers whose words are as burning lamps in troubled darkness, and whose energies have uplifted humanity, stand unprotestingly aside." A Los Angeles minister bemoaned the apparent injustice of sacrificing a valuable life "for an immigrant, ignorant, stupid, unkempt—a human clod, possibly," but then explained that such an "offering" is pure even though the "life for which the sacrifice is made may be poor and ignorant and foul." (On the other hand, a *Baltimore Sun* editorial noted that "if we start to weigh the relative value of lives lost, some emigrant child saved from the wreck may be or beget a second Lincoln.")[31] Class mattered and didn't matter; denying the existence of inequality functioned, paradoxically, to validate inequality. The wealthy proved their greater value by giving even the unworthy an equal chance to live.

With such lessons in noblesse oblige in mind, some commentators explicitly condemned those who continued to believe in conflicting class interests. According to the Boston publisher and philanthropist Edwin Ginn, the *Titanic* "should be a striking lesson to those who are constantly preaching the indifference of the rich to the condition of the poor." A former state's attorney in Maryland predicted that the "courtly gallantry of Mr. Astor as disclosed in the papers should go far toward the destruction of class hatred and establish, on firmest grounds, the world-wide brotherhood of man." A Baptist minister "spoke of the wrong done the millionaire passengers who, prior to this time, had been accused of having no feeling of sympathy or love for those less fortunate as to worldly goods." At a time when privilege was under assault by progressive reformers and the labor movement, the *Titanic* provided an opportunity to fling the rhetoric back in the faces of those who seemed to be advocating class antagonism. The antiunion *Los Angeles Times*, recently the target of a bomb attack allegedly carried out by the labor activist McNamara brothers, celebrated Butt, Astor, and other first cabin heroes for exercising the "privilege" of saving the weak, helpless, and undeserving and sacrificing their lives. "If these be some of the special privileges of the brave, the strong, the wealthy and the well-disciplined, then we pray that the day of absolute equality may be far distant that is going to rid us of so priceless a heritage."[32]

By dying for those lower than themselves in the class hierarchy, the first-cabin heroes demonstrated—again paradoxically—that class was a mirage. "Mistress and maid were as one," the *Independent* proclaimed; "the steerage women as the jeweled and guarded ladies of pampered wealth. All had the same honor and protection. The humblest woman, the most defenseless child, took place before the artist of world-wide fame, before the writer who has taught both continents, before the possessor of a hundred millions." Describing the effects of "such leveling disasters," a columnist put it more bluntly: "Going down to sea in ships makes Julia O'Grady sit right next [to] the colonel's lady in the lifeboat." The men on the *Titanic* brought home the idea of democracy in death—what the *Outlook* described as "the basic law that in the presence of death all men are on a level of humanity." "Paupers and potentates were brothers there, / Sailor and master one," mused the Bentztown Bard in a poem titled "Down to a Common Grave."

> *In that great moment of divine despair*
> *When larger manhood shone.*
> *The sabot-shodden emigrant drew round*
> *Her shoulders her poor shawl*
> *And went before those millionaires who died*
> *For her, as Christ for all.*

A Chicago minister eulogized, "They sleep tonight together, peasant and millionaire. What a democratic grave is this where its inmates are never to awake or weep!" "The rich died and the poor died alike," another minister observed, which was probably true in individual cases, though not in the aggregate. Another variation was the democracy of grief theme: "Wealth and society rubbed elbows with poverty in the crowd that besieged the steamship line officials, and both classes were in deep grief."[33] According to this myth of social consensus, there were no *real* class differences. Rich and poor men died together; rich and poor women wept together and then built memorials to the dead heroes.

Reassuring images of class harmony based on paternalism and deference alternated with unsettling counterimages. The specter of social disorder, which informed the democracy of death and grief motifs, also appeared in more direct ways—in stories of unruly behavior by "fear-stricken men" from the steerage and "grimed and frenzied" or "maddened" stokers. Washington Dodge, the millionaire financier of San Francisco, reported that there was "no panic of any description, excepting the steerage. I saw two frenzied men shot down by officers as they tried to fight their way into a lifeboat. That was the only outbreak I saw." Dodge then praised Major Butt and Colonel Astor for their heroism. A survivor from New York noted that "[e]verybody in the first and second cabin[s] behaved splendidly. The members of the crew also behaved magnificently. But some men in the third-class, presumably passengers, were shot by officers. Who these men were we do not know." Hilda Slater contrasted "touching scenes" of first-cabin men parting from their wives with the "indescribable scene" of steerage men trying "to seize one of the boats" and falling under "brisk revolver fire." A song pictured Astor, Straus, Hays, Guggenheim, Roebling, Butt, Stead, and Harris

> *Giving life to rescue others,*
> *Lab'ring hard 'mid frenzied throngs,*
> *Saving children, wives and mothers.*

All "disorderly conduct," the *New York Times* editorialized, "and there was enough to cause bloodshed, occurred among the steerage passengers. Some of the men were determined to save their own precious lives, in spite of the orders to let the women and children go first."[34]

Juxtapositions of heroism and cowardice, calm and panic, sacrifice and selfishness spilled over into other pairings of opposites: manly and unmanly, first cabin and steerage, eminent and anonymous, Anglo-Saxon and foreign. Few reports attributed panic to the circumstances of the steerage: its disadvantageous position within the ship, the smaller proportion of crew to passengers in the third cabin, the lack of information, language barriers, and perhaps less confidence in the ship's "superior" technology. Rather than be circumstantial, panic was a class, ethnic, and racial predisposition. According to the *New York Times*, "there would inevitably be men lacking courage among so many of so varied origin and training." The assistant city editor of the *New York Press*, recounting his boss's instructions for interviewing survivors, revealed that reporters expected such behavior—that they assumed different responses to the disaster based on class and ethnicity: "In getting the story of survivors and of those on the 'Carpathia' to whom the survivors told their story, find out how Astor, Stead, Straus, Millet, Harris, Butt, Futrelle, Guggenheim, and Smith died. Get every one to tell any story of heroism or cowardice he or she witnessed. Find out how the crew acted and the panic in the steerage, if there was one." A letter writer in Baltimore noted that "[f]rom reports those that gave the trouble were from other countries."[35]

While foreigners had a monopoly on panic, chivalry was an exclusively "Anglo-Saxon ideal"; adherence to the rule of the sea provided "evidence of the abiding chivalry of the Anglo-Saxon race." "Their chivalry and respect for the women and children showed that Anglo-Saxon men are made right," wrote another Baltimorean, while her fellow correspondent observed that the *Titanic* proved "the difference between men of the Anglo-Saxon race and the Latin, or any other for that matter." The *Louisville Courier-Journal* paid tribute to the men who "went down with the flags of our racehood flying," all of them "fit ambassadors of our Anglo-Saxon and Scotch-Irish stock before the Court of Heaven." Archibald Gracie, a first-cabin survivor, wrote that the "coolness, courage, and sense of duty that I . . . witnessed made me thankful to God and proud of my Anglo-Saxon race that gave this perfect and superb exhibition of self-control at this hour of severest trial." The poetic mayor of Toledo, Ohio, Brand Whitlock, described the "calm and all-sufficient answer / Of our intrepid Northern race!" to the disaster:

> *With lips*
> *Drawn tight, they look with clear, dry eyes on doom,*
> *And so confront the end, there in the night*
> *That was to have for them no pitying dawn.*
> *(Their kind alone of all intelligence*
> *Feels pity.)*

In the opinion of the *Atlanta Constitution*, the *Titanic* validated white supremacy and imperialism: "Outstanding in the Titanic disaster is the heroism that gives the lie to the croak of decay in the human race. The Anglo-Saxon may yet boast that his sons are fit to rule the earth so long as men choose death with the courage they must have displayed when the great liner crashed into the mountains of ice, and the aftermath brought its final test."[36] Wealth apparently transformed Isidor Straus and Benjamin Guggenheim into honorary Anglo-Saxons.

(In Britain George Bernard Shaw noted that the rules of romance demanded a contrast between Anglo-Saxon heroes and "foreigners, who must all be shot by stern British officers in attempting to rush the boats over the bodies of the women and children." Shaw and Arthur Conan Doyle argued in the British press over the proper response to the tragedy. Shaw perceived the *Titanic* as a "calamity which might well make the proudest man humble, and the wildest joker serious," but which instead made the British people "vainglorious, insolent and mendacious." All the talk about heroism and national honor struck him as "an explosion of romantic lying" and left him feeling "profound disgust." Conan Doyle testily answered that "we should indeed be a lost people if we did not honour courage and discipline when we see it in its highest form" and that this was more than mere chauvinism; the British, after

all, had "warmly eulogized" the "American male passengers"—especially "the much abused American millionaires"—
for their grand role "in the whole wonderful epic.")[37]

Commentators occasionally extended the sense of class and
ethnic difference into a distinction between men and animals.
Two "Chinamen" were "shot down like dogs," said one report. Another described "a frenzied mob of armed brutes."
Fifth Officer Harold Lowe recalled his impressions as his lifeboat was being lowered past the open decks: "I saw a lot of
Latin people all along the ship's rails. They were glaring more
or less like wild beasts, ready to spring." Most of these accounts
ended with the restoration of order through force, as first-cabin
heroes and the ship's officers put down the threat of dangerous workers and foreigners. "Manhood met brutehood un-
daunted, however, and honest fists faced iron bars, winning at
last the battle for death with honor."[38] Social Darwinism pulsed
through stories of combat between men and brutes, but it was
Darwinism with a curious twist. Instead of a struggle in which
the fittest survived, the disaster offered a "battle for death" in
which chivalric sacrifice for the weaker sex proved the superiority of Anglo-Saxon ruling-class men.

As Gail Bederman has shown, middle- and upper-class men
in this period defined manliness as a "white" trait. "Civilized"
men, meaning white men of the respectable classes, proclaimed
themselves more manly than those lower in the class and racial hierarchy. The coward or cowards in women's clothing
sometimes appeared as "Italian" or "Japanese," while men
suspiciously present in the lifeboats were "Italian," "Japanese,"
"Armenian," or "Filipino." Bederman also traces the process
by which the ideal of manliness, characterized by "civilized"
self-restraint and good character, was evolving into the ideal
of masculinity, characterized by "primitive" physical strength
and courage. Cultural spokesmen like Theodore Roosevelt
feared that American men were becoming manly at the ex-

pense of masculinity and urged them to find ways of combining these civilized and primitive virtues. By protecting women through both self-sacrifice and violence, the Anglo-Saxon heroes of the *Titanic* showed that they were both more manly and more masculine than the "brutes" from steerage. The conventional narrative of the disaster simultaneously bolstered gender, class, ethnic, and racial orthodoxies.[39]

Two tales in particular conveyed concerns and lessons about the violation of these orthodoxies. Jack Phillips, the *Titanic*'s wireless operator, became a hero thanks to his assistant, Harold Bride. Bride told the press how Phillips had remained at his post, alerting other ships in the area of the *Titanic*'s situation, until further transmissions were no longer possible. His efforts brought the *Carpathia* to the rescue of the survivors in the lifeboats. In Bride's telling he too had played a heroic role. Returning to the wireless cabin at one point, Bride found a man trying to steal Phillips's life belt. The first versions of the story made reference to "a stoker, or somebody from below decks, leaning over Phillips from behind." Bride struck the thief down. "I hope I finished him," he said. "I don't know." Almost immediately newspapers began embellishing Bride's account. The villain became "a grimy stoker of gigantic proportions," and Bride shot rather than hit him. In every version the stoker was mercilessly punished for his infraction. Finally, in Logan Marshall's book about the disaster, the tale assumed its full class and racial dimensions:

> An hour later, when the second wireless man came into the boxlike room to tell his companion what the situation was, he found a negro stoker creeping up behind the operator and saw him raise a knife over his head. He said afterwards—he was among those rescued—that he realized at once that the negro intended to kill the operator in order to take his life-belt from him. The second operator pulled

out his revolver and shot the negro dead.

"What was the trouble?" asked the operator.

"That negro was going to kill you and steal your life-belt," the second man replied.

"Thanks, old man," said the operator. The second man went on deck to get some more information. He was just in time to jump overboard before the Titanic went down. The wireless operator and the body of the Negro who tried to steal his belt went down together.[40]

Both literally and figuratively the stoker was a threat from below—from the lower decks, the lower class, and the lower race. Here was the specter of violence by a common laborer and a serious breach of racial etiquette, for which the punishment was swift and severe.

The second cautionary tale concerned the heroic exploits of President Taft's aide Major Butt. "There he stood on the deck of the sinking Titanic," read a typical account, "watching the lifeboats loaded and with a bravery unequalled, forcing crazy men to stand back and make room for the women and children." An accompanying cartoon showed Butt holding off shabby steerage men, presumably foreigners, with a gun. Subsequent versions changed the gun to an iron bar, but the meaning remained constant. Butt, the military hero, preserved order and kept the steerage men in their place. "Sorry," he said, "women will be attended to first, or I'll break every d——d bone in your body." The military's role in disciplining an unruly labor force was well known at the time. In the figure of Major Butt, whom Taft eulogized as a man who "never lost, under any conditions, his sense of proper regard to what he considered the respect due to constituted authority," readers witnessed military chivalry protecting women and children of all classes from the dangers of an assertive male proletariat. "With an iron bar in his hand, he is said to have stood at the steerage passage and defended the women and children from the maddened men in that part of the ship." In Elbert Hubbard's dramatic rendering Butt rescued the third-cabin women and children from their own selfish and unruly husbands and fathers: "Major Butt draws his revolver [we are now back to a gun]. He looks toward the crowded steerage. Then he puts his revolver back in his pocket, smiles. 'No, they know we will save their women and children as quickly as we will our own.'" The *Atlanta Constitution*, which spoke for the New South and its ideals of labor and race relations, called for a memorial to Butt—"an unassuming tribute to the courage and chivalry peculiar to the Anglo-Saxon, singularly peculiar to those traditions of the South which are among the most precious and fragrant inheritances that may be embalmed in the memory of a brave people." Two years later, at the dedication of the Butt Memorial Bridge in Augusta, former President Taft called his aide "the best type of the New South." In the ideology of the New South, white supremacy and a rigid caste and class system were justified as a defense of womanhood against the lusts of the lower ranks. When Archie Butt beat back the "crazy men" from down below, he acted to preserve a sacred but perpetually threatened social order.[41]

Images of a mob breaking "loose from the lower cabins" and a "fear-crazed throng" pouring up "like an overwhelming flood through the gangways" were strikingly similar to the specters of an immigrant tidal wave engulfing the United States in the early twentieth century. This version of the *Titanic* narrative offered a wish-fulfilling scenario in which the threats to traditional arrangements—feminism and suffrage, the labor movement, ethnic diversity, and demands for racial equality—were either negligible or easily suppressed. Anglo-Saxon men, declared an Episcopalian minister, were at their best in times of danger.[42] Yet there was an insistent, combative quality to the narrative that belied the assurances; the heroism was laid on too thickly. By evoking the "timeless" rules of social conduct—paternalism, noblesse oblige, deference—and by showing that these rules would be ruthlessly enforced when necessary, the disaster served to bolster a conservative conception of order and authority. Telling the story—making sense of the disaster and imparting its lessons—was itself a serious attempt to reassert authority.

Even the best efforts to establish a satisfying and coherent narrative could not eliminate uncertainty. The commercial press, not known for its modernist sensibility, had to confess that at least in this case the objective truth was elusive. While claiming to offer "A Complete Story" two weeks after the disaster, the *New York Times* felt obliged to add a qualification: "The stories varied widely and in their variances revealed how different may be the impressions received in different minds by the one occurrence. In the main features the recollections of a majority agreed. In detail they differed, one from the other, as the imagination of one who recounted them differed in quality from that of another." The *San Francisco Examiner* acknowledged that the stories were "incomplete and conflicting" but added that this did not preclude the construction of a seamless tale. "[T]hey form a wonderful human document when pieced together. . . . By combining the stories, some coherent idea is gained as to the manner in which millionaires act in the face of great emergencies and die on an equality with the other brave men of humbler class."[43]

Narrative ambiguities provided opportunities to advance competing claims of heroism. The fact that women boarded and rowed the lifeboats compelled the press to recognize "the heroism of weaker passengers." One report called the actions of the women passengers "an everlasting testimonial to the valor of the weaker sex in time of terrible stress." An account of the heroism of the rags-to-riches Denver socialite Molly

Brown seemed to make women into actors rather than the passive recipients of male protection: "Oftentimes it has been written that out of each great moment of history some man has emerged as master of the situation, some one hand and mind that has controlled where others held back. From verified statements and from circumstances explained by others the work of the women make them the central figures in the great sea tragedy." Women could, of course, be the central figures in the "women and children first" sense; they could be pedestaled as the objects of chivalric self-sacrifice. Some commentators domesticated the bravery of women passengers by distinguishing between a "quiet" female heroism and its more assertive male counterpart:

> In the clash of battle, with the elbow-touch of comrades; in the whirl of business competition with the rewards beckoning ever glitteringly—men develop heroism. Women are quiet in their heroism, persistent in their sacrifice, whether they go down into the valley of the shadow to bring children to the race; whether, alone, they fight the battle of survival with an unfriendly civilization; or whether, in other ways innumerable, they give of beauty and youth, strength and life itself, that children and husbands and fathers and brothers may live on in the sunshine.[44]

Here female heroism served to affirm sexual difference, but others assumed a more egalitarian view. One letter writer responded to the efforts of the Women's Titanic Memorial Fund by asking, "Why not, instead of having the memorial solely for the heroes of the wreck, have it also for the heroines!" Harriet Monroe, soon to be known as the editor of the modernist review *Poetry*, contributed "A Requiem" to the *Chicago Tribune* that combined conventional heroic imagery with gender inclusiveness:

Sleep softly in your ocean bed,
Ye brave who dared to die!
Your fathers, who at Shiloh bled,
Accept your company.

Ye sons of warriors, lightly rest—
Daughters of pioneers!
Heroes freeborn, who chose the best,
Not tears for you, but cheers!

Lovers of life, who life could give,
Sleep softly where ye lie!
Ours be the vigil! Help us live,
Who teach us how to die.[45]

Women occasionally made claims for their heroism at the expense of men whose class and ethnic origins were suspect. Cornelia Andrews complained that women were forced to demonstrate their physical strength because cowardly men had entered the lifeboats under the pretense that they knew how to row. "One of them was a Chinese," she felt compelled to point out. "[A]nother was an Armenian."

Yet there were also observers within the mainstream culture who realized the exclusivity of the conventional view. Some made specific demands for the recognition of the heroism of the children, second-cabin men, and engineers on board the *Titanic*. Others noted that the repeated references to a few famous names made heroism synonymous with privilege: "Naturally the survivors noticed particularly the action of the more notable of their fellow passengers who were known to them on that account, and it was of their conduct that they testified specifically, though it probably was only a fair sample of the conduct of many less conspicuous who died in the same noble company." After the initial celebration of prominent heroes had subsided, a *Washington Post* editorial suggested that "often the obscure hero is by far the greater."[46]

The same editorial offered the potentially subversive opinion that "Heroism knows no nationality." *Hearst's* magazine spoke of "a host of less known but equally heroic men of all classes of the *Titanic's* [sic] passengers and of the ship's company." The *Outlook*, which with Theodore Roosevelt on the editorial board was not immune to Anglo-Saxon boasting, observed in a sober moment: "There was no division of spiritual dignity between the classes into which the ship's company was divided; no monopoly of courage by sex or social privilege. Men and women, wealth and poverty, culture and ignorance, shared in common the peril and the courage." Everybody "played noble parts in the world drama, and impersonated neither race nor nation, neither sex nor condition, but humanity." "No race stock lacks its brave exemplars," said the *Christian Science Monitor*, "and no stratum of society is found wanting in idealists who will lose all in order to save all." The president of the Maryland Federation of Women's Clubs, soliciting contributions for the Women's Titanic Memorial Fund, said that the monument would be "a worthy remembrance of that splendid group, from the bellboy and the stoker to the army officer and capitalist, who faced death with the intrepidity which upholds our ideals and gives us fresh impetus for the life of our nation." According to an advocate of Pan-American solidarity, the women's monument should honor "those of many professions and trades" and "those of many nationalities" who perished.[47]

These voices spoke in recognition of the biases in the standard accounts of the disaster, if not the ideological purposes behind them. Conceding that "racial pride" can be "a mighty fine thing," an editorial from the multiethnic textile city of Lawrence, Massachusetts (the site of the IWW-led "Bread and Roses" strike from January to March 1912), warned that it becomes "a mighty bad thing when accompanied by racial blindness to the good qualities that belong to all races of mankind." Lawrence Beesley, the second-cabin survivor whose doubts about his own bravery we noted earlier, raised the question, "Major Butt and Col. Astor and Mr. Straus died as brave men died, but did not John Brown and Wilhelm Klein and Karl Johanssen? And yet they are not chronicled, and no newspaper has columns on their self-sacrifice and personal courage. But we know these things were true, and we can bear testimony now to every brave man who perished in the steerage, even if we knew not his name." The United Press actually did find a name—Nadji Narsani, an "Armenian peasant"—and described him as equal in heroism to Astor. A columnist for the *American* magazine went further by directly challenging the claim that "Anglo-Saxon courage" was "far superior to any other courage" and debunking the entire narrative as a retelling of "the old, old sea romance—the captain shooting himself on the bridge, the steerage in a wild panic armed with knives and being 'shot down like dogs' by the crew, the crew when not engaged in slaying the desperadoes from the steerage, either lining up with folded arms or working with machine-like regularity in lowering the boats."[48]

Skepticism, however, stood out as a rare exception in the commercial press. For every attempt to rewrite the romance, for every effort to present a more inclusive story, there were innumerable homages to the named heroes of the first class. The *Titanic* carried meanings that defined and shored up the status quo against disquieting change; in this way the conventional narrative served as a conservative critique of the incipient modern age. When it denounced uppity women, workers, blacks, and immigrants and invoked "commonsense" rules of social order, the critique defended privilege against threats both real and imagined. Still, the dominant culture contained tensions of its own, none more pronounced than the strain with which it confronted modernity. When it denounced luxury and materialism, as we shall see, it came dangerously close to subversion.

CHAPTER 3

MAMMON

℮ THE *TITANIC* CROSSED into the long career of the Reverend Dr. Charles H. Parkhurst for only a moment, but the intersection gives us another path into the meanings of the disaster. For thirty-eight years, from 1880 to 1918, Parkhurst held forth from the pulpit of the Madison Square Presbyterian Church in Manhattan—a pulpit that allowed him, as he put it in 1892, to bridge the gap "between the life of the church and the life of the times."[1] This was the concern that animated his career. A preacher of what came to be known as the Social Gospel—the application of Christianity to current social and political problems—Parkhurst contributed to the revitalization of Protestantism as a public language in the late nineteenth and early twentieth centuries. By making the Gospel current, he and his contemporaries opened up a wide range of issues and events, including the *Titanic*, to Christian interpretations.

The roots of Parkhurst's brand of Protestantism reached back into a rural New England childhood. Born in 1842, he grew up on a farm in Ashland, Massachusetts. His early training in self-discipline and piety stayed with him through Amherst College, several years as a high school teacher, a pastorate in the Berkshires, into his metropolitan ministry. "Under such conditions," he reflected, "there is very little opportunity for any kind of foolishness and no likelihood of disqualifying and debilitating luxury. It is not an elegant life, but a rigid one that calls for hard work and straight thinking."[2]

From the vantage point of New York, Parkhurst looked upon his upbringing as the antithesis of modern dissipation. Where the rural life built strong character, urban existence undermined it. Where the rural life was real, urban existence was artificial. "After one has become adult it is possible to be subjected to the artificialities of the city without serious detriment, but they make poor soil for the nurture of the *young* roots of human life." Modern civilization—enervating, artificial, bureaucratized, materialistic—attacked the integrity of the individual self. "People themselves grow to be artificial by prolonged companionship with what is not natural," Parkhurst observed. "They acquire a quality of demeanor that camouflages their original self." In place of the solid, self-disciplined, pious self of the past, modern civilization was producing a weak, unsteady, and hedonistic substitute. Like many of his contemporaries, Parkhurst phrased this contrast in terms of gender. The older self was masculine; the newer self was feminine. His parents, he recalled, respected the doctrine of separate spheres: "Father was the head of the house, the master, the court of last resort. Mother was always cooperant with him in her own sphere, where full authority was allowed her, and the spheres of operation were apportioned on the basis of sex. The line between masculine and feminine was recognized and definitely drawn; and from neither side was there any disposition to overstep that line." But modern civilization blurred the line. Far removed from the natural influences of the farm, the artificial existence of the metropolis bred effeminacy. Men needed a "thorough schooling in reality" to save them from becoming delicate and overrefined. They needed new kinds of strenuous activity to replace what had been lost in the move to the city.[3]

In his efforts to reconcile church life with real life, Parkhurst found such an activity. Between 1892 and 1894 he used his pulpit to wage war on municipal corruption involving the Tammany machine and the police. His sermons made him a public figure, an outspoken advocate of reform and muscular Christianity. "If your christianity [*sic*] is not vigorous enough to help save this country and this city," he warned, "it is not vigorous enough to do anything toward saving you. Reality is not worn out. The truth is not knock-kneed. The incisive edge of bare-bladed righteousness will still cut."[4] Parkhurst's martial rhetoric, his call for a crusade, recast Protestantism as an antidote to modern civilization. To embrace his brand of Christianity was to plunge into reality, to build character, to reclaim masculinity—to resist ease, artificiality, and weakness. Twenty years later Parkhurst's Protestantism still challenged these debilitating symptoms of modernity. He said of the *Titanic* disaster:

> The picture which presents itself before my eyes is that of the glassy, glaring eyes of the victims, staring meaninglessly at the gilded furnishings of this sunken palace of the sea; dead helplessness wrapped in priceless luxury; jewels valued in seven figures becoming the strange playthings of the queer creatures that sport in the dark depths. Everything for existence, nothing for life. Grand men, charming women, beautiful babies, all becoming horrible in the midst of the glittering splendor of a $10,000,000 casket![5]

The disaster, to Parkhurst, represented the catastrophic possibilities of the false values of modern civilization. The "sunken palace" represented the American metropolis with its facades, its unreality, its threat of meaninglessness.

Yet even Parkhurst displayed ambivalence toward what he ostensibly condemned. If the strenuous life and muscular Christianity suggested alternatives to modernity, they also indicated a form of adjustment to its values and demands. In his own quest for the strenuous life, Parkhurst explained in his autobiography, he took up mountaineering. Climbing the Matterhorn, like fighting the Tammany interests, served as the kind of real experience that the sedentary life of an urban professional conspired to deny. "I would like to encourage among young men the mountain habit," he remarked, "both because it is healthy and exhilarating." But mountaineering was a leisure activity, made possible by his congregation's "generous" allotment of vacation time. It was less an alternative to the sedentary life than a temporary escape from it, and Parkhurst's own description emphasized the therapeutic value of strenuous recreation. "When circumstances allow there is evident advantage in having a portion of the year detached from the twelve months and devoted to a distinct class of interests and activities. . . . People, like clocks, stand in need of periodic winding." His analogy of people and clocks conformed to the common image in American advertising of the body as a machine, which, through an array of commercial products, maintained its precision and efficiency. The escape into the mountains, like a healthy cereal or a good laxative, rewound the human mechanism for its return to the routine of everyday life. In a sense Parkhurst's intense two-year experience with urban reform served a similar purpose. Though he continued afterward to speak out regularly on public issues, he devoted his energies less toward saving "this country and this city" than toward expanding the bureaucratic organization of his church. He increasingly measured the success of his ministry in terms of the church's endowment and physical plant—its "wealth and volume"—and its proliferating committees. While condemning the enervating influences of modernity, he celebrated "church efficiency"—precisely the kind of modern, urban, materialistic value that he found so threatening to self and society.[6]

The same ambivalence that characterized Parkhurst's career permeated the language of Protestantism that he spoke. Thanks to Parkhurst and others, this language transcended denominations and extended beyond the churches into the culture at large. It was still available in 1912, when the *Titanic* disaster demanded an explanation, a way of making sense out of senselessness. And it still betrayed an uneasiness with modern civilization, simultaneously denouncing and making peace with it.

Does it matter whether or not the band was really playing "Nearer, My God, to Thee" in the *Titanic*'s final moments? (Experts now agree that it wasn't, though they remain at odds over what, where, and when the band did play; Walter Lord, after consulting hymnologists, believes that the band's last song wasn't a hymn at all but the popular waltz "Songe d'Automne," known as "Autumn." No reliable witnesses, he points out, remembered hearing "Nearer, My God, to Thee.")[7] Or does the significance lie in the popular belief, captured and conveyed in dozens of songs, hundreds of poems, and thousands of articles, that this is what happened? Nothing was more conventional in the conventional narrative than its ending: Christian death to the strains of a standard Protestant hymn. Whatever else it may have been, American culture in 1912 was not secular; the values associated with Protestantism—thrift, self-discipline, hard work—lingered in a tense relationship with the emerging values of corporate capitalism—consumption, self-fulfillment, leisure. Corruption, sin, and synonymous terms dominated public discourse; progress was as much a matter of anxiety and doubt as it was an article of faith. In this climate Americans derived religious messages about sin and redemption from the disaster—a "terrific and ghastly illustration of what things come to when men throw God out at the door and take a golden calf in at the window," as Parkhurst put it.[8]

Such interpretations drew on a long Protestant and republican tradition of associating luxury with moral, social, and political decay, mingled now with the concerns of progressive reformers about corruption and greed.[9] The specific context for the connection between the *Titanic* and degenerate luxury in the Progressive period was the rise of conspicuous consumption among America's ruling elites and the simultaneous burgeoning of mass consumption that threatened to blur the distinctions between luxuries and necessities.[10] In *The Theory of the Leisure Class* (1899), Thorstein Veblen had targeted precisely the "pecuniary culture" that was so well represented in the first cabin of the *Titanic*, and while Veblen may have been the most systematic critic of the consumption ethos, many others joined him in condemning these dangerous new ways.

Sermons on the Sunday following the disaster routinely treated it as a "grave warning" about "the undue passion for material welfare and mere earthly enjoyments." The *Titanic* served as a symbol of conspicuous display, and the fate of its elite clientele—the most conspicuous of consumers—provided a lesson about overvaluing comfort and self-satisfaction. "It was a huge ocean joy ride," said the Reverend James O'May of Chicago's Park Avenue Methodist Church, "and it ended where joy rides generally stop." "Our life in New York City is in a large degree marked by that same luxury which resulted in the loss of the Titanic," observed the Reverend Dr. Ernest M. Stires on the first anniversary of the sinking. "There are many warnings, but they are unheeded."[11] Wireless messages had failed to awaken the complacent to looming disaster; perhaps the tragedy would jar modern civilization into awareness of its own perilous course.

Protestantism offered a familiar moral vocabulary—and, in the jeremiad, a familiar form—for framing larger lessons about the disaster. Jeremiads were political sermons, brought to America by the Puritans, which ritualistically invoked the possibilities of decline and doom in order to promote spiritual and social renewal. The many jeremiads occasioned by the *Titanic* disaster linked conspicuous consumption to death by suggesting that the demand for luxuries was responsible for the lack of lifeboats. "The rich men" cannot give up "all the comforts and luxuries" even "for the few days of crossing the ocean," remarked a Baltimore preacher. Ministers bewailed the "sacrifice on the altars of Moloch" and the "God of Mammon," who was "master of that ship." The shipboard scene on Sunday night before the disaster "was a regular Belshazzar's feast," according to a Nashville Baptist, who completed the Old Testament analogy by describing the wireless warnings about icebergs in the vicinity as "the handwriting on the wall" that the revelers ignored. "Who Was to Blame?" asked the Methodist minister Fred Clare Baldwin in the title to a poem:

> *In part the spirit of this prideful age—*
> *Our blind, insatiate lust of luxury;*
> *Our false disdain of all simplicity;*
> *Our wild and senseless rage for speed;*
> *Our maddening haste*
> *That will not pause to reckon up the waste;*
> *Nor least of all—our gluttonous greed!*[12]

Conservative and liberal clergy—divided in theology and in their attitudes toward social reform—joined together in the attack on luxury and greed. For liberals "the thought of the fourteen or fifteen hundred lives which were sacrificed to the god of ambition, business, greed, and speed" proved the case for the Social Gospel; society needed to be saved by an activist Christianity. For conservatives the *Titanic* showed the dangers of forsaking the old ways and ignoring the state of the soul in the pursuit of worldly pleasures. The lesson was the same: The disaster exposed "the false sense of security, the commercial greed, and the demand for haste and luxury" that dominated and threatened modern America.[13]

Not just greed and self-indulgence but the hubris of a "progressive" age came in for attack. What more chastening example of the limits of technology and human intelligence could there be than the destruction of the "unsinkable" ship? What more striking metaphor for human arrogance in the face of nature and God? "Man's art came in contact with nature's gigantic forces and was naught," noted the *Christian Century*. "How suddenly, frightfully, overwhelmingly nature mocks the pride and puny strength of man," the *Christian Socialist* exclaimed. God and nature would not tolerate too great a confidence in progress and human powers. Deeper than admiration for the heroes and sympathy for the bereaved, said the *Bible Society Record*, was "an unwonted sense of the presence of God in His dread majesty—Creator, Redeemer, Judge of mankind. As in the beginning, the Spirit of God moves upon the face of the waters."[14]

The floating palace and the unsinkable ship—both mocked God. Luxury placed the material above the spiritual and created illusions about security. "If ever there was a time when the baubles of wealth were shown to be baubles, it is as we read of the richest men of earth along with the poorest, all of them swallowed up in one gulp of old ocean, regardless of their worldly holdings or their learning." Technological hubris created illusions of its own about security; the biblically enjoined mastery of nature had crossed the line into a defiance of death and a disregard for God. "There is no spot upon the face of the earth, nor [*sic*] upon the sea, where man is safe; there is no inch of surface of either land or water where he need not be prepared for death; there is no second of time throughout the seasons when he can say, 'I shall not die.' " Even if the disaster produced new safety regulations—suffering being "the price the race has always paid for progress"— no human inventions could "guard us from death." To stop building would be "foolish" and "even cowardly," but in the "soberer and more thoughtful" post-*Titanic* world, humanity would no longer allow its willfulness to obscure "the certainty of death." The purpose of the calamity was "to teach us" not to "put our whole heart into material things, or plans, or pleasures"—in short, "to number our days." Power, luxury, and security, the *Titanic* demonstrated, could dissolve "at a touch of the ice crag in the silence of the sea."[15]

Only rarely did a religious interpreter affirm progress unabashedly in the wake of the disaster. The most interesting departure from the consensus against hubris was the narrative of the fictional survivor Oscar, which focuses on a young couple named Elsie and Christian. After Christian is lost in the disaster, Elsie blames herself for urging him to travel on the *Titanic*; her obsession with participating in a transatlantic speed record, she grieves to Oscar, killed her lover. Oscar comforts her by explaining the tragedy's spiritual, perfectionist, and patriotic meanings: "The law could not prohibit the making of the record, for this is as old as the world. It lives within us and impels us toward progress and perfection." The "Breath of God," Oscar believes, "is ever renewing itself, expanding, crossing, returning, bursting into flame and becoming reincarnated in the minds of thousands of chosen beings and in the spirit of various nations." Elsie is the "incarnation" of the American "race," which "astonishes the world, and which is ever growing great and still greater by reason of its machinery, its railways, telegraphs and telephones, all of which constitute the transmitting nerves of its collective soul." The disaster is only a temporary setback on the divinely inspired path toward human and technological mastery.[16]

If, with few exceptions, the *Titanic* represented the sins of materialism and pride, was the disaster God's judgment? Here the agreement evaporated. As a lesson about greed, luxury, and arrogance, the disaster did seem to express God's displeasure. "How plain is this principle!" the *Christian Century* sermonized. "We know the end of the arrogant, the thoughtlessly pleasure-mad, the undisturbed sensualists. As they sail the sea of life we know absolutely that their ship will meet disaster."[17] But who was the object of His displeasure? The first-cabin passengers? The wealthy or "pleasure-mad" in general? The entire American public?

Only a few religious commentators were willing to identify specific targets of divine retribution. George Chalmers Richmond, a Philadelphia Episcopalian who had earlier denounced John Jacob Astor's divorce and remarriage, did not even wait for his Sunday sermon to explain God's judgment: "Mr. Astor and his crowd of New York and Newport associates have for years paid not the slightest attention to the laws of church or state which have seemed to contravene their personal pleasures or sensual delights. But you can't defy God all the time. The day of reckoning comes and comes not in our own way." The response to Richmond immediately established that such pronouncements exceeded the bounds of propriety. The *Washington Post* censured Richmond's "sensational preaching" and his "personal criticism of rich men." "Such methods merely encourage prejudice and hatred. Col. Astor died like a brave man. He showed himself a true American. He was entitled to his own opinion as to the best disposition of his money. It is not for Dr. Richmond, or any one else, to judge this man." Richmond learned a more dramatic lesson about boundaries two years later, when he stood trial before an ecclesiastical court. The ostensible charge was "conduct unbecoming a clergyman," but the real issue was his radicalism—what one of his defenders called "his views upon ecclesiastical, social, political and economic questions, and his fearless, direct and vigorous method of expressing them." After several appeals Richmond was suspended from the ministry. Rather than serve the suspension, he quit the Episcopal Church.[18]

While singling out individual sinners as emblems of a class was clearly off limits, treating the disaster as a more inclusive judgment on modern civilization was not. "To us the disaster is a judgment of God," the Greenville, South Carolina, *Baptist Courier* announced, but "not a judgment of those who suffered and perished." The idea of retribution did, however, provoke argument and dissent. Some conservative Protestant interpreters of the disaster objected to the invocation of divine judgment on the ground that it laid the blame on God. Ostensibly secular editorials and cartoons—like the one in the *New York World* that, above the caption "Reaching Out for His Prey," depicted the iceberg as a "scowling monster" raising "his clenched fists over the doomed vessel"—seemed to cross the delicate line between recognizing God's power and protesting its use. Edward J. Wheeler's editorial in *Current Literature* struck an Iowa Lutheran as "all but blasphemous" because Wheeler confessed that he felt "at first like lifting clenched hands toward high heaven in futile protest." It hardly mattered that he immediately shifted the blame from God to humanity: "Here is where we quit shaking our fists at high heaven and begin to consider our own shortcomings." In their "ravings against the Almighty," Wheeler and his ilk were preaching "a resentful despair." A Cincinnati Methodist argued that man's violation of "nature's laws" caused the wreck and that God was therefore not "at fault in this terrible catas-

trophe of the sea." It was "nothing less than sacrilegious—
yea, blasphemous—to say that an avenging God brought this
dire calamity to a world of suffering hearts."[19]

Beyond these theological disputes, America's Jeremiahs
spoke of the disaster with remarkable unanimity. Although a
Methodist editorial complained about the scarcity of references
to God in newspaper accounts of the disaster, secular voices
loudly joined the chorus condemning the sins that the wreck
had laid bare. The language of what Henry F. May has called
Progressive Patriotic Protestantism merged imperceptibly into
the language of progressive reform. Naval officers and engineers spoke out against "degenerate luxuries" in modern ships.
From Emporia, Kansas, the influential progressive journalist
William Allen White called the disaster an act of Providence
that would give the world pause before it resumed its "mad
chase after wealth and pleasure." Other journalists denounced
the "criminal folly of sacrificing safety for novelty and luxury"
and the passengers' obsession with "the fripperies of life." "The
cabins and decks were full of luxurious appointments—baths
and ballrooms, restaurants and gymnasiums and golf links—
but the davits were empty of life-saving apparatus. There was
everything for the joy of life except the adequate safeguard
against death." Marshall Everett, a hack journalist whose
Wreck and Sinking of the Titanic was one of several books rushed
out to capitalize on the disaster, lamented the "human sacri-
fices" to the "god of commercial greed" and prophesied, in
biblical language, that "[s]ome day, it is written, we shall cease
this heathen worship." Senator Isidor Rayner of Maryland
delivered a jeremiad to accompany the Senate's report on the
disaster. "We are running mad with the lust of wealth and of
power, and of ambition," he declared. "It takes a terrible warning to bring us back to our moorings and our senses. We are
abandoning the devout and simple lives of our ancestors, and
the fabric of our firesides is weakening at the foundation."[20]

Invoking the piety and simplicity of past generations was a common rhetorical strategy in the jeremiad tradition. At the very least, this kind of rhetoric implicitly challenged the presumptions of the wealthy and powerful. Even paternalism could undermine the smugness of privilege when it meant the "providential care" of a "righteous and loving Father" who "does not encourage men to think that they can find life and safety in their conquest of the forces of nature and the increase of material comfort and luxuries."[21] The vernacular of American Protestantism offered the possibility of a critique from within the conventional narrative.

Yet the attack on greed and luxury provoked by the *Titanic* disaster also suggests something about the limits of both the Protestant critique and mainstream progressive reform. Religious commentators and their secular counterparts in philanthropy, politics, and the press created a highly charged atmosphere of moral outrage that sparked the Senate investigation and produced a series of new regulations for ocean liners.[22] Moral outrage, however, turned into caution when it came to the delicate issues of class and structural reform. While the image of the "$10,000,000 casket" hinted at class disparities, the moral vocabulary of Progressive Patriotic Protestantism did not include class; its challenge to the first-cabin myth, and to the power and mystique of the ruling class, was muted and implicit rather than outspoken and direct. Most of the attacks on luxury blamed either the entire public or the White Star Line rather than the first-cabin passengers and the class they represented. The *Independent* lashed out at "[l]uxury and self-indulgence," "[w]ild extravagance, wanton waste, and bizarre display" but calmly blamed "the preferences, the working philosophy and the values which sum up the collective life of our age." "Humanity" had "sinned and must now repent and perform 'works meet for repentance' "—which meant demanding laws that would make ocean travel safer. An "impersonal thing" called "collective carelessness" was "the guilty party in this disaster." "The Public was to blame!" concluded the religious poet who had railed against the "lust for luxury" and "gluttonous greed." In the jeremiad tradition, the call to repent glossed over social conflict by reaffirming a collective identity and mission. For all their rhetorical violence, Protestantism and progressivism avoided confrontation and divisiveness by generalizing their outrage.[23]

Or, in the manner of the muckraking journalism of the period, they directed their criticism toward specific malefactors. The White Star Line and its chairman, J. Bruce Ismay, were singled out as emblems of greed, disregard for safety, and conspicuous waste. A Universalist minister described company officials as "inhuman monsters who seek to cover their moral deformity with the dazzling splendor of mammon's throne." Ismay made the perfect villain for American audiences. Not only had he put profits before safety, but he was also an Englishman, and most damning of all, he had survived the disaster. He was everything the first-cabin heroes were not: cowardly, selfish, and unmanly. As much a symbol as they were, Ismay made the disaster and the anxieties it stirred up manageable by reducing deeper conflicts to a struggle between good and bad men. The Hearst papers in particular condemned his "brutal economy" and suggested that he "must be glad he is an Englishman. He is no gladder than we are." To a Worcester preacher Ismay was "a skulking coward," while to the *Denver Post* he was "the Benedict Arnold of the Sea"— "the millionaire owner of the ship that to make big profits for him failed to protect the lives of its passengers." "Is it better to be a living Ismay or a dead Astor?" the *Post* asked rhetorically. "They were both millionaires." In Los Angeles Rev. Baker P. Lee tactfully declined "to judge" the "nameless official of the company" whom he proceeded to describe as "one of those human hogs whose animal desires swallow up all finer feelings" and "whose heart is atrophied by selfishness." The syndicated poet Walt Mason punctuated the heroism of the *Titanic* dead with the derisive refrain "and Ismay came ashore." Towns named Ismay in Texas and Montana decided to change their names but had difficulty finding replacements. The Texas town considered "Lowe" in honor of the officer who testified that he had "cursed out" Ismay. Most of the residents of the Montana town wanted to adopt the name of one of the famous *Titanic* heroes, but they did not "favor the name of Astor" and considered "Butt and Smith too insignificant a designation for a growing town like Ismay."[24]

As both the American and British inquiries determined, Ismay and White Star were responsible for the dangerous conditions that produced the huge loss of life. But focusing on particular malefactors was what allowed the conventional narrative to reconcile the attack on luxury with the celebration of first-cabin heroism. The *Titanic* revealed the distinction between heroes and villains, saints and sinners, not the disparities of class. An editorial entitled "The Lost and the Saved" blessed "the memory of those who, for the sake of others, were swallowed up in great waters" and condemned those who were "the objects of the wrath that is rising against every person responsible for this colossal tragedy." The *Denver Post*'s choice of covillains in the disaster suggests the boundaries of permissible discourse in the mainstream culture. "Next to J. Bruce Ismay, the meanest man developed by the Titanic disaster is George C. Richmond, the minister, who disgraced his calling by saying the wreck of the Titanic was a judgem[e]nt sent by God to punish Astor. Infinitely better to be a dead Astor, who voluntarily died that others might live, than a coward like Ismay or a defamer of the heroic dead like Richmond." To criticize the first-cabin passengers or offer an indictment of the ruling class as a whole was off limits, even in newspapers

that appealed to a working-class readership. The level of vitu-
peration against Ismay and the White Star Line was higher in
the "sensationalist" press than in the more staid and conservative papers, but the myth of first-cabin heroism obtained regardless of the class basis of the intended audience.[25]

When progressives made the connection between the first-
cabin passengers and social injustice, they usually treated injustice as a matter of ignorance or misunderstanding rather
than of class and power. A widely reprinted essay by Louis F.
Post, later assistant secretary of labor under Woodrow Wilson, linked "the beneficiaries of privilege" who remained so
"selfishly indifferent to the heartsickening perennial tragedies
of our industrial life" to "those of their own class who went
down with the 'Titanic.'" The "children of privilege" on "that
doomed vessel" showed themselves "as democratic and as brave
as any" and thus proved that what the privileged in general
lacked was "not democracy but imagination." Again in the
muckraking spirit, the key to reform was exposure and information:

> Let the privileged see the industrial tragedies they thrive
> upon, make them realize the tragical cost of their selfish
> luxury, and their icy greed will melt in the heat of their
> democracy. Real as their selfishness is, truly as it helps to
> make poverty and crime, it is no more basic or controlling
> with their class than with any other. Let their imaginations
> be fired, and they will feel their brotherhood and think of
> its responsibilities.[26]

And in the spirit of the Social Gospel, the lesson wasn't finally about class but about "brotherhood." The disaster's
"whole purpose," said the Reverend Price Alexander Crow,
"will prove humanitarian and Christlike." Its "promise and
prophecy" lay in the direction of kinship and harmony, not

difference and conflict.[27] To derive lessons from the gross disparity in survival rates about the depth of class differences and the reality of class conflict would have been to betray the serene and optimistic, if ultimately evasive, visions of social Christianity and mainstream progressive reform. The myth of first-cabin heroism allowed both conservatives and progressives to maintain their faith in an orderly, manageable, and peaceful society.

In both senses of the word, the conventional narrative *contained* tensions and anxieties. It *included* them, as the rhetoric about luxury suggests, by raising doubts about modern civilization. And it *controlled* them by resolving, at least in part, the same doubts it raised.

The transformation of American society around the turn of the century can be summarized in a number of ways. Warren Susman has described it as "a change from a producer to a consumer society, an order of economic accumulation to one of disaccumulation, industrial capitalism to finance capitalism, scarcity to abundance, disorganization to high organization." With the material changes came the shift in values that so disturbed Parkhurst—a shift that Susman and other cultural historians have represented with the terms "character" and "personality." Character was the model for the self that Parkhurst associated with the small-scale rural society of his childhood; character meant duty, work, morality, integrity, and manhood. Personality, on the other hand, was a model for getting along and getting ahead in a corporate, urban society; the key to personality wasn't duty or integrity but attractiveness and fascination.[28]

The *Titanic*'s first-cabin passengers were the personalities of the period; they were fixtures on the society pages, their exploits the stuff of spectacle, gossip, and "news."[29] They were famous for wealth, conspicuous expenditure, and fame itself rather than character and its attendant virtues. Mainstream interpreters of the disaster, in their discomfort with the values of a consumer society, insisted on recasting the passengers' images in traditional terms. Being merely rich, fascinating, and extravagant was an unacceptible criterion for celebrity. One also had to display character, which, according to the myth, was precisely what the first-cabin heroes did on board the *Titanic*. In this sense the myth raised doubts about the consumer culture; in this sense, too, it mediated between older and newer value systems and helped ease the transition into modernity.[30]

Since manliness and character were synonymous, the disaster was seen as a transformative moment in which luxury and effeminacy were simultaneously stripped away and the "true" nature of things was restored. "[T]hat rich, rushing, gay, floating world," with all its softness and sumptuousness, wrote a *Harper's* reporter, "suddenly shattered" when the iceberg tore open the ship. The feminine world of play and frills catastrophically gave way to a masculine world of seriousness, strength, and authentic experience. As in many antimodernist narratives, especially those of martial glory and the strenuous life, the moment of truth was violent and painful, but it was also welcome.[31] The *Titanic* destroyed veneers, brought men back to elemental reality, showed in the face of death how life ought to be lived.

It also demonstrated the compatibility of Christianity and masculinity. Thomas H. Mulvey prefaced his song "Just Whisper the Message" with the joyous news that the disaster had "route[d] those who say that Manliness and Godliness have become a negative quality." This linking of manliness and godliness was part of a broader cultural movement by and for men to reclaim Protestantism from women, who had played a dominant role in the churches throughout the nineteenth century. Reclaiming Protestantism, as Gail Bederman has argued, was a way for middle-class American men to reassert "their cultural dominance" generally. The disaster occurred at the height of the Men and Religion Forward Movement—William T. Stead, the British journalist and spiritualist, died on the way to address an M&RFM convention—which directly promoted the kind of muscular Christianity that the first-cabin men were said to display. As Mulvey put it, the *Titanic* heroes revealed that "in spite of our apparently frivolous ways, our moral and physical courage, our Godliness[,] is as virile, as ever in the history of humanity." Archibald Gracie testified to his own virile godliness when he recalled how with "God-given physical strength and courage" he had powered himself to safety. Thanking his "Maker" for his "Providential deliverance," Gracie boasted that he knew of no more splendid example of "the efficacy of prayer" and no greater proof of the Christian Darwinian adage "God helps those who help themselves."[32]

As a Christian narrative the disaster superimposed "masculine" images of courage onto "feminine" images of submission and thus contributed to the masculinization of American Protestantism. Americans should pay "reverend devotion to those brave men," exhorted an Episcopalian minister. "For there were not scenes of wild despair and hopeless panic. There were not the brutal struggles of those that believe with death all things end. Everywhere were prayers offered. The last thought of everyone was of God." The heroes met death with "unflinching courage, with the calmness of perfect submission, and hope inspired by faith." To Edward S. Reaves, a Baptist preacher in Honea Path, South Carolina, "the nobility of the brave men who faced death calmly while helping others" represented a specifically Christian kind of heroism. They were "martyr souls," animated by "courage, unselfishness and Christian fortitude." "Such a spirit of self-sacrifice as was manifested on board the Titanic that awful night could have been possible only among Christian people," remarked the *Baptist and*

Reflector, while an Iowa Lutheran linked Protestantism, Anglo-Saxonism, manliness, and civilization in paying homage to the heroes: "Evidently Anglo Saxon civilization, under the influence of Protestant Christianity, has developed a different fibre from that of Latin civilization." Racial superiority, patriarchy, and Protestantism went hand in hand. The *Christian Science Monitor* discovered in the heroism of the passengers and crew evidence that the morality of Christianity had triumphed over modern self-aggrandizement. "[T]he race is better today than it was, because it has stood off and viewed itself objectively as it were, and found itself not lacking in serenity, courage and self-sacrifice when a crisis comes and the gospels of Jesus and Nietzsche clash." Bishop Alfred Harding told a congregation that included President Taft, Secretary of War Henry Stimson, and the British ambassador Lord Bryce that the memory of the dead heroes "lives in thousands of Christian hearts. It is the memory of noble lives, cheerfully given in the service of the Master." After Harding's sermon the congregation sang "Nearer, My God, to Thee."[33]

Christian self-sacrifice indicated character—a core of convictions, a belief in more than pleasure and self-fulfillment. Conspicuous consumption had not eradicated the nineteenth-century virtues, which revealed themselves in times of crisis. An Atlanta minister who spoke of "the worthless women and children of the steerage" explained that character determined status in death and suggested too that class determined character: "A multi-millionaire and a man from the steerage stand side by side. Each has an equal place and chance, and yet they are not equal. Cowards and heroes are there. The issue of the hour reveals them. The trappings of life are swept away— men are equal, character abides, men are unequal. Thus they meet God."[34]

At such times, moreover, redemption was possible. "There stood upon her decks men who until their last moment had never known a spiritual thought," said the Reverend Dr. Hugh Birckhead, "but the call from God came to them out of the sky, and they were glorified in death." Katharine Lee Bates, the Wellesley College English professor who wrote "America the Beautiful" after a trip to Pikes Peak in 1893, asked and answered the question of whether in saving others, the *Titanic* heroes had saved themselves:

Did gleams and dreams half-heeded, while the days so lightly ran,
Awaken the glory seeded from God in the soul of man?
For touched with a shining chrism, with love's fine grace
   imbued,
Men turned them to heroism as it were but habitude.

(The little-known second stanza of "America the Beautiful" calls on the nation, through God, to exhibit character: "America! America! / God mend thy every flaw, / Confirm thy soul in self-control, / Thy liberty in law!") The *Western Christian Advocate* praised God "that in that supreme hour nobility of character arose to the surface with stalwart assertiveness."[35]

Religious interpreters noted the fact that the disaster gave the heroes just enough time to perform good works and rediscover their faith. They "knew that their hour had come" and that they had to hurry "to make their peace with God!" A Mennonite editorial created a tableau in which, amid the playing and singing of hymns, the "spirit of God had time to work on and prepare many to meet their Maker, who perhaps would have gone on in the mad race for gain, pleasure or fame." At the moment of death "there was the revelation of character," sacrifice redeemed sin, men "by their acts and deeds followed in the footsteps of HIM who suffered on the cross." The poet H. Rea Woodman was not alone in imagining what followed death:

Oh noble pain! Oh sacrifice
That level stands with God,
And in the weary, waiting dark
Shrinks not beneath His rod;
That stands before the Final Gate,
Patient, exalted, free,
And proves for every age and time
What love and death may be.[36]

Personality, Woodman's poem suggested, was false and fleeting. Character—"noble pain," godlike "sacrifice"—existed beyond "age and time," outside history, immune to change.

Was the point of these redemptive tales that the greedy and hedonistic were good Christians and responsible citizens after all? On one level they did mythologize elites and blunt class antagonisms. Forgiven now were Butt's foppish swagger and Astor's romantic entanglements, previously the subjects of society page gossip; both had proved themselves strong men of Christian character. Once "written down as a man without principle and with little character," Astor became for the *Religious Telescope* a reminder that "there is a slumbering nobility in the heart of every man which but awaits the supreme occasion to be called forth." "Men who were misunderstood are at last known for what they are. Men who were held in light esteem now bear upon us their very virility and moral weight. Men who had gone astray come back to the high path of honor at the last. And over it all the light of a human love which was yet divine shed a benediction that even death cannot destroy." A poem dedicated to Butt in the *Washington Post* even managed to elide the differences between redeemed and Redeemer in its sanctification of the first-cabin heroes. "For, like the Christ," went the last line, "they died for men."[37] In these ways the redemption theme fostered a kind of ruling-class mystique.

Among reformers and religious commentators, however, the *Titanic* served first and foremost as a vindication of reform and religion, not as an apology for corporate capitalism. "As we believe that they have acted when the ship was wounded to death," said the reformer Edward T. Devine, "so it is for us to act for the saving of lives, for the protection of the weak, for the rescue of the lost." Not only did the heroism of men "who at home were accustomed to have what they wished" demonstrate that "there is still good fiber in all classes," but according to a Quaker writer, their sacrifice conveyed the more important lesson that "there never was a more widely prevalent faith in God than there is now." The disaster, exulted the *Congregationalist and Christian World*, "honored and vindicated" religion. "This catastrophe at sea has not fostered atheism but theism" by showing "how inane and fruitless" was "the life in which luxury, ease and the appliances that minister only to the body are the principal elements" compared with the life of "duty, honor, service, sacrifice."[38]

Without sin there would have been no need for redemption, and until the transformative moment, many songs, sermons, and Protestant editorials pointed out, the heroes had been reprobates. W. B. Glisson's song ("for male quartet") condemned the passengers for being "out on the holy Sabbath" but concluded with their prayers, Jesus' forgiveness, and their safe passage "to eternity." In a Christian Socialist tableau the " 'emancipated' passengers," when the ship first struck the iceberg, may have "smiled with ill-concealed scorn at the peasant girl telling her beads, or scoffed in open anger at the prophet crying out for social righteousness. But in the last grim moments they were there with all the rest, peasant and millionaire, on their knees, with hands upraised and agonized face uplifted, singing 'Nearer, My God, to Thee.' " The lesson here wasn't about the benevolence of wealth; the lesson was that souls needed saving and that religion "is not dead." Through an extended *Titanic* metaphor, a Mississippi Baptist editorial made the case for renewed evangelical zeal: "The wireless call for help has come from hundreds of millions of men and women going down in the night from the sinking craft of false religion and no religion to the bottomless abyss of despair!" *Titanic* disasters "happen in God's world," said a Pittsburgh Methodist, not to gloss over greed but for "the moral and religious education of men."[39] If Progressive Patriotic Protestantism shied away from any sustained critique of corporate capitalism, it did not endorse the modern order unreservedly. Representing the first-cabin passengers as, in their final hour, men of Christian character made modernity more palatable by demonstrating the durability of older values.

When the Senate issued its report, the aged Isidor Rayner stirred the galleries to applause with his eloquent and impassioned words about the disaster's "lesson" and "moral." Warning that modern Americans were "defying the ordinances of God," Rayner attacked corporate monopolies and bemoaned the growing gap between the rich and poor. Then, having directly linked corporate capitalism, class inequities, and godlessness, he brought the disaster, the speech, and the critique to a glorious resolution by vividly describing "the sublime pathos of that awful hour." The band struck up "Nearer, My God, to Thee"; the victims stood "[a]lmost face to face with their Creator" and sang in unison. "As the sea closed upon the heroic dead, let us feel that the heavens opened to the lives that were prepared to enter." All was forgiven, all were redeemed, Rayner concluded. Unity and godliness prevailed. Yet the disaster remained "an admonition to the Nation," and its heroes would have died in vain if the "awe-inspiring" hymn, with its joyous return to God, failed to "reverberate" throughout the land.[40]

Nowhere are the tensions of the redemption theme more evident than in the Bentztown Bard's "Redeemed!," a poem that simultaneously castigated the ruling class for its past sins and celebrated it for its heroism on the *Titanic*. Nowhere too is there a clearer illustration of the pervasiveness of Protestantism as a public language than here, in a piece of verse in the *Baltimore Sun*:

> *They stand redeemed! They are not what we said.*
> *Or felt, or thought; they are the kingly dead.*
> *Who turned heroic after years of sloth*
> *To save the weak. No longer need we loath [sic]*
> *These rich whom slander oft has smeared with muck—*
> *God tested them, and there they proved their pluck. . . .*
>
> *With all their wealth they gave what few would give—*
> *Gave life and love and hope in the stern deed*
> *Sealed by Christ's love and deathless as His creed!*

While the poem—and similar claims that "[h]enceforth the world will speak somewhat more gently the phrase 'American millionaire' "—served purposes of legitimation, it did so in ways that denounced conspicuous waste and social irresponsibility. "Redeemed!" explicitly juxtaposed modern and traditional value systems: sloth and selfishness versus manhood and sacrifice. The poem's Protestant rhetoric functioned as both a critique and an apology. It contained tensions and anxieties by revealing them (there had been reason to "loath / These rich") and reconciling them ("They are not what we said. / Or felt, or thought"). The rhetorical strategy—of the poem and the conventional narrative as a whole—was to prove that the doubts and fears it invoked were ultimately groundless.[41]

Part Christian conversion narrative and part knightly adventure story, the conventional version of the disaster provided closure by showing how the ruling class redeemed itself when put to the test and, more broadly, how modernity was traditional after all. "When the twentieth century is called material, commonplace, sordid," said the Reverend R. L. McCready of Louisville, "we only have to point to the decks of the sinking Titanic and, behold, all the ages of the past have never surpassed its achievements of heroism and chivalry." By ending the story with redemption, the narrative contributed to what Christopher Lasch called "the moral and intellectual rehabilitation of the ruling class." American elites have traditionally seen themselves not as idle and leisured—Veblen didn't notice that the objects of his criticism also considered "leisure class" a term of opprobrium—but as vital and productive. The disaster evoked images of wastefulness and luxury only to counter them with pictures of active heroism and sacrifice.[42] But narrative closure could not fully resolve the tensions that revealed themselves along the way. The United States in 1912 was a modernizing society in which a secular ethos of materialism and consumption existed uneasily alongside Christian ideals of sacrifice and Victorian values of honor and chivalry. Those who felt this uneasiness tried to find in the *Titanic* disaster comforting signs of stability and reconciliation.

A Noble Structure of Enduring Stone

I HAVE AN ambivalent relationship with the Harry Elkins Widener Library at Harvard, which I find both forbidding and inviting. The stacks smell of mildewing books. The light, inadequate yet harsh, bears at least some responsibility for the gradual thickening of my lenses. I refuse to ride the elevators on Friday afternoons for fear that I'll be entombed for the weekend; they jolt and wheeze as if about to break down for good. Every ten minutes or so, sitting at a carrel, I am jarred by the sound of a mysterious explosion from deep within the library's bowels, somewhere below the dreaded D level. The torturous chairs have permanently wrenched my back. In the summer the heat dulls my mind. Sometimes I fall asleep and wake up with my face glued to the desk.

Of course there are millions of books, dozens of them about the *Titanic* disaster. On A and B levels there are periodicals in astonishing variety, and, through the tunnels, newspapers on microfilm—an underground mine of Titanica. I wouldn't be writing this book without the resources buried in Widener's crevices.

Like most visitors, I first experienced Widener Library as a tourist, which means I saw only the grand architecture of the public spaces and missed the functionalism of the stacks. Later this way of looking became reversed: I saw the stacks and missed the public spaces. Recently I've had reason to try to return to the original vantage point. Widener Library, for all its uses and meanings, is by name, design, and first impressions a *Titanic* memorial.

To recapture my sense of the building as a memorial, I hovered at the edges of the tour groups in Harvard Yard and listened to the guides talk about Harry and the *Titanic*. Some mentioned his chivalry in loading the lifeboats. All repeated the Harvard legend that undergraduates once had to pass a swimming test because Eleanor Elkins Widener stipulated so in her gift, though there is no evidence of such a stipulation. How could a survivor of the disaster have thought that being a good swimmer mattered in twenty-eight-degree water with the rescue ship *Carpathia* hours away?

Finally I slipped off, up the broad stone steps, past the massive columns, through the elaborate wrought-iron doors, and into the pink marble vestibule. I immediately encountered the *Titanic* on the tablet to the left:

HARRY ELKINS WIDENER

A GRADUATE OF

THIS UNIVERSITY

BORN JANUARY 3, 1885

DIED AT SEA APRIL 15, 1912

UPON THE FOUNDERING

OF THE STEAMSHIP

TITANIC

At the other end a matching tablet explains that the library

was "erected in loving memory" of Harry "by his mother."
From there I moved into the colonnaded hall, fifty feet long,
its walls lined with gold-gray marble. A staircase of the same
marble leads directly to the Widener Memorial rooms. I
strained not to be diverted by John Singer Sargent's murals,
added after the First World War. Through the entryway I
saw Harry's framed face in the distance and stepped into the
first of the memorial rooms—an octagonal hall of white
marble, a place to become contemplative and composed. I
circled the walls, gazed out the windows, and then crossed the
next threshold, into Harry Widener's library, paneled in dark
oak, his rare books encased along the walls and his portrait
centered above the fireplace. A guard gave me the once-over.
This was not the Widener Library of stacks and carrels. This
was a sacred place where I was supposed to pay quiet homage
to a *Titanic* hero, or at least refrain from touching his books.[1]

The most common way of dealing with the *Titanic* disaster—
of moving beyond grief and avoiding a sense of meaninglessness—was to point to the good that had come out of it. Usually
this good took the form of lessons about heroism, manliness,
and a revitalized Christianity. Harvard celebrated its own
Titanic heroes—Astor, the painter Francis Millet, and Harry
Widener—by following the conventional path from
"[s]orrow for their loss" to "glory that Harvard still has sons
who can die as well as live like noblemen." For the university
administration the good of the disaster took a much more tangible form. Harvard's library, Gore Hall, had been inadequate
to the needs of the expanding university for years. The director of the university library, Archibald Cary Coolidge, was
especially concerned about finding a solution to the pressing
problem of space. In May 1911 the *Boston American*, a Hearst
paper, printed a mock advertisement that played on Harvard's
frustrated ambitions: "WANTED—A MILLIONAIRE. Will some

kind millionaire please give Harvard University a library building? Tainted money not barred. Mr. Rockefeller, take notice. Mr. Carnegie, please write." The paper then created a scenario in which Harvard's president, A. Lawrence Lowell, connived with a press agent to issue an invitation:

> DO YOU KNOW YOU ARE GOING TO DIE?
> Well, you are. And do you want your name to go down into history as the man who got rich by selling Snoofer's Soap or Giggler's Ginger Ale?
> Of course you don't. Well here's a chance to get right with posterity.
> GIVE HARVARD A LIBRARY.
> Think of a beautiful marble building situated among the green trees in Harvard Yard, bearing over the door:
> GIVEN BY JAMES WHIFFLETREE SNOOFER.

The Widener and Elkins families had gotten rich not by selling soap or ginger ale but through street railways and real estate, mainly in Philadelphia. Harry Widener had stood to inherit part of a fortune estimated at seventy-five million dollars.[2]

By the time of the disaster a committee of architects had developed a plan for a new library to be built at an estimated cost of two million dollars, if a donor could be found. Lowell, through J. P. Morgan, tried to get Andrew Carnegie interested, and while some Harvard officials were squeamish about having a Carnegie Library on campus—Harvard was "too dignified" for it—Lowell recognized that there was no avoiding tainted money in the new era of philanthropy. The committee's Beaux Arts design, with its massiveness and symmetry, offered monumentality with nothing more particular to monumentalize than the aspirations of the modern university. Carnegie had already declined the invitation when the *Titanic* sank, Harry Widener left his rare book collection to Harvard, and his mother decided to fund a place to house it.[3]

Through delicate negotiation, Coolidge and Lowell convinced Eleanor Widener that the most eloquent tribute to Harry would be an entire library rather than a rare book wing, though to do so, they had to agree to her choice of architects. Horace Trumbauer had made his name and fortune by knowing that "only a magnificent setting could hope to satisfy an American with a magnificent income," and he had already imparted such magnificence to the Widener and Elkins mansions and an assortment of other palaces near Philadelphia and in Newport. Trumbauer did not stray far from the architects' committee's plans; the major revision, of course, was to replace the central circulation room with the Widener Memorial Rooms. But he also knew who his client was, so he gave elaborate attention to memorializing Harry in style. "Where the College could have spared expense," one critic has observed, "Trumbauer was lavish[;] where the Library needed essential conveniences, Trumbauer cut." Elevators, heating, lighting, shelving, and book delivery systems bore the brunt of his economizing, while the installations of marble in the memorial rooms went ahead as planned.[4]

Eleanor Widener, well aware that her gift was news, made certain that there was no doubt about its source and purpose. Whatever she thought of her late husband, also a victim of the disaster, it is clear that she resented being thought of as an appendage of his family and that she viewed the gift as *her* gesture. "In regard to the Press—," she wrote Lowell, "please use your own judgment—the only thing I would want emphasized is, that the library is a memorial to my dear son & be known as the 'Harry Elkins Widener Memorial Library' & given by me & not his Grandfather as has been so often stated." Wealth entitled her to take a subtle but forceful stand against patriarchy. In the struggle with her father-in-law, who had been credited for the gift in early reports, she emerged victorious. The *Dial* honored "the generosity of Mrs. George D. Widener of Philadelphia, mother of the late Henry [*sic*] E. Widener who with his father went down in the sinking of the Titanic" and noted that she "will make the long-needed building a worthy memorial to her son by expending two million dollars, if necessary, in its erection." Other reports recognized that the library was "entirely the gift of Mrs. George D. Widener" and that it would "perpetuate the memory of her son," "one of the heroic victims of the Titanic disaster" and "a loyal and generous son of Harvard." She was, of course, always described as the wife of George Widener, the daughter of the late William Elkins, the daughter-in-law of P. A. B. Widener, and "the mother of the young bibliophile who was lost in the sinking of the Titanic," but her major demand—that the act of giving be seen as hers—was respected. In addition to asserting control over the publicity surrounding the donation, she insisted on the validity of what Lowell called her "decided architectural opinions."[5]

Eleanor Widener's agreement with Harvard established the library as "a perpetual memorial" to her son and thus to the *Titanic*. To the irritation of Coolidge, who really just wanted a new library, she showed a pronounced interest in ceremonial events that repeatedly brought attention to the memorializing function of the building. She was ill, unfortunately, on the day of the groundbreaking in February 1913, but her son George wielded the shovel in her absence. One of Coolidge's colleagues described this as a "rather foolish ceremony." To soften the ground, it had been necessary to keep a bonfire burning for two days, while a tent shielded the spot from snow. Trumbauer made his presence known by "jollying the newspapermen and posing for their cameras." The cornerstone was laid on Phi Beta Kappa Day in June, with Eleanor Widener handling the trowel and Coolidge making the speech, the prospect of which, he had privately confessed, bored him "beyond words." Duty called, however, and he rose to the occasion, expressing "deep gratitude" while acknowledging that "our good fortune" had come "under the shadow of an appalling calamity." This "great monument," he intoned, would "commemorate a son of Harvard, who while still in his earliest manhood met a hero's end in one of the most touching tragedies of modern times." After a short strike based on a dispute over union affiliations between the exterior stone setters and the interior marble workers, work proceeded on schedule. Coolidge, mollified as the building neared completion, enthusiastically agreed to honor Eleanor Widener's wish to dedicate the library on Commencement Day, 1915. The occasion, he said, "should have as much éclat as possible."[6]

The monument that was unveiled on June 24 embodied the related, and ultimately conflated, themes of wealth and culture. "Conspicuous consumption of valuable goods," Thorstein Veblen had written at the turn of the century, "is a means of reputability to the gentleman of leisure." Harry Widener had made book collecting the object of his leisure—uninterrupted since he never had to work—so that by the time of his death he owned "the finest library ever gathered together by so young an American." In eulogizing him, the *Literary Digest* observed that he "numbered few peers among those of his age and large possessions." The Widener Memorial offered a public display of these possessions while reinforcing the private character of the wealth that purchased them. "His library was his bedroom," the *New York Times* remarked at the time that his bequest was announced, "and his waking gaze fell on his cherished companion." It would have been inappropriate to reconstruct Harry's bedroom, but the memorial did manage to convey the sense that visitors were entering an inner sanctum. "The portrait, books, flowers, and furnishings," wrote an early tourist, "reflect an atmosphere of realism[,] and it would seem that Harry Widener still lived among his books."[7] With its dark wood paneling, its glass cases, and Widener's gentle figure looking down from over the fireplace, the second of the memorial rooms unmistakably represented a gentleman's library—something, perhaps, from one of Trumbauer's Newport mansions. The books were there to be seen rather than used, and visitors received the impression that their presence was, if not an intrusion, an indulgence at the very least. But the library and the books *were* there to be seen; "reputability" required them to be both conspicuous and inaccessible. The room's semipublic display of rare acquisitions, its simultaneous creation and bridging of social distance, gave it its "private" (both personal and exclusive) character.

In Veblen's view the ruling-class mystique was rooted in the distinction between productive and unproductive activity. Through conspicuous consumption, Veblen argued, the leisure class brought attention to the fact that its members did not have to work. They consumed, in other words, rather than produced. As a book collector Widener embodied Veblen's distinction; collecting represented acquisition, not use. When the *Literary Digest* noted that "[i]t is counted one of the distinguished uses of large wealth to gather together the rarities among the world's printed books," it defined use *as* acquisition.[8]

Yet neither the eulogies for Widener nor the library celebrated leisure and consumption unambiguously. Veblen himself suggested that the leisure class, under the countervailing pressure to appear useful, engaged in "make-believe" productive activities, often of a "quasi-artistic or quasi-scholarly" nature. Widener, after all, collected *books*, which made him a man of culture. His library, said the *New York Times*, reflected "the knowledge, discrimination, and enthusiasm that formed it"—character, in a word—and so did the memorial. The most widely circulated story about Widener's death described how he had purchased an extremely rare 1598 edition of Bacon's essays in London and how he had "prized the volume so highly that he carried it in his pocket" on board the *Titanic*. He had even joked with the bookdealer that "if he was lost at sea the Bacon would go down clasped to his heart." (One of the tour guides told us that Harry's was the *only* copy of Bacon's essays. He had been about to board a lifeboat but scurried back below deck to retrieve the book and thus went down with the ship.) This was no dilettante; this was a young man who had died for great literature. "There was a certain poetic fitness in this association of books and collector even in death," noted the *Boston Herald*, "[f]or Harry Elkins Widener lived with his books as few men have ever done." Widener was no "mere spendthrift." His wealth did not lead him to sacrifice "his judgment of values." As one eulogist put it, he was "a man of almost unlimited means" who nonetheless knew "that the way to be happy" was "to have an occupation." A member of Veblen's leisure class, Widener acquired books as a kind of civilized duty rather than as self-indulgence. In the classic nineteenth-century language of culture and character, Widener possessed "rare judgment and an instinct for discovering the best."[9]

Thus the memorial couched what Veblen called "pecuniary" values in terms of older virtues—duty, knowledge, discrimination, stewardship, the appreciation of literature as uplifting and ennobling. Not only would Harvard students "have constantly before them a reminder of that noble company of men who from the decks of the *Titanic* looked death in the face without flinching and without thought of themselves," but they and the public would have a "noble structure of enduring stone" where students and visitors could, in a poet's words, "with the greatest thoughts of men commune!" By conflating wealth and consumption with culture and character, the monument offered a secular version of the religious theme of redemption, similarly fraught with inner tensions. As long as leisure was useful and ruling-class lives retained the trappings of virtue that luxury threatened, Harry Widener's memorial could stand as a testament to the permanence of values that the emerging ethic of consumerism was calling into doubt:

> *No useless monument is this we find*
> *To one who was beloved of many men:*
> *No empty tombstone where some denizen*
> *Of sandy earth may live and thrive confined:*
> *It is a palace beautiful where mind*
> *And heart alike exalted are. How long*
> *Will it protect the lyric lines of song*
> *And what the sage to every heart would bind!*
> *From age to age the youths throughout this land*
> *Will here delight themselves in Fancy's clime:*
> *From age to age before the picture stand*
> *Of him who died before he reached the prime*
> *Of his fair manhood—"Though we knew him not,*
> *A love for him is surely here begot."*[10]

The "palace beautiful" upheld moral and aesthetic standards, a genteel model of cultivated manhood, and idealism over materialism, acquisitiveness, and personal gratification. Ironically, the modern vices had laid the foundation for the timeless virtues.

At the dedication of the library on Commencement Day in 1915, Senator Henry Cabot Lodge spoke to these lessons in permanence. Widener was "the benefactor and the exemplar of a great host"—those "who have deep in their hearts the abiding love of books and literature" and who resist the "vast torrent of the ephemeral and the valueless." Following Matthew Arnold's definition of culture, Lodge distinguished between this love of literature for its uplifting qualities and the immorality of the mere collector:

> [T]rue lovers of books are a goodly company one and all. No one is excluded except he who heaps up volumes of large cost with no love in his heart, but only a cold desire to gratify a whim of fashion, or those others who deal in the books of the past as if they were postage stamps or bric-a-brac, as if they were soulless, senseless things, who speculate in them, build up artificial prices for great authors and small alike, and make the articles in which they traffic mere subjects of greed while they trade on the human weakness for the unique, even when the unique is destitute of any other value.

Conspicuous consumption, especially in the sacred sphere of literature, was still sinful. Though Lodge characterized Widener as a benefactor and exemplar, his speech suggested a less noble possibility and captured the ambivalence of the memorial itself: emblem of a civilization endangered by the modern vices of whim, fashion, speculation, and greed—all so much in evidence on board the *Titanic*.

As an attempt to shape the memory of the disaster, the library represented its first-cabin hero in terms of "enduring" values; Widener and the building that bore his name stood as custodians of culture. By the time of the dedication a more significant world event had entered the speakers' consciousness as a threat to the old order. Lodge ended his speech by pointing out the library's importance "just now," with the Great War raging in Europe, "when freedom of speech, and freedom of thought, when liberty and democracy are in jeopardy every hour." In this context the memorial was transformed into what President Lowell called "an arsenal of humane civilization," and Harry Widener became one of the first American war heroes— a young man who had given his life carrying civilization across the ocean into the arms of its new protector.[11]

Chapter 4

Unknown and Unsung

○○ Not long after the disaster Alma White, founder of the Pillar of Fire sect, leader of its model community Zarephath in New Jersey, and later a member of Alice Paul's National Woman's party and a supporter of both the Equal Rights Amendment and the Ku Klux Klan, wrote what may still be the strangest book about the *Titanic*. *The Titanic Tragedy—God Speaking to the Nations* was a patchwork of journalistic accounts of the wreck, biblical exegesis (specifically the story of Daniel and Nebuchadnezzar), anti-British and anti-Catholic diatribes, and an outraged puritanical travelogue of New York City. "In this volume," White summarized, "we have tried to impress upon our readers that there is a more serious and comprehensive side to this greatest of all marine disasters than the nations have yet conceived. IT IS GOD'S HANDWRITING ON THE WALL, foretelling the doom of those who are given to greed and pleasure in a world cursed by sin." The book described "the sinful indulgences upon the ship"—the profanation of the Sabbath by dancing, game playing, and other amusements among the first-cabin passengers—which "were enough to provoke the wrath of God." Men like Astor had "but little steel in their character" because of the "weakening influence of wealth." White "failed to see" any bravery in Astor's death: "He died as all men have to die where there is no chance for life." Major Butt was guilty of "communicating with the Pope" on his trip to Europe as Taft's representative, and God showed his displeasure both in the disaster and in the split in the Republican party. Butt's conduct on board—drawing a gun "on people in time of peril, after they had been kept in ignorance of their terrible fate until the last moment"—was "cowardly and dastardly." The first-cabin passengers, in White's view, were not Christian, manly, or heroic.[1]

A quarter century later Alan Lomax, the famous collector of American folk music, recorded a song called "Down with the Old Canoe." The song was performed by the Dixon Brothers, cotton-mill workers from Darlington County, South Carolina, who had adapted it from an older ballad. Dorsey Dixon's vocal was flat, almost deadpan, and the guitar accompaniment was spare. His brother Howard joined in on the chorus:

> *It was twenty-five years ago*
> *When the wings of death came low*
> *And spread out on the ocean far and wide*
>
> *A great ship sailed away*
> *With her passengers so gay*
> *To never never reach the other side*
>
> *Chorus:*
>
> *Sailing out to win her fame*
> *The Titanic was her name*

When she had sailed five hundred miles from shore
Many passengers and her crew
Went down with that old canoe
They all went down to never ride no more

This great ship was built by man
That is why she could not stand
She could not sink was the cry from one and all

But an iceberg ripped her side
And He cut down all her pride
They found the Hand of God was in it all

Chorus

Your Titanic sails today
On life's sea you're far away
But Jesus Christ can take you safely through

Just obey his great commands
Over there you're safe to land
You'll never go down with that old canoe

Chorus

When you think that you are wise
Then you need not be surprised
That the hand of God should stop you on life's sea

If you go on in your sins
You will find out in the end
That you are just as foolish as can be

Chorus[2]

There is no chivalry, no redemption for the passengers in either *The Titanic Tragedy* or "Down with the Old Canoe." There is only sin, and God's wrath, and death. These religious interpreters, who were to be called fundamentalists a decade after the wreck, were not uncertain about modernity; they condemned it unambiguously. Obscure as White's book and the Dixon Brothers' song may be, they suggest that not everybody agreed about the disaster—that although the conventional versions met the expectations of most Americans, they did not meet the expectations of all. They tell us that marginalized people and oppositional groups responded differently, that they drew their own implications from the narrative, that they constructed alternative narratives of their own. In the South Carolina upcountry, in New York suffragist circles, among midwestern socialists, in the black belt of Texas, at Pillar of Fire branches in Colorado, Montana, Nebraska, and Utah, the disaster took on different meanings. The *Titanic*, like American society, was contested terrain.

By 1912 the suffrage movement was gaining new momentum. After fifteen years of defeats and stagnation, suffragists were encouraged by the successful campaign in California in 1911 and by the revitalization of the National American Woman Suffrage Association (NAWSA) beginning in 1910. The parade in New York created such exhilaration that victory seemed imminent.[3] With this momentum came an ideological shift. The movement's earlier approach, dating from the Seneca Falls Convention of 1848, had been to argue for the vote on the ground of natural rights. Suffrage was a matter of justice, based on the assumptions of equality and common humanity embodied in the Declaration of Independence and later in the movement's Declaration of Rights and Sentiments. Near the turn of the century suffragists developed new arguments based on expediency rather than rights and "stressing what enfranchised women could do for the government and their communities." These arguments were compatible with prevailing conceptions of gender differences; women, as moral exemplars, had special gifts to bring to the polity. As one historian has summarized the shift, "the new era saw a change from the emphasis by suffragists on the ways in which women were the same as men and therefore had the *right* to vote, to a stress on the ways in which they differed from men, and therefore had the *duty* to contribute their special skills and experience to government."[4]

Although the *Titanic* provided fodder to the antis, it is not surprising that supporters of woman suffrage also accepted and fostered the chivalric myth. Suffragists who argued for the vote on the basis of difference easily defended themselves against claims that suffrage would destroy chivalry. The president of the Maryland Equal Suffrage League dismissed the antis' "supposition that the ballot makes men and women equal and that therefore neither should have preference in the recent maratime [*sic*] disaster" as "a misunderstanding of the position of the advocates of the vote for women." The sexes, she explained, "play a different part in the scheme of life, and to woman will ever be shown a chivalry and a respect that fittingly adorns her. I believe this spirit will make ever-unchanging the unwritten law of the sea, which recognizes the weakness of women in physical strength, but her worth in other directions."[5] From genuine belief and for strategic purposes, many suffragists made their own case for immutable gender differences.

While opposition to suffrage came, for the most part, from conservatives who read the *Titanic* disaster as a vindication of their beliefs, suffragists were also forced to defend themselves against an attack from the left. Emma Goldman, in Denver for a lecture when news of the *Titanic* arrived, used the occasion to denounce the "present-day woman" for her weakness and dependence, her willingness "to accept man's tribute in time of safety and his sacrifice in time of danger, as if she were still in her baby age." Like conservatives concerned about the deterioration of marriage, Goldman argued that the women on the *Titanic* should have died "with those they loved." Yet her concern was not for marriage (which she scorned) but for women's equality. In showing themselves unequal and un-emancipated, the women passengers had dealt the cause of women a severe blow. As an anarchist Goldman viewed suf-frage as a panacea; electoral politics could not produce mean-ingful change even if women were allowed to vote. As a feminist she rejected affirmations of inequality and difference regardless of the uses to which such affirmations were put.[6]

Denver suffragists answered Goldman by arguing that women "seemed to show their bravery as well as the men, though perhaps in different ways." Just as there was "an un-written law of the sea which makes it imperative for men to stand back," there was "also some intuitive principle which makes women, regardless of who or what they are, inclined to obey and not dally or complicate dangers by hysterics and argu-ment." By demonstrating that women were capable of "disci-pline" and "self-control," the disaster proved that they were "eligible for the ballot." Judge Ben Lindsey, the pioneer of the juvenile court system, insisted that even "if suffrage were the rule all over the world," the heroic response of the men would have been the same. "Men are better fitted physically [*sic*] than women to battle with wind and waves. Suffrage cannot affect this one way or the other." A former Colorado attorney gen-eral said that it was a simple "matter of the strong protecting the weak. If the theory of suffrage calls for strong men not to give way in time of danger, why I say give it up. But no such demand is made."[7] Suffrage, according to such views, posed no threat to essential gender roles.

Not all feminists were suffragists—Goldman is a case in point—and certainly not all suffragists were feminists. The term "feminism"—signifying opposition to sex hierarchy and a commitment to activism based on common experience—came into widespread use between 1910 and 1913.[8] Situated at the radical end of progressive reform, feminists redirected the *Titanic* disaster and its chivalric myth to their own purposes. Moving beyond the call for specific reforms concerning speed, the provision of lifeboats, and wireless transmissions, they read the disaster as a lesson in the need to extend protective legislation to cover all aspects of American life. To feminists memorializing the *Titanic* meant more than paying lasting tribute to the "noble altruism" of the first-cabin heroes.

Some accepted the chivalric myth but described it as the exception rather than the rule. Rheta Childe Dorr chose "Women and Children First" as the title of an article that described her experiences working in a "dismal" sweatshop in Brooklyn with its "foul odors" and "locked doors" that prevented mothers from going home to take care of their children. Her conclusion was blunt: "The law of the sea: women and children first. The law of the land—that's different." Dorr converted the claim that the men on the *Titanic* had sacrificed themselves for motherhood and childhood from celebration into criticism. "[I]t is known on land as well as at sea that the race is carried on by children and that women are needed to care for the children," yet only in a rare circumstance had men acted on this knowledge. Alice Stone Blackwell, editor of NAWSA's *Woman's Journal*, generously noted that "[c]hivalrous things were done even by men who had not been chivalrous in their past lives, as well as by those who had always been so," and she was touched "to see how many people were able to die bravely though they had not been able to live bravely." But Blackwell went beyond the conventional homage to call for a "new chivalry" that would transform protection into a general principle and apply it universally. The only way to achieve such a goal, she contended, was for women "to secure the ballot, the prime weapon in the modern warfare against oppression and wrong." Inez Milholland, an organizer of the New York parade, argued that the best way to extend the heroism and chivalry of the *Titanic* men was to give women the same freedom to exercise these admirable qualities.[9]

The chivalry displayed on the *Titanic*, which proved to many that women didn't need the vote and that American society was basically sound, demonstrated precisely the opposite to feminists such as these. Comparing the captain of a ship with a captain of industry, Blackwell observed:

> The "law of the sea" is quite different from the custom on land. The captain is expected to be the last man to leave his ship; all other lives must be saved before his. The captain of industry makes sure first of a comfortable living for himself, even if the workers in his employ die of tuberculosis through insufficient food and unsanitary conditions. The chivalry shown to a few hundred women on the Titanic does not alter the fact that in New York City 150,000 people—largely women and children—have to sleep in dark rooms with no windows; that in a single large city 5,000 white slaves die every year; that the lives and health of thousands of women and children are sacrificed continually through their exploitation in mills, workshops and factories. These things are facts.

An editorial in the *Progressive Woman* went further in contrasting chivalry at sea with exploitation on land by exposing the hypocrisy of the *Titanic* heroes themselves. "[M]ost of those men, no doubt, stubbornly opposed the idea of the rights of women in participation in governmental affairs. Exploited them in industry, voted for the white slave pen, sent the daughter to the street, the son to the army, the husband to tramp the streets for a job."[10] They may have redeemed themselves in the end, but their lives up to the moment of redemption had been anything but chivalrous. It was women, this point of view suggested, who were best equipped to universalize the self-sacrificing behavior that surfaced in men only in extraordinary circumstances.

Male chivalry, for example, had done nothing to prevent the disaster, only to mitigate its effects. Such "wholesale, life-taking disasters must almost be expected," wrote Agnes Ryan, as long as "the laws and the enforcement of the laws are entirely in men's hands." From Blackwell's perspective "[t]here was no need that a single life should have been lost upon the Titanic. There will be far fewer lost by preventable accidents, either on land or sea, when the mothers of men have the right to vote." Drawing an analogy from the *Titanic* to the ship of state, Ryan described the disaster as "typical" of the needless waste of life under the rule of men. "The need of women in all departments of human life to conserve life itself is pitiful. More than anything else in the world the Votes for Women movement seeks to bring humaneness, the valuation of human life, into the commerce and transportation and business of the world and establish things on a new basis, a basis in which the unit of measurement is life, nothing but life!" A member of the Women's Trade Union League (WTUL) rebuked male politicians for their "medieval minds" and their failure to recognize that "times have changed since the Knights of the Round Table rode out to protect the ladies fair." The "chivalry of today," she said, "will have to change its method if it is to do 'substantial justice' to women." Men who believed that their chivalry was sufficient in the modern world did "not know that women must protect themselves if they are to be protected adequately." The "new chivalry of this new day" would be "men and women working together for the good of humanity."[11]

Beginning by paying tribute to the *Titanic*'s heroes, feminists turned the chivalric myth against itself. Male chivalry

was exceptional and inadequate. To make care and protection
the rule required an active role for women in public life. Deference to men may have saved some lives on the *Titanic*, but
only empowered women could initiate the real work of life-
saving. In this version of the disaster the emphasis on gender
difference served radical ends. Women's special qualities—
described here as cultural more than biological—justified participation rather than paternalism.

Dorr and Blackwell invoked chivalry only to note its limitations. Other feminists praised the *Titanic* heroes and then
suggested alternative models of conduct. "Chivalry, no doubt,
has its attractive, romantic side," admitted the *Progressive
Woman*, "but just plain common sense would serve social
progress so much better!" Charlotte Perkins Gilman offered
an anthropological—and racist—interpretation of "the splendid record of human heroism" displayed on the *Titanic*. Chivalry was traditional among "the Teutonic and Scandinavian
stocks," she explained, because these civilizations had never
passed through a phase of polygamy and female slavery; from
an early "matriarchal state" they had moved directly into a
period of women's dependence on male providers through
monogamous marriage. Lesser races, according to Gilman's
evolutionary scheme, hadn't yet reached the chivalric stage,
while Anglo-Saxon civilization was ready to advance beyond
it. Elsewhere Gilman described women at this stage as "para-
sitic"—confined to roles that overstressed the "feminine" qualities of weakness and passivity. In her take on the *Titanic* she
was milder than usual. "The courageous and self-sacrificing
men who gave up their lives to save women are to be honored
truly," she wrote. But Gilman also demanded that "we honor
the women who waive this sex advantage and choose to die
like brave and conscientious human beings, rather than live
on a wholly feminine basis."[12] This was, in effect, a feminist
reading of the Ida Straus story, in which she chose to die with

her husband not out of deference to the sacred institution of marriage but as an assertion of equality. Where Emma Goldman, like her conservative counterparts, viewed the disaster as an unmitigated setback for women, Gilman saw it otherwise; some of the women passengers had proved themselves emancipated in death.

The most common response of feminists to the disaster was to accept the conventional narrative's version of events while redirecting it to an alternative set of conclusions. A few, however, rejected the narrative outright by debunking the chivalric myth. Letting women and children into the lifeboats was the least the men could have done. "After all, the women on the boat were not responsible for the disaster," and it would have been "gross injustice to decree that the women, who have no voice in making and enforcing law on land or sea, should be left aboard a sinking ship, victims of man's cupidity." A woman who called herself Daughter of Eve announced in the *Baltimore Sun* that she would "have nothing to say" about "how much of this heroism was due to the belief in the unsinkable qualities of the ship, or what part pistols played into converting cowards into brave men."

Perhaps the most subversive opinion of all was that of a Maryland suffragist who questioned the entire premise of extracting lessons from the tragedy. It was, she wrote, "a desecration to inject the question of woman suffrage into the Titanic disaster."[13] This was asking the impossible: for the public to express sorrow and grief alone, without looking for political and social implications. Feminists knew that political battles extended into the cultural realm. They knew too that to acquiesce in the disaster's lessons about eternal gender roles would be to concede a defeat at the height of their struggle.

Henry Louis Gates, Sr., met illiterate black soldiers in World War II who could reel off fifty verses of a poem—a "toast"—

about the *Titanic* disaster. His son, the future literary critic, encountered a *Titanic* toast in 1956, when a teacher in a newly integrated West Virginia classroom asked the African American students if they could recite any poetry. One of Gates's classmates stood up and began to narrate the story of Shine, a black stoker on the *Titanic*. The teacher, appalled by the poem's explicit language, cut him off. Gates calls the *Titanic* toasts "the most popular poem[s] in the black vernacular."[14]

At the time of the disaster, however, African Americans were as likely to greet the "Greatest of All News Stories" with silence as with eloquence.[15] In most of the African American press the *Titanic* wasn't news. Readers knew about the disaster; occasional editorials discussed it without elaborate explanation. It is possible that given the massive coverage in the commercial press, black newspapers decided that carrying the story would be redundant. It is equally possible that for many African Americans, there was no immediacy to the disaster. The black press continued to focus on matters that directly touched its constituency: the presidential campaign, state and local elections, Booker T. Washington, lynchings, church and lodge news, the International Negro Conference, the NAACP convention. What deeply engaged white Americans did not affect black Americans in the same way; what seemed universal to some—TITANIC DISASTER HITS HOME OF THE ENTIRE NATION read a typical headline—was actually a matter of perspective.[16]

Among the black editorialists who did address the subject of the disaster, some made universalist claims of their own about what the *Indianapolis Freeman* called the "catastrophe of the day, if not of all time," and they too were capable of embracing the chivalric myth. "The world of civilized peoples was profoundly shocked. It has in various ways showed [*sic*] grief on account of the lamentable happening, and respect and admiration for those—the men especially—who knew how to die when necessity presented." At a time when whites used "civilized" as a term of exclusion, testaments to shared shock, grief, respect, and admiration represented a desire or demand for inclusion. In this limited way, perhaps, black writers consciously or unconsciously shipped subversive messages into conventional eulogies. The *Chicago Defender* celebrated "the splendid lesson of self-sacrifice of those men who waved their last farewell to their loved ones upon that night of horror" as "a lesson in the equality of man, as Prince and Peasant alike met death dealt from the hand of Nature." The *Indianapolis World* observed hopefully that "the disaster has done much to enforce the lesson of universal brotherhood and the duty of love and sympathy and helpfulness for all mankind."[17] In the black press such lessons were assertions rather than descriptions. While the language was conventional, blacks may well have drawn lessons in equality different from those of class harmony. The disaster illuminated an ideal of universal brotherhood far removed from the realities of African American lives.

Where the *Titanic* resonated with blacks, it did so primarily in religious terms. Though the denominations were segregated, African Americans shared the language of Protestantism with whites, and it is not surprising that their interpretations of the disaster overlapped. Black sermons focused on an inscrutable God who worked through "great horrors as well as in the wonderful birth of the tiny flowers about us on every hand." At the Bethel AME Church in Pittsburgh, the Reverend P. A. Scott took as his subject "Ye Know Not What I Shall Do Now, but in a Little While," and the congregation followed with the hymn "God Moves in a Mysterious Way, His Wonders to Perform." Mattye E. Anderson's poem "The Titanic" noted the bravery of the men who "lingered with pride" but then described their

> *Poor souls so desolate*
> *Great wealth, the powerful and the strong,*

Cruelly death sweeps them all along;
To a sorrowful fate.

Lucian B. Watkins's "O Sea! A Dirge; the Tragedy of the Titanic, Memorable of 1912" sounded the theme of redemption—

Dear hearts there to baptism did repair
In this soul's triumphant hour of prayer,
In true nobility

—but ended on the note that "All was but vanity!"[18]

The empty pride of power and wealth, the illusion of security, and the deflation of pretensions were messages that black
readers and congregations could readily accept. God had
taught the rich and powerful a lesson in humility. "He is not
interested in the increase of millionaires," said the *Richmond
Planet*, "so much as He is in the increase of righteousness and
the well being of the poor of the earth, equally the objects of
His love as are the 'rich.' " While the *Afro-American Ledger*
advised its readers that "[n]othing but profound sorrow should
energize the breasts of mankind the world over in view of this
awful calamity," it also declared that the "Almighty is not
mocked."[19] Couched in general terms of man's pride and God's
majesty, many sermons and editorials indirectly but percepti-
bly addressed issues of race, class, and power. Despite the
Ledger's advice, more than sorrow energized the breasts of
black Americans.

Nowhere is this more evident than in the many African
American folk songs about the disaster. The black press—
middle-class, literate, self-consciously literary, and dominated
by Booker T. Washington's "Tuskegee machine"—tended toward conservatism. Folk songs, by contrast, were largely working-class, oral, and collective forms of expression. In many of
these songs the possibility of redemption is anything but cer-

tain. "De Titanic," which originated in Georgia and was sung by black troops bound for Europe in World War I, includes a standard image: "De people was thinkin' o' Jesus o' Nazaree, / While de band played 'Nearer My God to Thee!' " But the version that John Dos Passos heard in a New Jersey army barracks before shipping out to France ends with a dismal scene of "de women and de children / a floating and a sinkin in de cold blue sea." (The disaster must have had frightening resonance for soldiers about to make their first Atlantic crossing.) Rabbit Brown's Louisiana ballad suggests that the passengers were unprepared—"Not thinking that death was looking, there upon that northern sea"—though it too concludes with "Nearer, My God, to Thee."

Other songs were even more radical in their skepticism. In "The Great Titanic," from Northwest Alabama, the passengers call out to God in the first verse: "People began to scream and cry, / Saying 'Lord, am I going to die?' " Following the chorus (which includes the famous summer camp song line "It was sad when that great ship went down"), the lyric speaks directly to class discrimination. The rich refuse to ride with the poor, "So they put the poor below, / They were the first to go." God then demonstrates his power by destroying the unsinkable ship and killing sixteen hundred people who "didn't know that the time had come." A Texas version of the ballad "God Moves on the Water" asserts that though "the peoples had to run and pray," the archetypal first-cabin passenger went down unredeemed.

> *Well, that Jacob Nash was a millionaire,*
> *Lawd, he had plenty of money to spare;*
> *When the great Titanic was sinkin' down,*
> *Well, he could not pay his fare.*

With its doleful vocal, often accompanied by a wailing slide guitar, "God Moves" conveys genuine sorrow; lyrically, however, judgment and justice are the guiding themes. Jacob Nash—John Jacob Astor in some versions—was carrying too much baggage to get into heaven.[20]

Divine judgment was a common enough theme among African American interpreters of the disaster to provoke an angry response from more conservative blacks. A follower of Booker T. Washington criticized the "hysterical denunciations" that charged "the destruction of life to God's desire to punish the 'wealthy sinners' on board." Attempts "to definitely fix the object of God's wrath" bordered on "sacrilege." Was it God's wrath when a black church was struck by lightning? When a black hospital burned down? When the Mississippi flooded and killed five hundred blacks? The prevalence of religious interpretations of any kind disturbed and even embarrassed those who equated racial advancement with secularization. A chagrined writer for the *Pittsburgh Courier* mistakenly observed a "striking difference between the white press and the negro press" coverage of the *Titanic*. "Colored writers invariably infer or pre-suppose it to have been the work of God, or at least that God had some purpose in bringing it about. The white man discusses the matter with no such inference or prepossession." As long as the black man clung to "the silly belief that his misfortunes, defeats, reverses and tragedies were sent upon him by some God or Devil," progress was impossible.[21]

The central matter of interest and concern in initial black responses to the disaster was whether there were any African Americans on board the ship. (*Titanic* historians, despite diligent efforts, have yet to discover any.) Demanding inclusion even in disaster, some insisted that "the Afro-American must have been represented, as he generally is in everything in this country." While the conventional narrative had made heroism a matter of racial exclusiveness, black writers tried to broaden the chivalric honor roll. The "whole world" was properly "lauding the men on the ship for their heroism in their 'Women and children first' martyrdom," said the *St. Paul Appeal*, but "we can claim a few of the heroes" too. Though the "daily press has made no special mention of him, we know he was there, and that he died like the other men. And we shed tears to his memory as well as to the men of other nationalities who died with him." Like many suffragists, middle-class blacks accepted the Christian-chivalric myth only to expand it and, in their case, purge it of its racist connotations. "And when in the last day the sea gives up its dead," predicted the *Appeal*, the black hero, "like the others, will come into his crown of glory."[22]

The silence of the dailies on this heroic presence came as no surprise; white newspapers rarely reported on blacks except as criminals, and this prompted a wry comment about the coverage of the disaster from the black press. "There may have been a negro in the sinking of the great steamship Titanic off the Newfoundland coast last week, but the newspapers have not as yet discovered the fact. It is rather remarkable that there could be so great a tragedy without a negro somewhere concealed or exposed in it." When the apocryphal story surfaced of the black stoker who was "shot because he was about to stab a wireless operator," it conformed to the pattern in which blacks were either absent as heroes or present as villains in narratives of tragedy or disaster. As the *Philadelphia Tribune* sarcastically observed, "We thought it would be strange if there were no coloured persons aboard the fated ship. Of course, he had to be made to appear in the light of a dastard."[23]

Celebrations of the absence of blacks spurred a debate over what the proper African American response should be. The staid *Chicago Defender* chastised the *Louisville News* for its opinion that the disaster "is a grim incident upon which to levy recompenses from the inexorable law of compensation, but there is cause for racial congratulation that there were no Negroes aboard the ill-fated Titanic when she dived to her

doom." As Americans, the *Defender* declared, "we feel the loss
as keenly as our white brother. We do not want to adjust our
differences in such a matter. The Union soldier helped the
Confederate soldier bury his dead. Are we less gallant?" A
Philadelphia paper similarly spoke the language of brotherhood. While no blacks had died on the *Titanic*, "nevertheless
'one touch of nature makes the whole world kin,' and our sympathy goes out to the bereaved friends and relatives of the un-
fortunates who went to meet their Maker so suddenly and
unexpectedly." Yet not even the sober *Pittsburgh Courier* could
avoid an ironic comment: "The Negroes who consider their
poverty a curse may find consolation in the fact that they were
not wealthy enough to take passage on the Titanic. Every ad-
versity has its virtue."[24] Perhaps this wasn't divine justice, but
it was a kind of coincidental redress.

In more subversive ways absence and presence served as
the themes of the two most remarkable black folk versions of
the disaster: Huddie Ledbetter's blues ballad "Titanic" and
the various *Titanic* toasts. Boasting about being nowhere near
the scene of a disaster was a tradition of sorts in black folk
songs. A lyric transcribed in Mississippi in 1909 asks, "O where
were you when the steamer went down, Captain?" and answers, "I was with my honey in the heart of town." The *Titanic* replaced the riverboat after 1912 in places as far apart as
Mount Airy, North Carolina, and central Alabama:

> *O, what were you singing*
> *When the Titanic went down?*
> *Sitting on a mule's back,*
> *Singing 'Alabama Bound.'*

But Leadbelly's song, which he began performing with Blind
Lemon Jefferson in Dallas in 1912, names the absent person
and specifies the reason for his absence: the heavyweight cham-

pion Jack Johnson and racism. "Jack Johnson want to get on board, / Captain said, 'I ain't haulin' no coal.' " While the lyrics do not say that the *Titanic* went down *because* the captain denied Johnson passage, they revel in the irony that discrimination saved the black hero from death. The exclusion of Johnson, as Lawrence Levine has noted, makes the disaster "an all-white affair" and thus a source of "pleasure" and relief rather than grief and loss. The song ends with rejoicing: "When he heard about that mighty shock, / Might o' seen a man doin' the Eagle Rock." In one version Leadbelly not only describes a celebration but demands it: "Black man oughta shout for joy, / Never lost a girl or either a boy."[25]

The precise origins of the *Titanic* toasts, which made such a strong impression on Henry Louis Gates, Sr., during World War II, are uncertain. Some were collected in Louisiana and Mississippi in the 1930s, others in such diverse locations as Texas, Missouri, and New York in the 1960s, but there is evidence that they date back closer to the time of the disaster itself. Toasts were a "social genre," narrative poems performed in all kinds of settings. In the adventures of Shine the themes of presence and absence merge; Shine is on board when the ship hits the iceberg and long gone by the time it sinks. His story, through all its retellings and variations, manages to subvert nearly every feature of the conventional narrative. A worker from "down below," Shine is the first person to alert the captain to the magnitude of the accident. His reward for vigilance is a rebuke: "Go on back and start stackin' sacks, / we got nine pumps to keep the water back." After another attempt at warning the captain and another rebuke, Shine refuses to obey the order to return below deck. "Your shittin' is good and your shittin' is fine," he tells the captain, "but there's one time you white folks ain't gonna shit on Shine." (In some versions Shine responds derisively to the captain's faith in the *Titanic*'s unsinkability: "I don't like chicken and I don't like ham— / And I don't believe your pumps is worth a damn!"; "Captain, captain, can't you see, / this ain't no time to bullshit me"; "Well, that seems damned funny, it may be damned fine, / but I'm gonna try to save this black ass of mine.")

Realism and common sense reside in the black laborer, not in the white officer. The captain is a martinet—complacent and ignorant—a far cry from the newspaper hero who went down telling his crew to "Be British!" A "thousand million-aires" stare as Shine jumps ship and begins to swim. All they do is watch; Shine, not Butt or Astor, is the visible actor. The conventional heroes are passive and impotent, and their women appeal to Shine to save them. The disaster destroys the facade of Victorian respectability and all illusions of strong white manhood and pure white womanhood. First-cabin women, whether a "[r]ich man's daughter" or the "Captain's daugh-ter," need Shine rather than the "protection" of their husbands and fathers; they explicitly offer him sexual favors for his help, which he refuses. "Shine say, 'One thing about you white folks I couldn't understand: / you all wouldn't offer me that pussy when we was all on land.' " He also refuses money. The cap-tain, realizing his earlier mistake, pleads, "Shine, Shine, save poor me, / I'll make you richer than old John D," but Shine knows that money is worthless in these circumstances: "Shine turned around and took another notion, / say 'captain, your money's counterfeit in this big-assed ocean.' " Shine's code is anything but chivalric. He understands that the first-cabin passengers would do nothing to save him, and he cuts through the hypocrisy of their sudden kindness and generosity by de-manding that they live out their selfishness to the end. "A nickle [sic] is a nickle, a dime is a dime, / get your motherfucken [sic] ass over the side and swim like mine." In this Darwinian struggle, however, Shine is clearly superior; he has both the physical strength and the cunning to survive. He skillfully evades a shark attack and swims until he arrives safely in

America (in Los Angeles when the *Titanic* begins to sink and New York by the time it disappears, on "Main Street," in Harlem or Jacksonville, depending on the version). When he is present at the disaster, Shine is heroic: strong, shrewd, courageous, willing to resist white authority and its bribes. Once he is onshore, he celebrates his triumph and his absence by going to a whorehouse and getting drunk.[26]

The presence of the *Titanic* in folk songs and toasts indicates both the depth of its resonance and the diversity of its meanings. It also suggests something about cultural categories. For many years folklorists tried to preserve a rigid distinction between folk culture and popular culture. Folk expression was supposed to be local, organic, participatory, and pure, while popular culture was national, standardized, commercialized, and inauthentic.[27] Yet the *Titanic* was a national—in fact international—event that entered "folk" consciousness, directly or indirectly, through the standardized media of a modern industrial society. However obscure the origins of the *Titanic* folk songs and toasts may be, one thing is certain: They did not grow organically out of the pure southern soil. "Folklorists might have been purists," Lawrence Levine has written, but "the folk rarely were." They didn't insist on local subject matter, and they didn't object to making money from their songs. Charles Haffer of Clarksdale, Mississippi, who described himself as a "Noted Gospel Song Writer and Bible Lecturer," claimed that he wrote the first *Titanic* ballad and sold two or three thousand copies across the delta. Singers like Leadbelly and Blind Willie Johnson, who didn't literally *write* their songs, made money by performing them in public places.[28]

All news of the disaster came first through the wire services and the commercial press. What various audiences—including the "folk"—did with that news is another story. Though white and black performers and audiences interpreted them differently, songs like "The Great Titanic" often crossed racial boundaries and represented a regional and working-class alternative to the national consensus. White country singers like Roy Acuff and Loretta Lynn, rooted in "hillbilly" music, also sang of poor passengers being put below, where they were the first to go. The sources, in other words, may have been standardized, but the responses were not. Some "consumers" of the conventional narrative became active producers of alternative narratives, defying its tone as well as its content. Some even made the disaster into a joke.[29]

Seven months after the *Titanic* disaster Eugene V. Debs received almost a million votes as the Socialist party presidential candidate. The year 1912 was in many ways the golden day of American socialism and labor radicalism: the year of the Industrial Workers of the World's successful "Bread and Roses" strike in the textile city of Lawrence, Massachusetts (settled a month before the *Titanic* went down); the year in which twelve hundred Socialists held elected offices, including seventy-nine mayors in twenty-four states; the year in which Theodore Roosevelt and the Progressive party incorporated socialist planks into their national platform, cut into Taft's vote, and put Woodrow Wilson into the White House. The lines dividing socialism from mainstream American politics were never more blurred, nor was it possible to draw sharp distinctions between socialism and feminism, socialism and progressive Christianity, socialism and the more militant brands of middle-class reform.[30]

The American labor movement, of course, was not synonymous with socialism; it could not agree about the *Titanic* any more than it could agree on other issues. For the most part union leaders blamed the disaster on "modern business methods" and demanded new laws to protect passengers and crews in the future. They supported the Senate investigation and its recommendations for reform. The American Federation of

Labor boasted that it had been pushing for years for legislation that would require adequate lifesaving provisions on American vessels. Led by the International Seamen's Union, the labor movement denounced the lack of trained crew members on the *Titanic* and criticized shipowners for cutting costs and jeopardizing safety by using unskilled workers. As usual it had required "some great disaster" to expose corporate "mismanagement and incompetency" and "to arouse the public conscience." The campaign for passage of the Seamen's Act, led by insurgent Senator Robert M. La Follette of Wisconsin, was not above playing on the xenophobia that characterized large segments of organized labor, especially the conservative craft unions of the AFL. La Follette described the horrific prospect of getting "into a lifeboat in the crew of which there is a Turk, a Chinese, a Jap, a Greek, a Negro from South Africa, a Hungarian, and an Arabian."[31]

Workers of many persuasions found common ground in the belief that the *Titanic* was not an anomaly. The *Railroad Trainman's Journal* noted, for example, that "a half million a year pay death or disability tribute to industry" but that the "great world" found it easier to focus on a single tragedy than on the "steady grind" that "day after day, week after week, month after month, year after year takes life and limb." Why do "equally horrible but much costlier disasters in terms of human life," like mine cave-ins and explosions, get only passing attention? asked a Finnish newspaper in Fitchburg, Massachusetts. Another labor publication listed "Things That Are Worse," including mine disasters, child labor, prostitution, train wrecks, tuberculosis, poverty, sweatshops, and tenements—all of which, like the *Titanic*, were attributable to a greed that "puts profit above human rights and human welfare." The *Titanic*, according to a Teamsters' editorial, provided "another lesson in our every day existence where human lives were offered up as a sacrifice, and principally the lives of working people." "Speed and greed," summed up the *Black-smiths Journal*, "demand a frightful toll."[32]

When the crew of the *Olympic*, the *Titanic*'s sister ship, went on strike for safer conditions, the AFL defended the action and urged workers on land to make similar demands: "No locked doors to factories. No doors opening inward. No two-foot wooden staircases. No heaping up of inflammable materials regardless of life." The United Mine Workers could sympathize with the *Olympic* seamen, who were "enclosed for days and nights in a stuffy, heated room some fifty feet beneath the water line" and whose experience in the event of a disaster would not be enviable "even if accompanied by the band playing 'Nearer, My God, to Thee.'" The disaster only confirmed the need for a strong labor movement to protect workers and consumers from greedy or negligent owners. Union publicists seized on the *Titanic* as a rallying cry for workers to organize.[33]

Conservative craft unionists, however, tended to focus on the specific problems revealed by the disaster, and they phrased their attacks on greed in ways that avoided class antagonism. They too saw the *Titanic* as a great "illustration of the democracy of the human race; the millionaire and the peasant, the educated and the ignorant, all standing upon the same footing; the owner of diamonds and the wearer of 'homespun' on an equality as the end approached." A member of the International Brotherhood of Maintenance of Way Employes offered a verse rendition of the democracy of death motif that suggests the hazards of drawing rigid boundaries between secular and religious readings of the disaster:

> *Poverty and wealth went hand in hand;*
> *Side by side they sank.*
> *God showed no distinction*
> *In station, creed or rank.*

Many labor poems and editorials concluded with the band playing "Nearer, My God, to Thee." While noting that heroism was "not confined to any class or race," conservative unionists joined in the celebration of the first-cabin men —occasionally at the risk of inconsistency. James E. Kinsella, a postal worker who called himself the Post Office Poet, sounded positively radical when he wrote,

There were no lifeboats left on deck to save the steerage crew,
The toilers penned in the hold below wiped out by the billowy
blue;
This press agent guff, this savory stuff, of saving the rich and
poor,
The steerage died, swept down by the tide, in Neptune's
gripping lure.

Two stanzas later, however, "The Chevalier Bayard Major Butt died as young Sidneys die, / 'Women and children first,' he said, his ringing soldier cry." The end brought redemption: "By dying game you shed all blame—death wiped your 'scutcheon clean." The *Locomotive Engineers' Monthly Journal* reproached workers who took "satisfaction in the thought that for once the magnates could not buy their way out." Labor took a more expansive view of *Titanic* chivalry, opening the pantheon of heroes to include "the toiler strong" without necessarily challenging the predominant myths.[34]

Socialists and other labor radicals, on the other hand, constructed their own response to the *Titanic*—perhaps the most consistently subversive of all the counternarratives. They spoke directly to the silences in the conventional narrative, the class bias in its roll call of heroes, the conservative "lessons" it drew from the disaster. Only a few dissenting editorialists in the commercial press joined Charlotte Perkins Gilman in noting and criticizing the namelessness of the steerage victims and survivors. "In all that pain and grief and courage one bit of snobbery stands out," she wrote; "—among those saved from death we find Mrs. So and So 'and maid'! Had the 'maid' no name, no anxious relatives?" The Yiddish socialist poet Morris Rosenfeld inquired more generally into "the people without names who perished on the ship 'Titanic.'" While Gilman viewed this as an unfortunate omission, others argued that class determined the *Titanic*'s status as news; it was a disaster only because of the presence of the rich and powerful. "Had the Titanic been a mudscow with the same number of useful workingmen on board," the *Appeal to Reason* speculated, and had it "gone down while engaged in some useful social work[,] the whole country would not have gasped with horror, nor would all the capitalist papers have given pages for weeks to reciting the terrible details."[35] Consciousness of the *Titanic*, in other words, was itself the product of capitalism and its desire to legitimate itself.

Confronted with the myth of first-cabin heroism, radicals attempted to recast the disaster in terms that would undermine rather than bolster capitalism. Debunking was one strategy—that is, asserting that "[m]ost of this 'hero' business is rubbish anyhow." The "acts of heroism of the gilt rabble" were simply a "lie," declared a self-described "revolutionary" Italian newspaper in Paterson, New Jersey. Its anarchist counterpart in Lynn, Massachusetts, claimed that millionaires interceded to save their dogs ahead of "the plebeian rabble." Speaking to striking coal miners on the Capitol steps in Charleston, West Virginia, the radical labor activist Mother Jones posed a series of questions meant to expose first-cabin heroism as a transparent fraud:

I have been reading of the *Titanic* when she went down. Did you read of her? The big guns wanted to save themselves, and the fellows that were guiding below took

up a club and said we will save our people. And then the
papers came out and said those millionaires tried to save
the women. Oh, Lord, why don't they give up their millions
if they want to save the women and children? Why do they
rob them of home, why do they rob millions of women to
fill the hell-holes of capitalism[?]

Jones then launched into an elaborate anecdote about what
the Guggenheims and their "blood-hounds" had done during
a union organization drive in Colorado—ridden men out of
town, thrown "widows and orphans out on the highways in
the snow," jailed Mother Jones in a "pest house" when she had
smallpox. Was heroism, she asked, likely among such people?[36]

Jones's speech also provided an alternative version of events
in which it was the "big guns" who displayed their charac-
teristic selfishness and the "fellows" from "below" who acted
heroically. Her counternarrative, whether intentionally or
not, inverted the story of Major Butt with his iron bar beating back the crazed steerage men. Here it was the millionaires who had to be kept at bay by workingmen trying to
"save our people." While "the daily press has immortalized
the multi-millionaires as men of heroic mould," remarked a
writer for the radical Western Federation of Miners, it ignored "the common men who made up the crew of the Titanic, who with pistols in their hands kept back the patrician
mob, who yearned to seek safety in the life boats." In this
alternative scenario the first-cabin men were the "mob," and
Astor, begging to go with his wife, had to be waved back by
the "heroic crew whose chivalry towards women and children in the hour of peril and death, will immortalize them
as the bravest of the brave." The *Jewish Daily Forward* imagined a conversation among the *Titanic*'s dead in which an
"aristocrat" boasts that the "papers are full of our heroic
deaths" and the poor deride him: "Oy, that aristocrat fought

to get into a boat but was held back by pistols. Now the papers are filled with their heroism. We poor folk who died while stoking the fires in the engine room until the very last minute, we third-class passengers who truly showed heroism, about us they write nothing."[37]

Class shaped ethnic responses to the disaster too. Much of the immigrant and foreign-language press simply translated wire service stories and offered the usual combination of paeans to first-cabin heroism and jeremiads about speed and luxury—with important additions and exceptions, however. Irish Americans, for example, brought nationalism as well as class into their readings of the *Titanic*, debunking "the fake stories of heroism displayed by certain individuals and legends of the 'Be British' order," praising their "fellow-countrymen" for their "noble" behavior, excoriating the British crew for "lack of discipline and of fitness for their work," and exposing "the whole story" as "a bit of blooming English blundering."[38] Italian Americans challenged the allegations that their countrymen were shot down trying to force their way into the boats.[39] Jewish Americans not only decried the "tendency to limit the courage to dominant races and a dominant faith" but remade the Strauses, Guggenheim, and Henry B. Harris into Jewish rather than Anglo-Saxon heroes. The *Jewish Advocate* used the disaster to agitate against the pending immigration restriction bills: "The same people who sentimentalized over the actual death of those who lost their lives in the 'Titanic' are eager to kill off all opportunity for thousands who desire to come here."[40] Most significantly, in articles such as FINNISH PASSENGERS ON THE "TITANIC", WERE THERE CZECHS ON THE "TITANIC"?, IRISH VICTIMS ON THE TITANIC, COMPLETE LIST OF SHIPWRECKED ITALIANS, and MANY JEWS WERE PASSENGERS ON ILL-FATED S.S. TITANIC, the ethnic press constituted its readers as communities of mourning and gave identity and dignity to the nameless "foreigners" in the conventional narrative.[41]

Even when they did not specifically debunk first-cabin heroism, working-class advocates told a radically different story. Admitting that "what happened in the steerage quarters" was "clouded" by the fact that most of the testimony had been "gleaned" from first- and second-cabin survivors, the radical press insisted "that bravery and unselfish devotion was [*sic*] not confined to the staterooms and that most of the men in the steerage went down because they gave their wives and children the first chance to escape." The conventional narrative, with its biases and exclusions, had become the "truth" through sheer repetition. "We have been told a thousand times and with as many variations of the bravery of the rich and prominent men aboard, but very little has been heard about the bravery of *the men and women in the steerage*." The heroism of immigrants, "consigned to the bottom like bilge," was of "no consequence to the press," an Italian socialist complained. To compensate, the radical press interviewed survivors from the third cabin and celebrated "the heroes in the hold."[42]

This labor critique of the conventional narrative extended beyond the biases of the press into efforts to shape the historical memory of the disaster. At the intersection of socialism and feminism the *Progressive Woman* condemned the Women's Titanic Memorial Fund for trying to give permanent form to a distorted version of events.

> There is a movement on foot to build at Washington a monument to the heroes of the Titanic disaster. Said heroes are Messrs. Astor, Guggenheim, Butt, etc.—first cabin guests who "stood aside" to let first cabin women take the lifeboats in the wreck. It has developed that those who "stood aside" were unaware of the danger that threatened and are therefore less heroic than was at first supposed. However, there were men—stokers, engineers, etc.—who knew the exact situation they and the Titanic were in, who yet stood at their posts till the ship went down, never to

come up again. These are the real heroes of the Titanic. If there is a monument raised for Titanic heroes, it should be to these unknown, unsung toilers in the hold of that unfortunate ship.

A poem called "Fair Play" in an Indianapolis black newspaper made the point more generally:

> *A monument for millionaires*
> *A monument for snobs.*
> *No marble shaft for the men on the craft,*
> *Who simply did their jobs.*[43]

In the radical counternarrative heroism either transcended class or, as in this case, belonged exclusively to the proletariat. Class still determined conduct, but here ignorance and confusion described the "first cabin guests," while knowledge and fortitude characterized the workers.

Socialists joined in the ubiquitous warnings about luxury and greed and in the chorus calling for reform, but they did so in their own, more radical terms. They did not qualify their critique with the theme of redemption, nor did they accept the progressive belief in the basic soundness of the system. One radical writer wondered whether in their last moments, in the desperate knowledge that they would not be saved (or redeemed), the multimillionaires had thought of "the countless human beings whom they had wrecked and ruined in their mad gallop for wealth." Far from being heroic, the first-cabin men were implicated in their own fate. "So much space had to be given to the private promenades, golf links, swimming pools for the plutocrats aboard that there was no space left for life-boats when the crash came. Could misdirected ingenuity, perverted taste and mental and moral insanity go farther?" The *Masses* decried the "insanity of luxury, of foolish display and self-pampering even to the point of wrecking the safety and health of the luxurious themselves." In Charles Edward Russell's view "the true history of the Titanic disaster" resided in conspicuous consumption—"features that would attract wealthy persons willing to pay great prices" for "useless luxuries." The men of the first cabin were both perpetrators and victims, murderers and murdered in this "true history." The *Daily People* wryly observed that while the capitalist contingent on board had at least been able to enjoy the ship's attractions in exchange for the added danger, for the proletarian majority "the increased risk of drowning was thrown in for good measure" and nothing more.[44]

For Americans of many political persuasions, the cause of the disaster was the greed of the White Star Line; for socialists, however, that greed represented systemic corruption rather than an isolated transgression. "Greed and speed are the characteristics of the capitalist system," proclaimed Victor Berger, the Socialist congressman from Wisconsin. "They caused the disaster and are causing disasters almost as appalling every day in the industrial world." A writer with the fitting name (pseudonym?) of John M. Work, while sympathetic to "the suffering and heartache caused by the wreck of the Titanic," offered the opinion that it was "a very slight tragedy" compared with the "millions upon millions who are enduring a living death under capitalism." Blaming the disaster on sin generally was also "humbug," said a poet in the anticlerical Polish humor magazine *God's Whip*. The clergy who saw it as God's "punishment for human pride" rather than a crime of capitalism were "trying to befuddle" the masses.[45]

Socialists were willing to identify specific villains but only as representatives of an evil system. It seemed almost too fitting that "Money Baron" J. P. Morgan, with his "ghoulish grasp for dividends," controlled the White Star Line. "So the Titanic was driven on lest Morgan might have to economize in his fleet of private yachts." He "had fattened his pockets from the conditions that made inevitable this feast of death." Ismay too could serve as "the epitome of capitalism"—with the added attraction of being almost universally loathed—and elicited some wishful thinking on the part of socialists and the syndicalists of the IWW. "Years ago, Ismay would have been painted a hero. Now even capitalism finds it hard to stomach him. There's a reason: capitalism is reaching a stage where its shortcomings are literally killing off and hurting its best supporters, a la the Astors and Strauses. Let the good work go on!" Others, however, refused to join in the "hounding" of Ismay on the ground that fixing the guilt "upon some particular individual" diverted the "public wrath" from the real culprit, capitalism. Piecemeal reform and committee investigations were similarly diverting. "Any remedy will be absolutely futile no matter how ably applied so long as we retain the system," Russell argued. The time had come to move beyond "superficial thinking," "bromidic and tiresome reflections" to discover deeper causes and genuine solutions. Socialists were "out to abolish capitalism—and the necessity of investigating committees that land nowhere."[46]

In the conventional narrative the story of the *Titanic* functioned as a parable of the natural goodness of class, racial, ethnic, and gender hierarchies. The left too treated the *Titanic* as an object lesson, with the difference that the disaster was a metaphor for capitalism. "The tragedy of the month, the sinking of the Titanic," said the *Ladies' Garment Worker*, "is typical of the constant tragedies which occur in our industrial life." Like the ship of state, the *Titanic* sailed with "proud boasts" and illusions. On the upper deck "comfort and luxury," "[f]easts, cards and gallantries" occupied the rich and beautiful. "Sounds of revelry" drowned out "the cry of the sick baby in the steerage," while "stokers far below in the stifling under-world" toiled and sweated "day and night." In the final moments the first-cabin men awakened "from their orgies of self-indulgence" and realized "their manhood obligations," but their redemption was hollow—"too late for this life." As a visual metaphor for class hierarchy the *Titanic* "illustrated in herself and in her destruction" the "contempt for human life which under capitalism inspired and presided over her creation." The *Masses* grieved over "Our 'Titanic' Civilization," while *Pravo*, a Czech socialist paper in Cleveland, observed how the ship and the disaster reflected "the attitude of the entire governing capitalist world of today. 'They' never fail to arrange for the most luxurious items . . . , yet to take care of people's lives does not cross their minds." The "ship of life" would continue to "sink millions and millions of people," predicted the *Jewish Daily Forward*, as long as it was "commanded by the capitalist captains of industry."[47]

While the equation of the *Titanic* with capitalist society served as an indictment of the status quo, it also pointed hopefully toward the future. According to the metaphor, after all, capitalism was a sinking ship, and by extension the proletariat was an iceberg. "The will of the vast working class is forming and hardening; obstructions to capitalism are cropping up in the most unexpected places; the collective mind of the working class may crystallize overnight, massive and unrelenting." (Neither icebergs nor class consciousness actually "crystallize overnight," of course. Inflated rhetoric was one thing that radicals shared with their enemies.) In a different metaphor "the iceberg of capitalist profit" floated "in the pathway of human progress, awaiting many more thousands of victims." The problem here was that icebergs are natural phenomena—hardly something that the IWW would have wanted to say about capitalism; thus the metaphor shifted abruptly, to the "humane heart" mourning the tragedy while the "humane head" worked "to end human misery by ending capitalism." What confirmed the permanence of a certain vision of social order for conservatives represented the opposite to radicals. "Just as the Titanic went down in wreck and disaster so will

capitalism[,] which she so tragically typified[,] also go down."
Here too there would be casualities, "but it is to be hoped that
when the crisis comes there may be life boats enough to carry
humanity safely into the Socialist Republic."[48]

Paradoxically, visions of the classless future led some on
the left to embrace the myths that they tried elsewhere to
debunk. The *Appeal to Reason* described the steerage passengers as "penned in like cattle" and kept back "with loaded
revolvers" so that "the rich passengers" could "make sure of
their escape," yet somehow rich and poor alike had done the
"fine thing" of observing the rule of the sea. Chivalric behavior, unfortunately, was the "extremely rare exception"
rather than "the rule of life." By contrast, socialist society
would be organized "on the basis of women and children
first" and would prevent such tragedies from ever occurring.
"Had the Titanic been constructed under social supervision
and in social service, instead of being privately owned and
launched and operated for private profit this appalling disaster would never have blackened the annals of humanity."
Socialists and anarchists also redirected the "democracy of
death" motif to their own purposes. Images of "rich man and
poor man, millionaire and stoker" standing together as
"equals and brothers, without a barrier between them, going down to death together" did not suggest to the left that
the status quo was all brotherhood and harmony. But in a
moment of crisis they provided a glimpse of the classless future and confirmed "the faith of the Socialist, that all are
children of the earth together, all members of one great family, all of a common origin, all sharing a common destiny, and
all by every right entitled equally to light, happiness, opportunity and the bounty of the earth, our common mother!" In
that moment the artificial distinctions of the capitalist system
were swept away, and Astor and the stokers *"stood on one common basis of equality in the democracy of death."*[49] Catastrophe

exposed the socialism at the core of every human being—the "realities" beneath the capitalist facade.

By laying bare human nature, the *Titanic* demonstrated the viability of socialism. Critics who disparaged socialists for their utopianism—their naive disregard for the fundamental selfishness of human beings—needed only to be reminded of the disaster. "For we might rest our whole cause upon what happened that night on the Titanic," proclaimed Charles Edward Russell. To those who insisted that socialism required "a change in human nature," we "point to that night on the Titanic and say that for human nature so noble and good to be perverted and dragged in the mire and slimed in the filth and hardened in the fires of Capitalism is the most unspeakable of crimes and that the race had never better friends than those that are trying to rid the earth of such a monster." The readiness with which even rich men sacrificed their lives for others showed that selfishness resided in the profit system, not in the human heart. Abraham Cahan declared that the disaster proved social Darwinism a lie: "Is this not the greatest evidence of the falsity of the claim that only the possibility of making money serves as an incentive for people, that that is human nature and cannot be altered?" Socialism, argued Jozef Sawicki in the *Polish Worker*, "will create conditions to obliterate the bad and nurture the good aspects of human character," such as those revealed on board the sinking ship. Emma Goldman made the same case in a different way. Inverting the myth of noblesse oblige, she envisioned the workers dying "for those far removed from us by a cold and cruel social and material gulf—for those who by their very position must needs be our enemies—for those who, a few moments before the disaster probably never gave a thought to the toilers and pariahs of the ship." Self-sacrifice of this kind was "so wonderful a feat of human nature as to silence forever the ridiculous argument" that the classless society was unnatural and therefore impossible.[50]

Human nature, in the context of the *Titanic* disaster, proved remarkably malleable. Americans across the political and social spectrum seemed actually to agree that the disaster carried lessons about what was and wasn't natural, but their agreement stopped there. When it came to the content of those lessons—was woman suffrage natural? feminism? racial equality? socialism?—consensus evaporated. As a social drama, as a public performance in which American culture thought out loud about itself, the *Titanic* disaster produced a cacophony of voices rather than a chorus. The conventional narrative tried to represent itself as common sense, to put itself beyond critical demystification, to treat the truths of the *Titanic* as self-evident, to allow for only one way of comprehending the event and its meanings. Yet dissenting voices responded to the conventional narrative, revised it, and in some cases overturned it completely. The insistence that a certain "picture invariably presents itself" failed to convince those who well understood the meanings that such a picture conveyed. They preferred to draw their own.

The *Titanic* disaster was historically not intrinsically meaningful. While we like to think that the disaster's resonance is timeless—that it has to do with universal themes of humans against nature, hubris, false confidence, the mystery of the sea, hydrophobia, heroism, and cowardice—the *Titanic* seared itself into American memory not because it was timeless but because it was timely. Americans in 1912 made it speak to the concerns of contemporary politics, society, and culture. Although many of them claimed to have found transhistorical truths in the disaster, such claims were themselves historically grounded in their own present circumstances and ideological purposes. No more than any other event was the *Titanic* inherently memorable. Making rather than finding its significance, people worked and fought to shape how the disaster would, they hoped, be remembered.

A decidedly male "spirit of heroism" uses a megaphone to inspire and cajole the passengers. (Marshall Everett, WRECK AND SINKING OF THE TITANIC)

IN MEMORY OF TITANIC HEROES

Charles Dana Gibson's poster for the Women's Titanic *Memorial Fund. The monument reads "To the men who gave their lives that the women & children might be saved."* (NEW YORK TIMES)

The Women's Titanic Memorial at its present site, Fourth and P streets SW, in Washington, D.C. Fundraising for the memorial began immediately after the disaster. Designed by Gertrude Vanderbilt Whitney, it was unveiled in 1931 and stood on the banks of the Potomac until it was relocated to make room for the John F. Kennedy Center for the Performing Arts in 1967. (Historical Society of Washington, D.C.)

THE GUARDIAN ANGEL OF THE SEA PAYS TRIBUTE TO THE MARTYRED HEROES

Though the "guardian angel of the sea" lays wreaths for the sailors and the band, the named heroes belong exclusively to the first class: Archibald Butt, John Jacob Astor, Isidor Straus, and Henry B. Harris. (Marshall Everett, WRECK AND SINKING OF THE TITANIC)

Critics of rising divorce rates seized upon the story of Ida Straus, who chose to stay and die with her husband, Isidor. (DENVER POST)

The Denver Post *hired a theater troupe to reenact scenes from the disaster. Here, as the caption explains, an officer shoots down "panic-stricken Italians" who tried to board the lifeboats.* (DENVER POST)

Major Archibald Butt, in a crisply pressed uniform, prevents shabbily dressed steerage passengers from taking women's places in the boats. In some versions he used an iron bar instead of a gun. (Denver Post)

The democracy of grief motif: Rich and poor women wait and mourn together. (Detroit News)

Before radio, sheet music and parlor singing were major forms of middle-class entertainment. More than one hundred Titanic *songs were published in 1912 and 1913. The cover of this piece shows a heavenly light shining on the* Titanic *heroes as they go to their deaths.* (LIBRARY OF CONGRESS)

Christianity provided consolation and redemptive meaning, even in "secular" commercial newspapers like the St. Louis Globe Democrat. *(Marshall Everett, WRECK AND SINKING OF THE TITANIC)*

Many commentators blamed the huge loss of life on the era's penchant for luxury and self-indulgence. In a Detroit News *cartoon, elegantly dressed first-cabin passengers search in vain for a lifeboat. A sign in the empty davit advertises the* Titanic's *tennis courts, Turkish baths, gymnasium, ballroom, concert saloon, and billiard room. (Marshall Everett, WRECK AND SINKING OF THE TITANIC)*

A portrait of Harry Elkins Widener looks down on his collection of rare books in the memorial room at Harvard University. (Harvard University Archives)

Suffragists compared the Titanic *to the ship of state. With the vote, they argued, women would steer the ship clear of all sorts of dangers. The sea monsters are labeled "smallpox," "saloons," "fire traps," "graft," "sweatshops," "white slavery," "poverty," "gambling," "social diseases," "diptheria [sic]," "child labor," "impure food," and "consumption."* (State Historical Society of Wisconsin, negative number N13283)

The Strauses, transformed into honorary Anglo-Saxons in mainstream versions of the disaster, are reclaimed as Jews on the cover of a Yiddish song. (Library of Congress)

In an early attempt to profit from the disaster, a magazine ad explains that any man can be heroic if he protects his women and children with Travelers Insurance. (SURVEY)

EXTRA, TUESDAY, MAY 14
SAVED FROM THE TITANIC

ECLAIR'S WORLD SENSATION

MISS DOROTHY GIBSON, a survivor of the sea's greatest disaster, tells the story of the shipwreck, supported by an all-star cast, on the film marvel of the age ❖ ❖ ❖ ❖

TUESDAY MAY 14	ECLAIR FILM CO. FORT LEE, NEW JERSEY SALES COMPANY, SOLE AGENTS	TUESDAY MAY 14

The first film made about the Titanic *starred actress Dorothy Gibson, an actual survivor of the disaster.* Saved from the Titanic, *a melodrama, was released exactly one month after the sinking. No copies of the film survive.* (Old Mill Books)

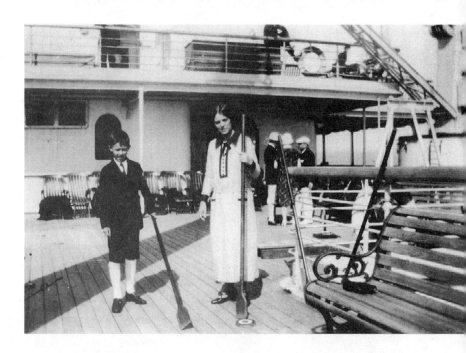

Nine-year-old Walter Lord plays shuffleboard on the deck of the Titanic's *sister ship* Olympic *in 1926.* (Walter Lord)

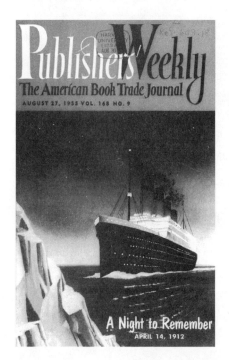

The doomed ship steams toward the iceberg on the original jacket of Walter Lord's A Night to Remember, *advertised on the front cover of* Publishers Weekly. (Henry Holt and Company)

Mrs. Brown
refused to sink

"Keep rowing or I'll toss you all overboard!"

The threat came from a redhead in corset and bloomers, with a Colt .45 lashed to her waist. And as the lifeboat marked *S.S. Titanic* lurched into the waves, she rowed too, rowed until her hands bled.

Mrs. Margaret Tobin Brown had come a long way to take charge of that crowded lifeboat. Once penniless, she now had millions. Once semi-illiterate, she now knew five languages. Once spurned by Denver society, she now hobnobbed with nobility.

But, as she said, "You can't wear the social register for water wings." Her $60,000 chinchilla cloak covered three children; her other outer garments she had given to elderly women. She swore, threatened, sang grand opera, joked—and she kept her boatload of wretched survivors going till rescue came.

Asked how she'd done it, she replied, "Typical Brown luck. I'm unsinkable." But it wasn't luck. It was pluck. And Americans have always had plenty of that smiling, hardy courage. When you come to think of it, that's one reason why our country's Savings Bonds rank among the world's finest investments.

For 160 million determined Americans stand behind those Bonds.

The surest way to protect your own security—and the nation's—is through United States Savings Bonds. Invest in them regularly—and hold on to them.

★   ★   ★

It's actually easy to save money—when you buy United States Series E Savings Bonds through the automatic Payroll Savings Plan where you work! You just sign an application at your pay office; after that your saving is done *for* you. And the Bonds you receive will pay you interest at the rate of 3% per year, compounded semiannually, for as long as 19 years and 8 months, if you wish! Sign up today! Or, if you're self-employed, invest in Bonds regularly where you bank.

Safe as America—
U.S. Savings Bonds

The Unsinkable Molly Brown is pressed into Cold War service to promote personal and national security. (Ad Council)

The consummation of the Titanic's *maiden voyage represents a victory in the Cold War in this comic strip version of Clive Cussler's* Raise the Titanic! (Universal Press Syndicate)

The discovery of the Titanic *in 1985 became an emblem of the buoyant Reagan years. Lee Iacocca, the decade's premier entrepreneurial hero, salvages the ship with a Chrysler tow truck.* (James Margulies)

A 1993 tabloid demonstrates that the Titanic *defies conventional notions of time.* (WEEKLY WORLD NEWS)

PART II

MEMORIES

CHAPTER 5

A NIGHT TO REMEMBER

∾ HOWARD MILLAR CHAPIN may hold the distinction of being the first *Titanic* buff. Chapin and his wife, Hope, daughter of Governor D. Russell Brown of Rhode Island, were honeymooning on board the *Carpathia* when, early in the morning of April 15, 1912, the survivors of the disaster began arriving on deck. As the day broke, Hope snapped a photograph of a huge iceberg—perhaps the one that had collided with the *Titanic*. The *Carpathia*'s return to New York cut the newlyweds' trip short.

Back in Providence, Howard launched his career as librarian at the Rhode Island Historical Society. In his spare time he helped preserve the memory of the *Titanic*. He arranged a visit by Arthur Rostron, the *Carpathia*'s heroic captain, to Brown University. He also recorded his experiences, first as an article in a London magazine, then in the *Brown Alumni Monthly*, and finally in a short pamphlet called, simply, *The Titanic Disaster*. Meanwhile, he began collecting other pamphlets and books about the tragedy. By 1926 his collection included thirty-nine items. Reminding his fellow bibliophiles of the "sudden-ness and extent" of "the greatest maritime disaster not inten-tionally caused by human beings" (the Great War had been fought in the interim), Chapin published his "Bibliotheca Ti-tanic." Among his annotations he described Henry Fredricks's *The Tragic Story of the Titanic* (1912) as a "sensational account with interesting illustrations," including one of Howard and Hope Chapin.[1]

In the years after 1912 people commemorated the disaster in a variety of official and unofficial ways. Survivors and par-ticipants—Captain Rostron of the *Carpathia* in 1931, Second Officer Lightoller in 1935, John B. Thayer in 1940—published memoirs. Others gave interviews. Every year a Coast Guard cutter from the International Ice Patrol, created as a result of the *Titanic* sinking, visited the site, fired volleys, and sounded taps. Sailors held annual memorial services at the Titanic Tower, a lighthouse built atop the Seaman's Church Institute on South Street in lower Manhattan. On the twentieth anni-versary a seamen's choir sang "Nearer, My God, to Thee," and a chaplain read from a sermon originally delivered at the tower's dedication in 1913. "The world," he warned, "has a short memory even for the things which thrill and shock it most deeply, and it is well for us to stop and stand and look and remember." To commemorate the disaster was "to refresh our soul in the presence and inspiration of heroism"—an in-clusive heroism in this case, given the venue.[2]

When Mrs. William Howard Taft unveiled the Women's Titanic Memorial in May 1931, the speakers took the occasion to rejoice that at least as of 1912 chivalry wasn't dead. Repre-sentative Robert Luce of Massachusetts told an audience that included President and Mrs. Hoover that the difference be-tween men's and women's survival rates was "the reason for this memorial and our presence here today." The speakers didn't mention the Depression, now in its second year, but the ability of men to protect their women and children was under particular strain as the Hoovers stared at the pink granite statue on the bank of the Potomac. "Heightened concern for family stability" during hard times and "conflict over women's paid work," Barbara Melosh has written, "found cultural expression in a reaffirmation of traditional gender ideology." Melosh is concerned with New Deal art and theater projects, but her argument that public iconography both mirrored and shaped Depression-era attitudes holds for the Titanic Memorial as well. With the family order threatened yet again, the disaster worked to remind men and women of how things should be. "[A]s we stand before this beautiful Titanic Memorial, depicting the figure of a man with outstretched arms in the form of a cross, as a symbol of sacrifice," one woman wrote, "we recall again the heroism displayed on the great ship *Titanic*, where men forgot self and offered their own lives that women and children might be saved."[3]

Away from public occasions and official ceremonies, commemoration took many different forms, both sacred and secular. Theologian J. Gresham Machen invoked the *Titanic* in 1923 as he laid the intellectual foundations for fundamentalist Christianity. Arguing that men do not redeem themselves but achieve salvation only through the suffering of Christ on the Cross, Machen challenged the popularity of "Nearer, My God, to Thee." While there was nothing wrong with this hymn, he explained, its meaning was extremely limited; it meant only that "our own crosses or trials may be a means to bring us nearer to God." It said nothing about Christian salvation, which was "altogether rooted in the Christian doctrine of the deity of Christ." Machen felt "sorry that the people on the *Titanic* could not find a better hymn to use in the last solemn hour of their lives," and he left the clear implication that they were not, after all, redeemed.[4] In a small way, then, the *Titanic* figured into the contest between religious fundamentalism and liberalism that culminated on a popular level with the Scopes trial in 1925.

In the unlikely locale of St. Meinrad, Indiana, a would-be Dante named Henry Brenner published an epic called *Titanic's Knell: A Satire on Speed* (1932), in which the narrator is given a tour of "the dark and terrible abyss" by Christopher Columbus. Columbus—presumably chosen to represent a prelapsarian America—bemoans the "cruel frenzy of modern progress" and an array of other sins, including vanity, lechery, and luxury; jewels and expensive clothing still cling to the passengers' bones at the bottom of the Atlantic.[5]

In Joplin, Missouri, a gambler named Alvin Clarence Thomas was rechristened Titanic Thompson because of "the way he's sinking everybody around here," though it was rumored that he got his nickname by dressing in women's clothing to escape from the actual ship. Thompson became a celebrity for testifying as a material witness in connection with the 1928 murder of Arnold Rothstein, the gangster who fixed the 1919 World Series.[6]

Gamblers and the *Titanic* also figured into Wilson Mizner's tale "You're Dead!" published in the appropriately titled 1936 collection *Stories for Men*. As Mizner's unnamed narrator tells it, Harry Rodney and Little Bert were inseparable partners who decided to work their "ocean graft" on the *Titanic*. Harry survived by taking his chances in the freezing water and getting picked up by a lifeboat; Little Bert, he told everyone, had died. Ten years later a mysterious man shows up at the narrator's hotel room, identifies himself as Little Bert, and explains that he escaped from the ship by stealing clothes and jewelry from a woman's stateroom and sneaking into a boat. Aboard the *Carpathia* and from then on, Harry insisted to Bert, "You're dead," ostensibly to protect him and his stash of jewelry from the law but really because Bert had violated the masculine code of honor, which even criminals were supposed to adhere to, and was no longer fit to live in the world of men. In Damon Runyonesque language Mizner updated the *Titanic*'s gender lessons for a less genteel Depression-era male readership.[7]

We have already seen how rural and urban "folk," especially African Americans, passed along and revised *Titanic* songs, which folklorists like the Lomaxes recorded in the 1930s and 1940s and spread to urban white audiences. Blacks also carried their versions of the disaster from the rural South to southern and northern cities during the Great Migration between the world wars. Folklorists, who began collecting southern versions of the adventures of Shine in the late 1930s, found a much richer variety when they turned their attention to the urban North in the 1950s and 1960s; Langston Hughes and Arna Bontemps published a version Hughes heard on a Harlem street in their *Book of Negro Folklore* (1958).

The disaster, then, continued to do important, if sporadic, cultural work, from reminding men and women of their proper roles and responsibilities at the onset of the Depression to asserting racial equality and exposing racial injustice in the dismal climate of the interwar years. It would have been strange had the *Titanic* not endured in American lore and memory. The ubiquity of the disaster in April and May 1912 and its mythic power—the "timeless" themes of hubris, fate, and heroism—carried the memory along into the 1920s and beyond. But if the *Titanic* (the memory, that is, not the ship) never disappeared, its presence after 1913 was occasional or marginal until it was rediscovered for new audiences in the 1950s as a commercial phenomenon.

For all its other meanings, the *Titanic* functioned in 1912 as a commodity; it sold newspapers and books and encouraged a variety of entrepreneurial schemes. The Travelers Insurance Company advertised its services by celebrating the rule of the sea and urging men to buy policies to protect their women and children. Theater owners showed glass lantern slides of the disaster's aftermath—photographs sold by the American Press Association and Underwood & Underwood and then marketed by the firm of Hinton-Fell-Elliott, which also offered posters to draw in viewers. Exhibitors across the country displayed footage of what they claimed—some truthfully, some fraudulently—was the *Titanic*. (The only genuine footage showed the *Titanic*'s keel at the Harland & Wolff shipyards in Belfast, though several advertisements implied that audiences would see actual scenes of the disaster.) The most fascinating attempt to profit from the disaster, as well as an early example of what Frank Thompson calls the "instant transformation from news to drama," was the film *Saved from the Titanic*. Rushed into theaters only a month after the wreck, the film starred Dorothy Gibson, a movie actress who had actually survived the disaster, and built the incident into a romantic plot about how Dorothy overcomes her fear of the sea to let her fiancé do his duty and stay in the navy. Like the newspapers but more transparently, *Saved from the Titanic* combined authenticity and fabrication for commercial purposes. Gibson used her real experience to authenticate and promote the movie.[8]

The *Titanic*'s commercial possibilities lay dormant from this initial outpouring of entrepreneurial energies until after World War II, when the disaster again reached mass audiences. In 1936 David O. Selznick launched a well-publicized movie project about the *Titanic*, intending to make the film Alfred Hitchcock's Hollywood debut, but immediately ran into a multitude of obstacles. Howard Hughes and a French company owned *Titanic* scripts and threatened lawsuits. British censors refused to permit a film that might criticize British shipping and so deprived Selznick of lucrative overseas markets. Then the war came, closing off still more markets and raising serious doubts about the appropriateness of a movie about a horrific ship disaster.[9] Hollywood didn't sink the liner on-screen until 1953, when Twentieth Century-Fox released *Titanic*, directed by Jean Negulesco and starring Clifton Webb and Barbara Stanwyck.

British obstructionism had the ironic result of ceding the *Titanic* to German filmmakers. Herbert Selpin's *Titanic* transformed the disaster into Nazi propaganda in 1943; the hero of the film is the fictitious German first officer, who must combat the selfishness and stupidity of the British shipowner and passengers. Film historian Harry Geduld notes that as a result of Nazi propaganda minister Joseph Goebbels's artistic differences with Selpin, the director was "garrotted with his own suspenders." Two earlier German films about the disaster, E. A. Dupont's *Atlantic* (1929) and Arnold Fanck and Leni Riefenstahl's *S.O.S. Eisberg* (1933), "introduced the now familiar disaster-movie formula" of melodramatic plots and impressive special effects. (Germany also produced a novel about the disaster, Robert Prechtl's ponderous *Titanensturz: Roman eines Zeitalters*, published in 1937 and translated into English as *Titanic* in 1940. John Jacob Astor, the hero of Prechtl's book, speaks more like a German philosopher than an American tycoon. "Would this conception of a state of ecstasy lifting the mystic out of this world also explain divination?" he asks in a discussion of the Beyond among the first-cabin passengers.)[10]

The fate of Selznick's project suggests that the *Titanic*'s forty-year absence from American commercial culture was simply a result of mundane circumstance. But if we look at the particular ways in which the *Titanic* story was told in the 1950s, we can understand its rediscovery in more significant cultural and historical terms. Nobody deserves more credit for this rediscovery than Walter Lord, whose 1955 best seller *A Night to Remember* gave the disaster its fullest retelling since 1912 and made it speak to a modern mass audience and a new set of postwar concerns. In the creation of the *Titanic* myth there were two defining moments: 1912, of course, and 1955.

Lord's interest in the *Titanic* reached back to childhood. In 1926, when he was nine, he traveled to Europe on the *Titanic*'s sister ship, the *Olympic*, where he spent his time "prowling around" and trying to imagine "such a huge thing" going down in the middle of the Atlantic. At ten or eleven he was drawing pictures of the ship—"masses" of them, he recalls—and when he started collecting *Titanic* memorabilia, "people began to take notice of this oddity." After majoring in history at Princeton, serving with the Office of Strategic Services during World War II, and getting a degree from Yale Law School, Lord went to work as an editor of legal and business newsletters and then as a copywriter at the J. Walter Thompson advertising agency. He wrote *A Night to Remember* in his spare time.[11]

Published by Henry Holt in November 1955, the book was an immediate success. By January 1956 it had sold sixty thousand copies and climbed onto the best seller list, where it stayed for more than six months and briefly edged out Anne Morrow Lindbergh's *Gift from the Sea* (which had been at the top of the list for forty-four consecutive weeks) to take the number one spot. Without a doubt *A Night to Remember* owed much of its popularity to Holt's aggressive marketing campaign and—though Lord rightly observes that "there was virtually nothing on the subject between 1913 and 1955"—to the 1953 Webb-Stanwyck film and some recent *Titanic* articles in *Coronet*, *Cosmopolitan*, *Life*, and *Holiday*. Holt announced the book with a full-page ad on the cover of *Publishers Weekly* that showed the dust jacket illustration of the *Titanic* steaming toward the iceberg; the next page boasted that with ten thousand dollars' initial advertising and a fifty-thousand-copy first printing, it was a "sure best seller!" Lord published an account of the leadup to the crash in the December *American Heritage*; condensed versions of the book appeared in the November *Ladies' Home Journal* and the January *Reader's Digest*, and the Book-of-the-Month Club offered its own edition in June 1956.

Kraft sponsored a live NBC-TV version on March 28, directed by George Roy Hill and narrated by Claude Rains, which attracted twenty-eight million viewers and helped boost hardcover sales over the hundred thousand mark. (Lord later remarked that "[m]ore people probably learned about the *Titanic* that night than at any time since 1912." The broadcast was "the biggest, most lavish, most expensive thing of its kind" yet attempted, involving thirty-one sets, 107 actors, seventy-two speaking parts, and three thousand gallons of water and costing ninety-five thousand dollars.) Bantam issued a paperback edition in October 1956 and celebrated its fiftieth printing in 1988; the book has never been out of print.[12]

It would, however, be a mistake to say that marketing entirely—or even primarily—explains the resonance of *A Night to Remember*. Lord sees much of its appeal in its "breezy" style and "freshness" of form: short paragraphs, reconstructed conversation, anecdotes, and what he calls "the minute-by-minute idea." One reviewer perceptively described Lord's technique as "a kind of literary pointillism, the arrangement of contrasting bits of fact and emotion in such a fashion that a vividly real impression of an event is conveyed to the reader." The fact that the book so readily translated to television is important. The narrative is highly visual—it begins with *Titanic* lookout Frederick Fleet peering "into a dazzling night" and ends with the sun catching "the bright red-and-white stripes of the pole from the *Titanic*'s barber shop, as it bobbed in the empty sea"—and aural—full of dialogue, music, crashing, screaming, and silence.[13] Lord plunges his readers into the moment with the immediacy of a live broadcast or a television documentary. *A Night to Remember*'s appearance was bracketed by the four-year run (1953–1957) of the CBS show *You Are There*, in which actors re-created historical events (including the *Titanic* disaster, broadcast in May 1955) and Walter Cronkite interviewed the participants.[14] Though Lord claims

that he hadn't seen the approach used before, Jim Bishop beat
him to the best seller list in 1955 with *The Day Lincoln Was
Shot*. Both authors successfully repeated the formula in 1957,
Lord with *Day of Infamy*, Bishop with *The Day Christ Died*.
Blurring history into news and drama, these books all collapse
historical duration into intense moments of lived experience.

I mentioned earlier how the *Titanic* disaster confirmed a
distinctly modern sense of time and space—the ability, through
wireless communication, to experience events simultaneously
across long distances. While this insight belongs to Stephen
Kern rather than Walter Lord, *A Night to Remember* implicitly conveys much the same idea. Simple and chronological
only on the most superficial level, Lord's narrative takes an
imaginative approach to time and space in which hours and
minutes prove extremely malleable, the ship itself seems almost infinitely complex, and the disaster assumes order and
unity only from far away.

Fleet gazes from the crow's nest just before 11:40 P.M. on
April 14, but before we can see the iceberg, Lord has shifted to
the rich passengers' dogs and then back to Fleet at 10 o'clock.
By the time the berg has passed from view, we have experienced the collision from the after bridge, the first class dining
saloon, the galley, eleven passenger cabins, and the first class
smoking room. After stopping time (or, more accurately, expanding it) for this tour through the ship, Lord moves to the
bridge, repeats the collision, inspects the damage in the boiler
rooms, repeats the collision again (this time from the aft boiler
rooms), jumps ten miles away and half an hour back to the
bridge of the *Californian*, and ends the scene with the
Californian's second officer watching a "big ship suddenly stop
and put out most of her lights" at 11:40.[15]

Lord, in short, constructs a modernist narrative around a
modernist event. While the subsequent chapters move the
story ahead in discrete chunks of clock time, *A Night to Re-*

member routinely manipulates and violates this simple chronology. Moments are extended outward through space—to the *Californian*, to the survivors watching and listening from the boats, to the "wildly excited" New York City—and drawn out within the ship's expanse through the recurrent narration of simultaneous events. The narrative manages in this way to juggle an enormous cast of characters and convey a sense of the *Titanic*'s magnitude. "This book is really about the last night of a small town," Lord writes. "The *Titanic* was that big and carried that many people." As news of the collision spreads, as passengers put on their life belts, as the boats are uncovered and the loading begins, Lord shifts the action from port to starboard, from the upper to the lower decks. The Strauses stop to reminisce about their lives together: "the ashes of the Confederacy . . . the small china business in Philadelphia . . . building Macy's into a national institution . . . and now the happy twilight that crowned successful life." But time moves differently for Second Officer Lightoller on another part of the boat deck: "His gauge showed time was flying. The pace grew faster—and sloppier." For a group of steerage women and children, the pace is agonizingly slow; their "long trip" to safety takes them "up the broad stairs to the Third Class lounge on C Deck . . . across the open well deck . . . by the Second Class library and into First Class quarters. Then down the long corridor by the surgeon's office, the private saloon for the maids and valets of First Class passengers, finally up the grand stairway to the Boat Deck." Every moment—the last boat departing, the rising of the water toward the stern, the final plunge, the boats adrift, the *Carpathia* steaming to the rescue, the rescue—Lord splits into multiple perspectives. For the women in the boats, there is "an agonizing stateliness" when the band plays "Autumn" (the hymn, not the popular song) at 2:15; for the men on deck, there is too much happening to pay attention.[16]

The book's main character is the *Titanic* itself, which Lord portrays in all its vastness and intricacy. While the story has an obvious beginning and end, he resists easy closure by suggesting that the multiple perspectives could be multiplied several times more; despite his painstaking research, including interviews with sixty-three survivors, to "tell everything that happened is impossible." Here again, *A Night to Remember* embeds a modernist event in a modernist form: fragmented, uncertain, open-ended. At the end of the book Lord pauses in his account of the *Carpathia*'s arrival in New York to present a list of ifs about the weather, the wireless ice warnings, the direction and timing of the collision, the construction of the ship, the number of lifeboats, the failure of the *Californian* to respond. The whole event hinges on these ifs—on alternatives and contingencies, any one of which could have radically changed the outcome.[17]

But there are limits to Lord's modernism. He doesn't actually call the ifs contingencies; they are "fate," and the disaster is "a classic Greek tragedy." More significantly, he interrupts the narrative at 2:20, just when the stern has disappeared into the ocean, for an extended piece of historical analysis. In addition to the book's style Lord attributes its appeal to "a new point" that *A Night to Remember* makes at this break in the story: that the sinking of the *Titanic* represented the end of an era. Admitting the class and ethnic "prejudices" of the "old days"—Lord's politics in these pages is a kind of genteel liberalism—he celebrates what he takes to be their disappearance after 1912. But he also expresses regret for "this lost world." Whether causally or symbolically, the disaster "marked the end of a general feeling of confidence." Uncertainty replaced the belief in "a steady, orderly, civilized life." The *Titanic* was "the first jar" in an "unending sequence of disillusionment. Before the *Titanic*, all was quiet. Afterward, all was tumult."[18] Not only has Lord stopped time here, but he has imposed an entirely different temporal scheme. The end-of-an-era theme grafts world-historical significance onto the minute-by-minute drama. The disaster becomes an epochal dividing line. The modernist narrative dissolves into nostalgia.

There is, of course, no inherent opposition between nostalgia and modernism (Henry Adams, the *Titanic* ticket holder, was a nostalgic modernist), and their compatibility in *A Night to Remember* goes a long way toward explaining the book's resonance in 1950s America. By then modernism as a literary form had become part of the mainstream, even if it was (and remains) rare in history books. Lord's narrative, moreover, offered a modernist style without a crucial element of modernist substance: irony. The disaster lends itself to irony—to a depiction of characters caught up in a frustrating and absurd situation—but Lord preferred to call it a tragedy. Faced with fate rather than absurdity, the characters finally gain full knowledge of their predicament and act accordingly. In the end they do things rather than have things done to them. Established usages do not elude or fail them; they are not, like Hemingway's Frederic Henry, blown up while eating cheese.[19] There was nothing in Lord's book to jar its readers' sensibilities. He placed them in rather than above the action, at eye level rather than at ironic distance. Irony would have precluded Lord's kind of nostalgia.

What was *A Night to Remember* nostalgic *for?* Certainly not class or ethnic prejudice. But Lord also mentioned the disappearance of "some nobler instincts"—chivalry and noblesse oblige—and recognized, in retrospect, that "the women and children first idea was still very stirring" at the time he wrote the book. Tales of old-fashioned chivalry possessed obvious appeal in a postwar culture that celebrated the "traditional" family and sacralized the roles of male breadwinner and female homemaker. These roles, as Elaine Tyler May has shown, "represented a source of meaning and security in a world run amok."[20] Lord sounded a common Cold War theme when he waxed nostalgic about confidence and certainty, and though he debunked the most egregious myths about Butt and Astor, *A Night to Remember* told a new generation about how men protected women in times of danger. (Five years later, in *The Good Years*, he refined the end-of-an-era idea to give it more of a reformist bent and made the Great War rather than the *Titanic* the watershed event. "These years were good," he wrote, "because, whatever the trouble, people were sure they could fix it," an attitude no longer possible after the experience of world war. As alternatives to "Good," he suggested "Confident," "Buoyant," "Spirited," and "Golden.")[21]

Above and beyond its stated objects of nostalgia, Lord's narrative yearned for time itself. Review after review linked the book's excitement to its profusion of characters and, more specifically, to the ways in which Lord depicted "[w]hat they saw and felt and did at a particular moment"—"the human side of the Titanic story." Unlike the 1912 accounts, which described heroism and cowardice in terms of gender, class, and ethnicity, *A Night to Remember* revealed a spectrum of behavior among "men and women, rich and poor, officers and crew." How people "acted," said the *New York Times*, "is the core of Mr. Lord's account, and explains its fascination, a pull as powerful in its way as the last downward plunge of the ship itself." If what another reviewer called "legendary acts of gallantry" stood out most dramatically, what really mattered was the ability—the time—to think and feel and act in any way. "What would it be like to be aboard a sinking ocean liner?" began a *Newsweek* piece titled "The Fabric of Disaster." The night was "a mixture of overconfidence, heroism and stupidity," or, in a slightly different trinity, "devotion, gallantry, and stupidity." While noting Lord's "restraint," the *Christian Century* observed that "the terrible drama of this existential situation par excellence"—the fashionable Jean-Paul Sartre had even made his way into book reviews—"comes smashing through all the author's reticence."[22] In place of irony Lord posed a mimetic challenge to his readers: How would I have acted in the same situation?

Time to act: This is what links *A Night to Remember*'s modernism and nostalgia. Lord's method of stretching time to leap from point to point in space postponed the inevitable so that readers could see, over and over again, that the *Titanic* disaster happened slowly. Lord maintained "suspense . . . against a known conclusion"—suspense in the most literal sense, interruption and delay.[23] The *Titanic* took two hours and forty minutes to sink, and Lord's narrative, with its combination of quick jumps and recurrence, managed to move at a fast pace while dramatizing the disaster's full duration. The minute-by-minute, multiple-perspective technique and the end-of-an-era theme fused to create a double sense of lost time. Simultaneously wistful and anxious, *A Night to Remember* spoke of a bygone age in which disasters gave people time to die.

In the 1950s there was good reason to be nostalgic for this older kind of disaster. Nostalgia, as Fred Davis has noted, "thrives . . . on the rude transitions wrought by such phenomena as war, depression, civil disturbance, and cataclysmic natural disasters—in short, those events that cause masses of people to feel uneasy and to wonder whether the world and their being are quite what they always took them to be."[24] The *Titanic* resonated in the fifties because it provided a nostalgic alternative to a world in "rude transition" to the atomic age. Just as the "return" to the nuclear family and "traditional" gender roles seemed to offer security amid the constant threat of nuclear war, so did the *Titanic* provide shelter in the "memory" of a safer time and even in the recollection of a quainter kind of disaster. In addition to observing that *A Night to Remember* depicted the passengers and crew in a range of emotions and a variety of actions, reviewers uncritically accepted Lord's idea that the disaster marked a point of radical discontinuity. "It was," wrote one, "the end of an era of security and the beginning of a time of danger and disbelief." A technological catastrophe, despite all reassurances about its impossibility, ushered in a new era of anxiety and fear; "the unpredictable undid the most confidently predicted"; nothing was fail-safe.[25]

The real rude transition had occurred more recently. A truly modern technological disaster would not give its victims time to die, would not necessarily allow for survivors, might not even have an aftermath. The *Titanic*, like all objects of nostalgia, was at once current and distant—a "means for engaging the present" and an emblem of discontinuity. "There is an even-keel, golden-mean gentility about most of the action which makes the whole event far more remote than 44 years would ordinarily make anything," the *Christian Century* shrewdly observed. "But the desperation in the context of the action makes it contemporary enough to keep you up as long as it takes to finish the book the night you start it." Time to die was something remote; desperation was contemporary.[26]

Few directly mentioned the bomb, but it loomed nevertheless. *The Reader's Digest* condensation was bracketed by articles entitled "Inside the H-Bomb Plant" and "The Fearsome Atomic Submarine." The most intriguing reference appeared in the last line of *Time*'s review of *A Night to Remember*: "This air age, when death commonly comes too swiftly for heroism or with no survivors to record it, can still turn with wonder to an age before yesterday when a thousand deaths at sea seemed the very worst the world must suffer."[27]

The popularity of *A Night to Remember* coincided with an interest in disasters among social scientists that was in its own way as nostalgic as Lord's. Under government and academic auspices, "disaster research" came into its own during and after World War II. Many institutions conducted "disaster projects" in the late forties and fifties; scholars studied disasters at the RAND Corporation, a consortium of New York universities, the University of Chicago, the University of Maryland, the University of Michigan, Cornell University, the U.S. Strategic Bombing Survey, the National Research Council and the American Association for the Advancement of Science (in 1951 the Defense Department asked the NRC and the National Academy of Sciences to establish a Committee on Disaster Studies), the University of Oklahoma, the New School for Social Research, Columbia University, the Institute for Research in Human Relations, Civil Defense Research Associates Inc., the Washington Public Opinion Laboratory, and Johns Hopkins University. Though the research covered a range of disasters from revolutions to hurricanes, the "specific impetus," as one survey of the literature put it, was "the threat of air attack on American and British cities." The expertise of social scientists, the argument went, would play an essential role in the atomic age; sociologists, psychiatrists, psychologists, and anthropologists would apply their knowledge of disasters to the problems of survival.[28]

Behind such work lay the assumption that past disasters could provide the necessary data for formulating policy and devising the proper therapeutic responses. But as the critic Philip Wylie observed in the *Bulletin of the Atomic Scientists*, this assumption was based on flawed analogies and a false sense of continuity. Even though many of the victims and witnesses of an explosion in Houston and a tornado in Worcester believed that they were experiencing an atomic bomb blast, the "successful" therapeutic responses to these disasters would be inappropriate or impossible in the event of a real nuclear attack. "Pragmatic investigations into 'familiar' calamities, whether fire, flood, explosion, hurricane, epidemic, earthquake or church social food poisoning," wrote Wylie, "will not furnish dependable data for adducing human behavior under totally unfamiliar nationwide atomic onslaught." *A Night to*

Remember's nostalgia for an older kind of disaster implicitly acknowledged the gaping differences between the *Titanic* and nuclear war; if it took refuge in the past, it didn't do so as a matter of policy. The nostalgia of the "disaster studies" movement—Wylie's review appeared a year after Lord's book—was far more dangerous. To Wylie the claim that we could take comfort in the lessons of "familiar" disasters resembled efforts to soothe the American public about hydrogen bomb testing with assurances that testing would make for a "cleaner" H-bomb. It also resembled the government-sponsored civil defense movement's attempts to normalize nuclear disaster through air-raid drills and fallout shelters. As Paul Boyer has shown, public officials, experts, and books like *How to Survive an Atomic Bomb* (1950) tried to convince Americans that preparing for a nuclear attack was not only possible but actually simple as long they dressed correctly, kept their cool, and didn't "forget the facts."[29]

Lord's book took a particularly imaginative approach to the time-to-die and end-of-an-era themes. The TV version, with its huge cast and elaborate staging, similarly stretched time by juxtaposing simultaneous moments throughout the ship's expanse. A reviewer summed up George Roy Hill's technique: "A narration delivered by Claude Rains was used to bridge the almost limitless number of sequences that made up the comprehensive picture of life aboard the doomed liner." Rains announced the time—11:40, 11:45, midnight, 12:15, 12:20, 12:24, 12:42, and so on until 2:20—as scenes shifted from first class to steerage, from the bridge to the wireless room, from the *Titanic*'s boiler room to the *Californian*'s radio cabin. (Commercial breaks also added to the suspension of time, if not to the suspense of the drama.) As in the book, there were no dominant characters; the show displayed a range of responses. Unlike the book, the broadcast ended with the ship going down rather than with the *Carpathia's* arrival. It focused exclusively on the slowly dawning awareness of the disaster's seriousness: the preparations for escape or death. "With no fixed policy to guide them," Rains explained, the passengers "behaved as the moment and their characters dictated." In 1956 preparation no longer necessarily meant making things right with God, though the band played the hymn "Autumn" in the TV version. Now it was the mere possibility of preparation—loading boats, saying good-bye, contemplating, brooding, even panicking—that gave the broadcast its dramatic intensity. *Variety* observed how the "[s]killful interlacing of shots from every quarter of the ship delineated the initial confidence in the ship's unsinkability and then captured the varied moods of resignation, panic, cowardice and heroism as the truth became known." After the "freezing waters of the North Atlantic closed over the grave of the *Titanic*" came the denouement. Rains, seated at a book-covered desk, ran down the list of contingencies and declared with consummate British authority, "Never again has man been so confident. An age had come to an end." Fade out.[30]

The 1958 British film production of *A Night to Remember* (which was more successful in the United States than was the Hollywood *Titanic*) economically covered the gamut of behavior from Ismay to the Strauses to a composite steerage hero named Murphy, but it also featured a central character, Second Officer Charles Lightoller (Kenneth More), whom the script called upon to announce the end of an era while sitting atop an overturned collapsible lifeboat in the black and freezing Atlantic. "I know what the sea can do. But this is different," Lightoller tells Colonel Gracie. "Because we hit an iceberg?" Gracie inquires. "No," explains Lightoller. "Because we were so sure. Because even though it's happened, it's still unbelievable. I don't think I'll ever feel sure again. About anything." While these pronouncements of the Age of Anxiety gave the broadcast and film their currency, their poignancy came from the elaborate dramas of awareness and prepara- tion. The movie took what Lord thought was the enormous liberty of allowing the band's cellist to sing "Nearer, My God, to Thee," but what mattered more than absolute accuracy was the tempo of the music—unhurried, deliberate—and the pos- sibility of resolutions. (In contrast with its content, promotional strategies for the film were distinctly modern. American ex- hibitors were encouraged to try a variety of tie-ins, including souvenir books, contests through local radio and TV, "quiz mats" about the disaster in newspapers, swizzle sticks in the shape of the *Titanic*, and department store window displays featuring movie stills and posters and juxtaposing 1958 fash- ions with 1912 fashions. For all its ambivalence about moder- nity, *Titanic* nostalgia was also a shrewd marketing ploy.)[31]

The possibility of resolutions spoke not only to the threat of nuclear annihilation but also to the related ideology of domes- ticity. Experts in the 1950s frequently linked the atomic age, the Cold War, and the specter of sexual chaos and urged the "containment" of women in traditional gender roles. One of the stories told in all the versions of *A Night to Remember* in- volved a young Philadelphia couple, Mr. and Mrs. Lucien Smith. In the TV broadcast the Smiths enjoy the consummate modern marriage, based on loving companionship and con- sumption. The gender theme is introduced early, when the ship's designer, Thomas Andrews, complains to his steward, Alfred, that nobody is retiring to the ladies' writing room af- ter dinner. Alfred observes that "the ladies of the twentieth century are not as retiring as formerly"—in other words, that they are now attractive and entertaining companions to their husbands rather than quiet exemplars of duty and sacrifice. After the collision Mrs. Smith's first concern is whether the coat she has chosen to wear is "all right." Her ignorance of the real danger they face is portrayed as natural; it is Mr. Smith's role to know about the world beyond the protected site of consumption and marital bliss. He assures her that the collision will mean nothing more than a minor change in their travel plans and tells her only that "it might be wiser not to bother with trifles" like jewelry. She cheerfully agrees to "just take these two."

The subtext here is that Mrs. Smith is not consuming wisely. She seems to be teetering on the edge of overconsumption, female frivolity, and delusional self-indulgence. According to 1950s gender ideology, the balance between domesticity, consumption, and social health was delicate. Up on deck Mr. Smith continues to withhold the truth while acting firmly to protect his wife. "Dearest, I never expected to ask you to obey," he says apologetically, "but this is one time you must. It is only a matter of form to have the women and children first. The ship is thoroughly equipped. Everyone on her will be saved." She asks if he is telling the truth, and he replies yes. Then, according to the stage directions, "[h]e kisses her and she steps obediently into the boat." Mr. and Mrs. Smith occupy the "equal" roles of breadwinner-protector and consumer-protected in a marriage built on love and satisfaction rather than obedience, though power ultimately resides with him. The commercials reinforced these roles by giving Mom recipes for Kraft products that were sure to please her family, including a kidney bean rarebit spiced with "the tantalizing flavor of Cheez Whiz." Women's fulfillment was supposed to come by pleasing their husbands and children through agreeable personalities and wise consumer choices.[32]

In the television broadcast the Smiths' story provided no more than a subplot, but domesticity furnished the central melodrama of the 1953 Hollywood *Titanic*. An American aristocrat and playboy, Richard Sturges (Clifton Webb), sneaks his way into steerage to prevent his wife, Julia (Barbara Stanwyck), from running off with their children, Annette and

Norman. Julia wants to save the children from a "rootless, superficial," and decadent international life and return them to the wholesomeness of midwestern America. In a desperate moment she informs Richard that Norman is not his son but the result of a one-night stand with a kind man who seemed to promise relief from her bitterness and depression. Because Richard has sought the pleasures of excessive consumption outside the home, Julia has been driven to find sexual fulfillment outside marriage. When disaster strikes, Richard redeems himself from his foreign and unmanly ways by saving many women and children. (His manliness stands in contrast with the behavior of a character appropriately named Meeker, who cross-dresses his way to safety.) Norman also acts heroically, and Richard proclaims him "my son." Richard's behavior reconciles him with Julia; in their parting moment they remember the simpler times of their courtship, and he offers a "restatement" of his "eternal devotion." This divorce and remarriage plot domesticates the disaster by making it into the means by which middle-class nuclear family tensions are resolved. The family wouldn't have found itself in such a fix had Richard and Julia been content to stay in the safety of the Midwest and avoided unwholesome social and sexual adventures. But at the critical juncture Richard finally assumes his proper role as protector—"Webb becomes a man in the crisis," said a reviewer—and, by dying, "saves" the family, though only Julia and Annette survive.[33]

(Christopher Durang parodied the Webb-Stanwyck film in a 1974 play. At dinner on the *Titanic* Durang's Richard learns from his wife, Victoria, that their son, Teddy, is actually the product of Victoria's affair with a derelict. Richard, who has always ridiculed Victoria's Indiana pig farm upbringing, then informs her that their daughter, Annabella, is actually the product of his affair with Harriet Lindsay; using mirrors, he and Harriet had tricked her into thinking that she gave birth.

Victoria, in turn, tells Richard that there is no Annabella; she and Harriet were having an affair and, using mirrors and white bread, faked Annabella's birth to deceive Richard. The play ends without a family reconciliation. As the orchestra plays "Nearer, My God, to Thee," Teddy shoots and kills his parents.)[34]

Though the 1953 film exposes the hollowness of Richard's aristocratic pretensions, its ultimate effect is to efface class disparities. Richard buys his ticket at an inflated price from a Basque immigrant named Mr. Uzcadam and thus inadvertently saves Uzcadam's life while supplying him with a nest egg for his American future. When the ship is sinking, Richard returns to steerage to rescue Mrs. Uzcadam and her children. His duty done, he parts with the family, and the steerage disappears from the film. *Titanic* provides no signs that class played a major role in the disaster. Instead the film affirms the classlessness of the universal middle class by sending the Uzcadams on their way to solid bourgeois citizenship and containing Annette in a healthy marriage to the gee-whiz Purdue tennis player Giff Rogers (Robert Wagner), who courts her aboard the ship and survives after heroically untangling a lifeboat and falling into the ocean.

Class figures much more prominently in *A Night to Remember*. In the film Murphy must use force against the crew to save women from the steerage, and many steerage passengers remain on deck to die singing "Nearer, My God, to Thee." The TV production depicts the travails of a German family named the Clasens who don't arrive on deck until the last boats are gone. Lord himself discusses class discrimination quite explicitly. After giving the survival statistics, he notes: "Neither the chance to be chivalrous nor the fruits of chivalry seemed to go with a Third Class passage." But in tallying what was lost in the disaster, he conveys a good deal of sympathy for the "wonderful intimacy" of the "little world of the

Edwardian rich." Meanwhile, he suggests, a bit regretfully, that social class vanished with the *Titanic*. "The Titanic somehow lowered the curtain on this way of living. It never was the same again. First the war, then the income tax, made sure of that." *A Night to Remember* speaks from the vantage point of the supposedly classless (i.e., middle-class) American fifties and its assumptions of homogeneity and consensus.[35]

Other "rediscoveries" of the disaster conveyed the time-to-die theme with less creativity than *A Night to Remember*. Jack Weeks's "tragic saga of incredible folly and incredible courage"—a nonfiction piece in *Holiday* magazine that coincided with the release of the Webb-Stanwyck movie—simply listed "the customary performances of confusion, inadequacy, stupidity and selfishness," and, of course, "beautiful courage." Richard O'Connor's *Down to Eternity* had the double misfortune of being published less than two months after *A Night to Remember* and not being nearly as good a book. With its glossy cover painting of Clifton Webb, it tried to capitalize on the resurgent interest in the disaster generated by the film. O'Connor too emphasized the variety of "human behavior" and the possibility of human drama—the long opening chapter was called "Dramatis Personae"—though his cast of characters was smaller than Lord's and he sacrificed credibility by repeating the old legends about Astor, Butt, and a heroic Newfoundland that dog-paddled for hours to help guide the lifeboats to the *Carpathia*. Still, *Down to Eternity* shared with other fifties Titanica the dual sense of continuity and discontinuity. The book was advertised with the slogan "The Night a World Ended," and O'Connor explicitly stated that the disaster marked a sharp historical break: "Even across the comparatively short interval of four decades, the Edwardians seem almost like a lost tribe to be studied from the viewpoint of an anthropologist, so little did they apparently have in common with the tense and fearful man of the present." The disaster brought out the contrast between Edwardian confidence and modern anxiety, but it also signaled the realization that unimaginable technological catastrophes were still possible. Here again the *Titanic* was both unlike and like the bomb, a far cry from its threat of instantaneous destruction yet its ancestor in terms of misplaced assurance and extraordinary hubris: "So the Edwardians contemplated, when they were not completely deaf to, a warning signal that they and their works—no matter how massive, how convenient, how defiant of the forces that have always waited at the world's edge to remind man of his frailty, whether an iceberg or a man-made device that can destroy cities in a flash of solar energy—were only of the earth, earthly."[36]

The politics of nostalgia are ambiguous. A deep feeling of dissatisfaction with the present combines with a sense of historical disjunction so absolute that there is nothing to do but regret the loss. Lord sealed off a compelling discussion of historical contingency by chalking everything up to fate. Later he regretted the loss of faith in the possibility of human-directed change and reform. Despite such fatalism, the rediscovery of the *Titanic* served at least in part as a political critique—an implicit challenge to the Cold War gospel of progress. The fascination with an archetype of technological hubris indicated serious doubts about the equation of technology and advancement. While many fifties Americans were reading about or watching the *Titanic* disaster, the atomic establishment was telling the public about "the sunny side of the atom." More broadly, the nostalgia for security reflected an ambivalence about the achievements of the "affluent society" and the burgeoning national security state. Locating security in the remote, pre-*Titanic* past called into question the claims that defense-based abundance had provided Americans with permanent safety and comfort.[37]

The *Titanic* steamed into the Cold War in less ambivalent ways too. Here the improbable figure was Margaret Tobin Brown—the Unsinkable Molly Brown—who also happened to be rediscovered in the 1950s and early 1960s. Molly Brown had been a minor legend since the time of the disaster, especially in Colorado, which proudly claimed her as a local hero. She appeared in popular historian Gene Fowler's *Timberline* (1933) as a regional type—a "vital Amazon" of hard-drinking Irish stock who grew up in Hannibal, Missouri, fished with Mark Twain and shocked him by swimming naked, and lit out for the mining camps of Colorado, where she met and married "Leadville Johnny" Brown. Johnny struck it rich but burned up the three hundred thousand dollars he had earned for his claim by setting a fire in the stove where Molly had hidden it, then went out the same day and struck it even richer. Molly made him move to Denver before setting off by herself for Europe to join international society. Next she bought a seventy-room mansion near New York City. On another trip home from Europe she traveled on the *Titanic*. When the ship went down, she took charge of a lifeboat, rationed her abundant furs and clothing among the other passengers, barked commands while standing dressed only in her corset with a Colt pistol tied to her waist, threatened to throw complainers overboard, told tales and sang songs, and directed the boat to safety. She spent the remaining twenty years of her life traveling. She and Johnny stayed separated.[38]

Coronet reprinted Fowler's rags-to-riches tough-gal story in 1949 as "The Unsinkable Mrs. Brown." Lord and O'Connor gave her cameos in their books in late 1955 and early 1956. At the same time the Advertising Council and the Magazine Publishers of America sponsored a full-page ad for U.S. savings bonds headlined MRS. BROWN REFUSED TO SINK. The ad featured a photograph of Molly wearing an elaborately textured dress, a silk cloak, and an enormous hat, leaning against a chair with one arm, her other hand confidently on her hip, smiling brashly away from the camera. The text borrowed freely from Fowler's account, except that it replaced the vaguely bawdy "Keep rowing, you ———, or I'll toss you all overboard" with the tamer "Keep rowing or I'll toss you all overboard!" After three paragraphs about Molly's lifeboat exploits, it moved into the sales pitch:

> Asked how she'd done it, she replied, "Typical Brown luck. I'm unsinkable." But it wasn't luck. It was pluck. And Americans have always had plenty of that smiling, hardy courage. When you come to think of it, that's one reason why our country's Savings Bonds rank among the world's finest investments.
>
> For 160 million determined Americans stand behind those Bonds.
>
> The surest way to protect your own security—and the nation's—is through United States Savings Bonds. Invest in them regularly—and hold on to them.

This Molly, uttering threats and ready to shoot if necessary, was less a feminist heroine than a symbol of a triumphant nation, and her story had evolved from regional Americana to Cold War parable. Pluck, courage, and determination would ensure personal and national security. Faced with peril, America "refused to sink." Through Molly's adventures, the disaster was made to illustrate American strength and to affirm prosperity and progress. The Ad Council spoke the language of what the historian George Lipsitz calls corporate liberalism, which envisioned a suburban society based on private investment and consumption and directed by big business and the national security state. The Molly Brown marketing strategy for savings bonds embodied this ideology by urging Americans to "protect" their security by investing— literally and figuratively—in national defense.[39]

The *Titanic* scene in Meredith Willson and Richard Morris's 1960 Broadway musical *The Unsinkable Molly Brown* is short but pivotal. With the sinking ship in the background, Molly (Tammy Grimes in the play, Debbie Reynolds in the 1964 movie) enforces order in the lifeboat by whipping her .45 out from her chinchilla coat, firing into the air, and then pointing the gun at a hysterical man: "I said, sit, 'fore I color the Atlantic with your yellow guts." The scene is pivotal because it comes at a moment when Molly's American sense of determination is ebbing away. According to the stage directions, "The years she has been drifting through Europe have taken a terrible toll." She has just accepted and then rejected a marriage proposal from the Prince DeLong, who wants to make her "a citizen of the world." She has resisted internationalization—"Nope, I'm stamped American from stem to stern"—but in her separation from Johnny and America, she finds herself slipping into a debauched cosmopolitanism. Returning to America on the *Titanic*, she regains her pluck when she is confronted by disaster. She threatens and encourages the passengers who fear that the lifeboat will sink. "Not with Molly Brown aboard," she says. "I was born in a cyclone in Hannibal, Missouri. That was my start and this sure in hell ain't gonna be my finish." Molly arrives back in Denver a hero. In the end she is reunited with Johnny in Leadville, where they settle into their new home, "a big baronial hunting lodge—a castle really, the biggest ever built out of the red rock of Colorado. Many American flags fly from its turrets." They reprise the show's theme song, "I Ain't Down Yet."[40]

The Unsinkable Molly Brown brought home the theme of American resiliency and exceptionalism, in this case with an isolationist undercurrent. While Molly vividly demonstrated American strength overseas, the play and movie also suggested that becoming too entangled in international affairs threatened American sovereignty and identity. (In the Webb-Stanwyck *Titanic* Julia tells Richard that she is "rescuing" their children because "We're Americans. We belong in America.") The Iowa-born Willson had already shown his attachment to small-town American ways circa 1912 in *The Music Man* (1957), and in *Molly Brown* he followed the conventions of musical romance and postwar gender relations by concluding the play with a scene of domestic bliss—the home as castle, an American fortress in a dangerous world. Again, somehow, the *Titanic* came to represent the promise of security in a well-protected, unsinkable nation.

From the nascent nuclear anxiety of *A Night to Remember* to the flag-waving patriotism of the Ad Council's Molly Brown, the Cold War informed the rediscovery of the *Titanic*. Playing off the omnipresent themes of security and insecurity, these versions of the disaster ranged between questioning and celebrating progress. None amounted to a full-fledged critique, and none displayed the genuine subversiveness of the songs and toasts that continued to circulate in African American communities and, in the case of the songs, reached white youth subcultures as well during the "folk revival" of the late fifties and early sixties. In 1953, four years after Huddie Ledbetter's death, Folkways Records released a version of "Titanic" on the LP *Leadbelly's Last Sessions*. Pink Anderson of Spartanburg, South Carolina, recorded "The Ship Titanic" for a 1956 album on Berkeley's Riverside label. Dorsey Dixon sang at the 1963 Newport Folk Festival, which starred twenty-two-year-old Bob Dylan, and RCA rereleased his "Down with the Old Canoe" the following year. Mance Lipscomb, who learned "God Moves on the Water" from Blind Willie Johnson in Navasota, Texas, sometime around 1916, performed the song at the Berkeley Folk Festival in 1961, recorded it in 1964, and sang it again in 1965 at Newport, where Dylan shocked the crowd by playing electric guitar.[41]

Dylan acknowledged debts to performers, including Leadbelly and Roy Acuff, who invoked the *Titanic* to expose the injustices and hypocrisies of race and class. As a teenager in the 1950s he may have heard their *Titanic* songs on his pilgrimages to a black disk jockey in Virginia, Minnesota, or in the coffeehouses of Minneapolis's Dinkytown. Whether or not these songs exerted a direct influence, in 1965, the year after *The Unsinkable Molly Brown* appeared as the last of the grandiose MGM screen musicals, Dylan's "Desolation Row" implicated the *Titanic* in a satirical indictment of modern America. Described by his biographer as a "rock vision of contemporary apocalypse," the song takes a grotesque tour through the world of the oppressed and marginalized and updates the earlier class critique by showing how a bureaucratic society ignores its outcasts while policing its dissenters. "Nobody has to think too much / About Desolation Row," Dylan sings. Meanwhile, "the riot squad they're restless"; the

> *agents*
> *And the super human crew*
> *Come out and round up every one*
> *That knows more than they do*
> *Then they bring them to the factory*
> *Where their heart attack machine*
> *Is strapped across their shoulders.*

A deluded and complacent America speeds along to disaster:

> *Praise be to Nero's Neptune*
> *The Titanic sails at dawn*
> *Everybody's shouting*
> *Which side are you on?*

From Dylan's perspective, this last question is absurd. Sides don't matter on a sinking ship; there are no genuine political differences among the denizens of the corporate state. One critic suggests that the song's images of the moon and stars hiding and a fortune teller taking all her things inside point to the desolation of nuclear holocaust. In any event, Dylan's imagery went far beyond latent unease to make a frontal assault on the Cold War consensus and its illusions of benign progress. Even as Molly Brown sang and danced about American pluck, the countercultural *Titanic* surfaced again. The Ad Council had revised the disaster to serve the imperatives of national security and the American Way. Dylan revised it to undermine those same imperatives.[42]

But it wasn't the counterculture that staked the main claim to the disaster in the 1960s. While new audiences were encountering the underground—or submerged—*Titanic* in clubs, at concerts, and on records, a much different and more concerted effort to preserve the memory of the ship and the disaster began to take shape. There may have been individual buffs like Chapin before the sixties, but buffdom as a widespread and organized phenomenon grew out of Lord's book, the television broadcast, and the movies. Lord's nostalgia proved contagious. Responding to what they perceived as the deficiencies of the modern world, buffs translated "a night to remember" into a call to action.

Chapter 6

Enthusiasts

e∽ Only a small sign in the window alerts visitors that Henry's Jewelry Store on Main Street in Indian Orchard, Massachusetts, is also the home of the Titanic Historical Society. Henry's stands directly across the street from the former Grand Theater, which was once owned by Edward Kamuda's father and grandfather and was where, in 1953, Ed watched showing after showing of the Clifton Webb–Barbara Stanwyck version of *Titanic*. To the right as you enter the store, framed pictures of Jesus and other pieces of religious and inspirational art are arranged for sale. To the left, rings, bracelets, necklaces, and watches line the long display case, behind which autographed glossies of celebrities, including Tiny Tim, Jonathan Winters, and Chad Everett, beam from the wall. Through a doorway in the back are the modest headquarters of the THS. The Titanic Museum, described as "the world's largest private acquisition of *Titanic* (pre-discovery) artifacts," features several cases of "authentic *Titanic* relics[,] including a third-class menu, a wool carpet remnant cut from a first-class stateroom floor on C-deck, the Marconigram ice warning from S.S. *Amerika*, and *Titanic* lookout Frederick Fleet's rendition of the fatal iceberg," as well as newspapers, postcards, sheet music, photographs, models, and "survivor keepsakes." Paintings of the ship and other liners decorate the walls. Books and inauthentic Titanica—board games, key rings, dishes—crowd the corners of the room. In a cramped office adjacent to the museum Ed and his wife, Karen, oversee the operations of the THS, the most time-consuming of which are the publication and distribution of the society's quarterly, the *Titanic Commutator*. (A commutator is an instrument used to measure the list of a vessel.)[1]

Ed Kamuda is the reason why the THS is in landlocked Indian Orchard, a suburban neighborhood that Ed thinks is falling apart as its composition changes and it becomes less and less isolated from the problems—especially crime and declining property values—that Springfield has faced for years. Ed does not hide his politics; an "Impeach Clinton" bumper sticker announces his views to jewelry shoppers and museum guests. After getting hooked on the *Titanic* in the 1950s by the movie and Walter Lord's book, he began corresponding with survivors and "some other fellows" who, like him, "were just interested—we had no relatives or anything" on the ship; one of them, Joseph Carvalho, had published a picture of his *Titanic* model in *Mechanics Illustrated* with the goal of attracting people to start an organization. When Walter Belford, the *Titanic*'s baker, died and his landlady threw out all his mementos, Ed knew he had to act. "I said this is a rotten shame," he recalls. "This is history that's being thrown away." In July 1963 Ed and his correspondents met at his house and decided to band together formally to preserve the memory of the *Titanic*. They chose September 6, the anniversary of the incorporation of the White Star Line, as the official launch date of the Titanic Enthusiasts of America (TEA).

The Enthusiasts struggled for the first few years. Putting out the newsletter, originally called the *Marconigram*, ate up most of the group's resources. (Marconigrams were wireless messages bearing the brand name of radio inventor and entrepreneur Guglielmo Marconi.) Kamuda cut costs by using his National Guard unit's mimeograph machine and expanded the newsletter from two to fifteen pages. But in 1968, with little publicity and a membership of only about 160, the organization came close to folding. The savior was William Tantum, who ran a publishing company called 7C's in Riverside, Connecticut. Tantum began reprinting old books about the *Titanic*, with forewords by the officers of the TEA and full-page ads soliciting new members. The Enthusiasts became a sales outlet for 7C's, marketing the books through the *Commutator* and receiving half the profits. Membership grew from 250 in 1973 to more than 1,500 by 1977, thanks to publicity in an Entex *Titanic* model kit and newspaper coverage of the group—now the THS—and its conventions. The discovery of the *Titanic*'s remains in 1985 helped boost membership even more dramatically. The THS now claims 5,000 members, and the *Commutator* is a glossy, lavishly illustrated magazine of more than fifty pages with full-color covers and advertisements for a wide range of *Titanic* and related merchandise.[2]

Just as Civil War buffs form a unique subset of those who like to read, know, and think about the Civil War, so too are *Titanic* buffs involved with the ship and the disaster in ways that a serious, though perhaps less dedicated, observer can only try to comprehend by exploring the concerns and practices of this distinctive group of historians. Fortunately the desire of buffs to get to know one another provides a way to develop a rough sketch of who they are. Until 1985, when the numbers became too large, the *Commutator* printed short biographies of all new THS members, which can at least serve as a point of departure for an informal ethnography of *Titanic* buffdom.[3]

Buffs are overwhelmingly male—almost 90 percent, according to my survey.[4] They are also overwhelmingly "white." While new members did not identify themselves by race, many of them did send in photographs. On the admittedly problematic basis of appearance, I identified two African Americans and one Asian American out of more than 650 pictures published in the *Commutator* between 1963 and 1985. The THS claims members from many countries, but the vast majority (roughly eight out of ten) live in the United States, with the largest concentrations in the Northeast and Midwest.

One- or two-word job descriptions make it impossible to talk about the occupations of THS members with any precision. Students clearly form the largest group. Kamuda explains that they often join in a flurry of excitement "because of school projects" involving the *Titanic*, but they are the least stable part of the membership; many drop out after a year or two when their interest wanes.[5] Otherwise, buffs run the occupational gamut from lawyers and doctors to truck drivers and short-order cooks. Most new members listed jobs that could be classified as blue-collar or low-level white-collar: "laborer," "mechanic," construction foreman, custodian, policeman, firefighter, pipe welder, binder, packer, lithographer, longshoreman, window washer, systems analyst, financial management trainee, "clerk," audiovisual technician, legal secretary, paralegal, hospital orderly, nurse, "salesman," assistant credit manager, waiter, and Fuller brush dealer, for example. Elementary and secondary school teachers, small-business owners, and (among women) homemakers were also well represented.

Not surprisingly, given that many of them learned about the organization from a model kit, the new members were devoted hobbyists. Many listed hobbies other than the *Titanic* in their biographies. Yet whether the *Titanic* shared time with stamp or coin collecting, model railroading, the Civil War, or *Star Trek* or functioned as a full-time hobby, it occupied a significant space in their lives. Not surprisingly, too, its significance was generally assumed and unspoken rather than fully elaborated and articulated. Dru Schillow, a teacher in Philadelphia, compared his interest in the *Titanic* to his students' hobbies: "I asked one boy this year why he collected football cards. He looked at me and smiled and said, 'I just do.' 'Well,' I responded, 'That is why I like the Titanic. . . . I just do!' "[6]

Ed Kamuda believes that the appeal of the *Titanic* resides in "the story itself. It's things that don't exist today: honor and heroism and men stepping back from the boats and letting the women and children go. With women's lib today you wouldn't have anything like that. . . . It just doesn't happen anymore. That's the end of the Edwardian Age—the class system. The millionaires were up on the upper decks, and the lower class were down on the lower decks, near the boilers more or less. Today everything's tourist class." Kamuda's condemnation of feminism and his puzzling dismay at the "end" of the "class system"—puzzling because he is a hardworking store owner of modest means—speak to a cultural conservatism rooted in perceptions of social turmoil and decline. He acknowledges the influence of Walter Lord and *A Night to Remember*, which another THS member has described as the enthusiasts' "Bible"; buffs frequently echo Lord in regretting that a "wonderful, carefree era" came to a catastrophic end when the *Titanic* plunged into the Atlantic.[7] The revised *Titanic* myth, with its plaintive sense of the disaster as the last gasp of the good old days, lies at the heart of Kamuda's understanding of its emotional resonance. But his statement also reveals a depth of antimodernism that goes well beyond Lord's more cheerful nostalgia.

Ken Marschall, an artist and a THS member who has made a career of painting the *Titanic*, first became interested in the ship and disaster as a junior high school student in Southern California in the mid-1960s. After seeing the 1953 movie on TV and reading *A Night to Remember*, he built a model of the ship and then did an oil painting for his high school art show in 1968. But the judges rejected the painting for being "too photorealistic"; in their view it wasn't "art." The following year Marschall went to pay tribute to the Apollo 11 astronauts at a local stop on their national tour. "Ken was appalled at the treatment they received from a portion of the crowd," his friend Don Lynch wrote in a tribute to Marschall in the *Commutator*. "The 1960s was an era of social unrest and some people jeered the astronauts and the space program. They felt the funding should have been put into social causes." Marschall sent his first *Titanic* painting and a letter of support to Neil Armstrong, whose technological triumph contrasted, as Ken pointed out in his letter, with the *Titanic*'s failure but whose courage seemed reminiscent of the disaster's heroes.[8]

Both Marschall's countercounterculturalism and Kamuda's nostalgia for the Edwardian class system reveal a conviction, shared by other buffs, that important institutions and roles are under attack or in decline. Many new THS members pointed with pride in their biographies to their military experience. By highlighting their service, the society's officers—called "The Men on the 'Bridge' " in a 1974 *Commutator* portrait—indicated their patriotism and respect for the military at a time when values such as duty and honor carried the taint of Vietnam. Robert Gibbons, the president, worked as a technician for the Atomic Energy Commission and NASA, served in the U.S. Army Reserve in the late sixties and early seventies, and was employed by the Springfield, Missouri, Air Pollution Control Authority in 1974. He was also president of his local historical society, where he was trying to establish a Bicentennial museum. William Tantum, the vice-president, had served in the military from 1943 to 1956, working his way to first lieutenant. Before starting the 7C's Press, he had been a public school teacher in Trenton and a gun company sales manager in Ithaca, New York. He was the former membership director of the National Shooting Sports Foundation and a member of the American Legion, the Retired Officers Association, the American Ordnance Association, the U.S. Armor Association, and several military history organizations. Kamuda, the society's secretary and acting treasurer in 1974, had served in the Massachusetts Army National Guard from 1961 to 1967. His cofounder, Frank Casilio, had served in the Guard from 1965 to 1971.[9]

For many buffs the *Titanic* represents a lost "golden age" of order, certainty, and authority. THS member Jack Finney is so unabashedly nostalgic that in his 1995 novel *From Time to Time* (the sequel to his acclaimed *Time and Again* of 1970) he contrived to stop the twentieth century from happening. Naturally this involves intervening in the *Titanic* disaster. Finney's hero, Simon Morley, is sent on a time-travel mission to save Archibald Butt from going down with the ship. Morley learns that Butt—returning from a diplomatic mission to Europe somehow coordinated by the warring Taft and Roosevelt—was carrying secret documents that would have prevented the Great War. By interrupting the chain of events at a point when they were "still small, still manageable," Morley can preserve the "pleasant peaceful world" of 1912, "a time worth protecting." As his boss explains:

> You've got to go back, Si, because—we've researched this—
> the sinking of the *Titanic* seems to have been an event that
> changed the course of the world it belonged to. Even more
> than the loss of the people who went down with her was an
> *attitude* lost with it. A way people thought about the world
> and the century. After the *Titanic* things were never the
> same. It was a kind of Big Bang that changed everything.

And the world veered off in another and wrong direction,
the century that could have been, derailed.

People who deride nostalgia, another character remarks, are
"time patriots" who fail to recognize that "there just might have
been better times than here or now." The novel is driven by the
urge to reverse the wrong turn and return to a better time.[10]

Making their case for the ongoing significance of the disaster, buffs speak directly about its usefulness as a point of com-
parison between the present and the past—a source of
inspiration and valuable lessons. Character—the older model
of selfhood that *Titanic* heroism seems to embody—is disap-
pearing, they believe, and needs to be conserved or recovered.
"[M]ost of all," observes Charles Haas, a high school teacher,
onetime president of the THS and founder of a splinter group
called Titanic International, "the legacy of the Titanic was the
opportunity it gave for displays of heroism. And I am not sure
that those opportunities exist today. At least, not on the scale
of the Titanic. We are intrigued by these demonstrations of
love and loyalty, and total devotion to duty." George Behe, a
pest controller and frequent contributor to the *Commutator*,
explains that "one reason we need to remember the *Titanic*
disaster is because we need certain honorable standards of behavior against which to measure our modern-day society."
Behe points specifically to materialism, selfishness, and an
unwillingness to take responsibility for one's own actions as
signs of decline. "By comparing present-day human behavior
with the behavior of those men who stood back from the
Titanic's lifeboats," he says, "we have an excellent and telling
way of gauging whether modern man is as worthy of respect
as were those men who faced death at sea eighty years ago—
and didn't flinch."[11]

Perhaps this opportunity for didacticism is what draws so
many teachers to the subject. (THS member Bruce Trinque

shrewdly notes the disaster's pedagogical value in making social change "more graphic and intelligible." Students can understand historical processes more easily when they are
encapsulated in a single dramatic event.) Haas, whose school
has adopted *A Night to Remember* as part of its ninth-grade
English curriculum, explains that the disaster offers alternatives to "today's world," where the "evening news" presents
nothing but "mayhem" and "inhumanity." By demonstrating
the "timeless qualities of human beings at their finest moments," the disaster reflects "what lies within each one of us"
and "shows people what we can be capable of." Joseph Ryan, a
teacher at an Ohio vocational school, wrote to the *Commutator* in 1979 to discuss his classroom use of the disaster. It wasn't
enough to teach students a trade, he observed; it was essential
to teach them character as well, and "where could character
be better related than in the sinking of the *Titanic*?" Echoing
Lord, Ryan regretted that "[n]one of us are really sure of anything at all any more." People had become self-interested and
"jaded." When he asked his students in a "sense of values test"
how they would have responded on board the *Titanic*, "[t]heir
reaction was 'every man for himself.' " But "*true* students" of
the disaster learned its real message: the importance of character—steadfastness, self-discipline, "regard for others," in
short, "manhood."[12]

These "timeless" values and the prospect of reclaiming them
to stop the downward spiral of modern history account for
the *Titanic*'s pull on Kenneth Bilbo, a soldier from Mississippi,
and W. F. Moshier, a teacher from California. "The *Titanic*
expresses in that era the eternal achievement of humankind,"
Bilbo proclaimed when he joined the THS in 1983. Moshier
pronounced himself "in favor of keeping alive the spirit and
the times of the *Titanic* and the world which seemingly vanished with it." Chad Audinet lectures to third-grade classes
about the *Titanic* as a way of "helping our future generations."

He is concerned that "modern ways could destroy or erase the history of this great ship." Geoffery Evers sums up his involvement by reflecting that the *Titanic* "represents a way of life which I and others long for."[13]

Remembering the *Titanic*, then, is a moral undertaking—a way of reasserting the authority of older values. For buffs, memory becomes a refuge from modernity by invoking a series of oppositions: self-sacrifice and self-indulgence, standards and relativism, certainty and uncertainty, order and chaos. Their nostalgia for the late nineteenth century, or for the time before the social unrest of the sixties, might explain the organization's limited appeal to African Americans and to women. (It also suggests why some women *are* buffs. Karen Kamuda approvingly cites a *National Review* article by Linda Lichter called "The Lost Luxuries of Ladyhood" that describes the disaster as "the last gasp of Victorian chivalry." Lichter reveals that she finds the obscure Women's Titanic Memorial more moving than the popular Vietnam Veterans Memorial. Karen Kamuda agrees that gender relations have changed "for the worse" since "the time of the *Titanic* disaster when women were placed on a pedestal.")[14] But for all its limitations and blind spots, there is nothing frivolous about buffs' attraction to a mythic past, their concern for character in a time of materialistic excess and therapeutic self-obsession. They may not offer a fully formed conservative critique—they rarely, if ever, articulate the causes of the erosion of character—but they approach the *Titanic* with the honorable conviction that their interest in the subject is a serious matter.

When history functions as a kind of moral catechism, the distance between past and present—ironic or otherwise—collapses. The *Titanic* becomes more than a subject for study; it becomes a way of life. Responding, in effect, to *A Night to Remember*'s invitation to answer the question, "How would I have acted?," buffs seek to participate in the events they study, not only to know about but to *live* the experience. "If it were possible to travel back in time and actually see the *Titanic*, walk upon her decks and sail the Atlantic," Ronald Klubnik wrote to the THS, "I would begin to realize the basis of such an inspiring legend of the sea. I'm sure the Society is the best alternative." Robin Wehrlin has tried to imagine what the passengers "must have been thinking. 'Will I be one of the lucky ones that I might see the sun rise again? Or is this where the road of my life comes to an end?' " At THS conventions the main attraction is the survivors, there in person, living connections to the *Titanic*, a way of touching the past directly without the mediating presence of the written word. Artifacts, though inanimate, similarly offer a material link to the disaster.[15]

Titanic buffs, unlike Civil War buffs, don't do reenactments; it would be too expensive, dangerous, and wet. Still, they find imaginative ways to conquer time and space. A few even harbor suspicions that they really were there. A new THS member mentioned "three or four" dreams in which he "was a passenger experiencing the actual sinking" and concluded that "quite possibly I could have been on board the *Titanic*." Another new member, describing himself as "a very rational person," confessed to "an unexplained closeness and oneness with the *Titanic* and the people on her, as though I were there on the maiden voyage." Sheri Calvert, who has "never been one to believe in reincarnation," recalls an uncanny experience. Leafing through a new book on the disaster, she came across a photograph of some crew members. Suddenly she pointed to one of the men and, without "conscious control over [her] hand or [her] words and thoughts," exclaimed, "I know him!": "It's as if I can feel what it was like to be on the ship; like I am there, standing on the deck and looking out at the ocean. I have questioned in my mind whether this could just be imagination since I have read so much about it, but I feel that it is something more." Where words and pictures must suffice, the preferred technique is a well-crafted sense of immediacy, the nearest possible imitation of reality. Robert Ballard, the wreck's discoverer, praised Don Lynch's minute-by-minute account and Ken Marschall's photorealistic illustrations in *Titanic: An Illustrated History* (which prompted Calvert's "strange occurrence") for bringing "the great lost liner . . . magnificently back to life." The book, he wrote, was "the next best thing" to visiting the ship itself.[16]

To bridge historical distance in these ways is to recast oneself as an actor in a great event. Perhaps this explains the vehemence with which some buffs throw themselves into the *Californian* controversy, where marshaling evidence to convict or vindicate Captain Stanley Lord of negligence in not coming to the *Titanic*'s rescue is to become a character in the disaster's ongoing narrative. It is, in other words, to enact a transformation from being a historical object (the modern world is alienating and debilitating) to being a historical subject. Participating, however vicariously, in the *Titanic* disaster is a protest against powerlessness—an assertion of autonomy.

While buffs are engaged in a quest for moral authority, they are also driven by a passion for fact. They want to know *everything* about the *Titanic*. "I can't learn enough about her," exclaimed new THS member David Peterson, whose interest in the ship "spanned 53 years." Edward Levin joined because of his "absolute fascination and excitement with all the aspects of *Titanic* history, people (passengers and crew as well as builders, etc.), details of the tragedy, etc." Fred Miller hoped that the THS would open up new opportunities for knowledge since he had "virtually exhausted all sources available to me." Charles Sachs, founder of the Oceanic Navigation Research Society and host of an annual black-tie dinner to commemorate the disaster (featuring the menu from the ship's fatal night), convinced an interviewer that he had "read, collected, studied, and memorized everything to do with the great ship and its captain, passengers, and crew." Other buffs described their interest as "insatiable" or an "obsession."[17]

For someone hooked on the *Titanic*, the pursuit of facts is its own reward. It doesn't seem necessary to ponder the larger purposes of this pursuit; the significance of the ship and the disaster is assumed, unspoken, deeply felt, and widely shared. Still, just as the interest in character speaks to concerns about moral authority, so does the passion for fact address concerns about epistemological and personal authority. If Walter Lord's canonical version describes the disaster as the source of modern uncertainty, studying the disaster becomes a way of combating that uncertainty. "One yearned for something that would present a more factual presentation of what really happened," Kamuda recalled in explaining the appeal of *A Night to Remember*.[18]

Kamuda's yearning for fact is strong enough to make him hostile toward novels about the disaster. Yet he wrote the introduction to a book called *Titanic: Psychic Forewarnings of a Tragedy*; interestingly, his objections to *Titanic* fiction do not extend to that curious subgenre of *Titanic* writing that explores the disaster's paranormal dimensions. Many books about the disaster mention the uncanniness of Morgan Robertson's 1898 novel *Futility*; Lord discusses it in the first paragraph of *A Night to Remember*. In *Futility* a ship called the *Titan*, almost exactly the same length and displacement as its real-life counterpart, with the same number of propellers, the same maximum speed, the same passenger capacity, the same shortage of lifeboats, similar engines, and comparable watertight compartments, collides with an iceberg on its starboard side and sinks. "Prediction and premonition?" ask John Eaton and Charles Haas. "Who can say?"[19]

In *Titanic: Psychic Forewarnings of a Tragedy*, George Behe arranges several hundred premonitions of the disaster into five categories: "curious coincidences," "mistaken accounts and deliberate hoaxes," "phenomena connected with W. T. Stead" (famous at the time for his explorations of the paranormal), "possible psychic phenomena," and "probable psychic phenomena." Dismissing "an uncritical, fanatical belief in paranormal phenomena," Behe also rejects "the attitude of the dyed-in-the-wool sceptic." He submits all the accounts to critical analysis before concluding that enough witnesses heard about people's fears and nightmares *before* the disaster to lend credence to many of these premonitions. Behe's THS colleague Rustie Brown takes a less rigorous approach and reaches a similar conclusion in *The Titanic, the Psychic and the Sea*. The evidence, according to Behe, Brown, and other investigators, is too plentiful to suggest "mere chance." Brown approvingly quotes Alan Vaughan, who wrote the foreword to her book: "The coincidences or synchronicities that link our lives are manifestations of a universe so highly organized that literally *nothing* happens by chance. Like some incredibly complex clockwork, the universe unfolds in time and space its inner plan that does not allow for accidents. . . . Chance is but an illusion fostered by our incomplete knowledge of the universe's greater plan." Like Lord's ifs, premonitions and related paranormal phenomena replace contingency with fate. H. Wayne Summerlin's article on astrology and the *Titanic* purported to "show evidence of forces governing the lives of people and objects, reaching beyond our logic" and "the perimeter of chance."[20] The disaster, so shocking because of its unpredictability, proves to have been predictable after all. Foreknowledge imposes certainty on an event that symbolizes uncertainty. Human error and imperfection are subsumed by "destiny." Order prevails after all.

The paranormal is a long way from cold, hard fact, and not all buffs go in for this sort of thing. The *Titanic*, after all, remains a powerful symbol of the inability to predict events. But there are intriguing similarities between the belief in precognition and the impulse toward positivism. Both represent a quest for certainty. If, for those who remain doubtful about psychic forewarnings, the disaster represents the limits of prospective knowledge, the relentless pursuit of fact represents the triumph of retrospective knowledge—the sense that if we can't prevent the disaster, we can know so much about it that we somehow gain control over it. "No doubt some of the 'unexplainable' connected with the *Titanic* will become clearer as years go by and research into psychic phenomena continues," Brown predicts. "Maybe there is not much one can do to control one's fate, but paradoxically, maybe there is."[21]

Brown shares with more skeptical buffs the desire to leave nothing about the disaster unexplained. At the same time the seemingly infinite proliferation of detail offers what Eaton calls "the challenge of the hunt, the pleasure of contributing something new." The pleasure lies in the combination of definitive knowledge and the possibility of uncovering still more facts. In Eaton's marvelous phrase "there will always be that additional nine to the right of the decimal point"—an endless increment of tiny, apparently insignificant new pieces of information. Jay Browne, a career navy man, has accumulated so much information that he now maintains a computerized data base; he hopes "someday . . . to do some computer modeling of the event" to add to the "map work" he has already done "to try to sort out just where ships were on the night" of the disaster. Browne's fellow THS member Darwin Rizzetto, disturbed that two television documentaries failed to present the "most important information," researched, wrote, and circulated his own "Titanic Report," which purports to prove that the iceberg "did not cause a mortal wound," that Captain Smith could have saved the ship by steaming to port instead of stopping, and that "[t]here never should have been any loss of life." Rizzetto's report, to which he attached the relevant pages from a physics textbook, uses a series of equations to represent the disaster as a matter of mathematical certainty: Had Smith known enough to proceed onward to New York at precisely 17.7 knots, the first four compartments would have taken on 42.2 feet of water, the bow would have dropped 21 feet, but the ship would not have sunk and tragedy would have been averted. In a later report Rizzetto demonstrated that constructing six rafts out of the *Titanic*'s thirty-six hundred life jackets (when one takes into account the jackets' buoyancy and the average passenger's weight), maximizing the capacity of the lifeboats, and rationally organizing their loading would have saved everyone on board, with room for 319 to spare.[22]

Facts like these are stable and solid, authoritative and sure. They impose a mastery over events. To possess them is to have a kind of power that even—especially—the heroes on the *Titanic* didn't possess: if not prescience, if not quite omniscience, then expertise. Facts too produce a remarkably democratic form of history. Anyone who wants to participate in the pursuit of "the additional nine" can do so; no credentials are required. Truth demands nothing more than the right facts, equally accessible, presumably unmediated by messy interpretations and ideologies, free from hierarchical standards of review and esoteric methodologies.

Buffs may not hate their jobs any more or less than the rest of the population, but mastery of Titanica is a path to authority outside work. When Eaton, once the official historian of the THS and later the cofounder with Haas of Titanic International, was asked what inspired him and his fellow buffs, he answered with the Latin motto *Studium omnibus habendum est*, which he translated as "Everybody needs a hobby." The *Titanic* is particularly well suited to fulfilling this need by redressing the deficiencies of modern work. Studying the ship and the wreck is a self-chosen, self-directed activity—an autonomous kind of "work" performed for its own sake at a self-determined pace.[23] Talking and writing about the *Titanic*, members of what Haas calls the "movement" convey a sense of pure joy in their activities. Behe offers a typical account of the development of a buff. As a boy in the 1950s he found Logan Marshall's 1912 book about the disaster on his grandmother's shelf. Troubled by the inconsistencies and contradictions in Marshall's account, he wondered "which version—if any—might be the true one" and "hoped one day to discover the answer." When he grew up, Behe recalls, "I began devoting my leisure time to seriously researching subjects that interested me. The *Titanic* came first, and has predominated ever since." His goal, he explains, is "to gain as much accurate, first-hand information about the disaster as possible."[24] In other words, like most buffs, he used his leisure time to transform himself into an expert whose cultivation of a specialized body of knowledge takes him beyond the workaday world of externally driven and routine activity.

While they take pride in their role as leisure time or amateur historians, buffs also point to the seriousness of their work. Even mild *Titanic* jokes on an episode of the TV sitcom *The Munsters* and on a record called "You Don't Have to Be Jewish" could strike a sensitive nerve. On *The Munsters*, Grandpa pulls the vaudeville stunt of flinging odd items out of an old steamer trunk, including a *Titanic* life preserver, until he finds what he is looking for. On "You Don't Have to Be Jewish," a woman yells at an elevator operator, "Stop, stop, you're going down without my husband." The operator replies, "Don't worry, lady, this isn't the *Titanic*." In response Stuart MacDonald urged his fellow Enthusiasts to assert their proprietary interest in the disaster: "*Titanic* is a name which we should all be proud of. It stands for something great in men[']s minds. We the members of T.E.A. should try to stop the constant ridicule about the *Titanic*." (Buffs concerned about ridicule may have also had in mind the habit of summer camp singers to replace the line "Husbands and wives, little children lost their lives" with "Uncles and aunts, little children lost their pants.") Kamuda explained to a reporter at a THS convention that the society's activities weren't "for kids who just built a model or did a history project."[25]

In some ways buffdom simulates a profession—a far-flung community of experts with its own organizations, journals, and conventions. Like most professions, it produces substantive conflicts that outsiders would find baffling or insignificant, such as the *Californian* controversy or the matter of the band's last song. Like most professions, it has produced personal and political conflicts, such as the one between Kamuda on one side and Haas and Eaton on the other that led to the formation of their rival organization, Titanic International. (The dispute involved charges that THS officers' elections were undemocratic and that Kamuda presided despotically over the society.)

More important, buffdom provides the sense of identity and belonging that professions confer on their members, but without the elaborate process of accreditation that makes professions exclusive. Whether one comes to the *Titanic* through reading, movie watching, model building, family lore, or some other route, membership in the THS or Titanic International is a move from idiosyncrasy and isolation to an awareness of shared interests and common practices. Tarn Stephanos described the THS as a "godsend" for showing him that he was not "alone in my Titanic obsession." Meeting others who shared his interest at THS conventions, he learned that "many of them had also languished as the only Titanic buff in their community, & many had long believed that only they were fascinated in the unsinkable Titanic!" Kenneth Westover aspired to advance the collective knowledge on the subject while experiencing the satisfactions of participating in a common enterprise. "Everything about that great ship holds a fatal fascination for me. I just can't get my fill and I want to 'rub shoulders' with those who feel the same." But he hoped "to do more than receive. Someday I want to contribute something (original, I hope) to the club which will add to the lore of this beautiful ship, and to the knowledge of my fellow members."[26] Buffs, in short, find the "professional" benefits—community, authority, expertise, the chance to make original contributions—in their leisure time that most of us don't find in our jobs.

Charles Haas may be exceptional in what he has achieved through his interest in the *Titanic*, but his career vividly illustrates how some buffs literally (and literarily) gain authority: by becoming authors. As a student Haas spent his spare time in microfilm rooms researching the ship and the disaster. After joining the THS, he quickly became a major contributor to the *Commutator*; his articles on other White Star ships, meticulously documented, occasionally took up entire issues. In 1982 Haas and Eaton received a grant from two other buffs to visit Nova Scotia, where they uncovered documents and photographs that allowed them to write "the first published, comprehensive look" at the place of Halifax in *Titanic* history. Four years later, when the picture book they envisioned "ballooned up" with their new findings, they published *Titanic: Triumph and Tragedy*. Two other books followed. Haas, still a high school teacher, and Eaton, a hospital administrator, are now internationally renowned authorities on the subject. In 1993 they were invited to accompany researchers and salvagers on dives to the wreck, which they recounted in a second edition of their book.[27]

For most buffs, of course, the rewards of authorship are more modest. While Don Lynch, who succeeded Eaton as the official THS historian, parlayed his expertise on the *Titanic*'s passengers and crew into a handsome coffee table book, many other enthusiasts seem content to share their passion and expertise through articles in the *Commutator* or Titanic International's *Voyage* or, occasionally, books published by small specialty presses. Like Clara Warchol or the winners of the THS's first annual William Harris Tantum IV Writing Competition in 1982, they write about "Heroes and Heroines of the Titanic Disaster." Warchol, explained the *Commutator*, was an "invalid, whose world would be limited" to her apartment if not for the "insatiable curiosity" and "creative imagination" that went into researching and writing her biographical portrait of architect and *Titanic* hero Edward Austin Kent. They write about survivors, "whose very private lives and fortunes," according to the *Commutator*'s survivors' issue, "were changed in a few moments in time by a tragic accident that, in effect, changed all our lives as well." They write about *Titanic* memorials, model building, the ship's larder, the history of the Harland & Wolff shipyards, and the iceberg. They debate the *Californian* controversy and the issue of salvage.[28]

In painstaking detail they describe the design and construction of the *Titanic* and other classic ocean liners. They provide technical information to fellow ship enthusiasts, many of whom are also members of the Steamship Historical Society of America. This elaborate attention to what Haas calls "the mechanical side" of buffdom is nearly impossible for a nonbuff to comprehend. To the extent that buffs explain why they are captivated by the workings of engines, screws, rudders, boilers, and funnels, they do so in aesthetic terms. The old liners, they point out, were beautiful. "I have a deep feeling for the beauty and grace that was the *Titanic* and her sister ships," wrote a new THS member in 1978. Another new member, an auto mechanic, confessed that he was "amazed at the beauty and elegance she possessed." Grace and elegance extended beyond the opulent furnishings to "its size and styling and the beauty of its construction." The *Titanic*, said an electronic technician who joined the THS in 1982, "holds—what would you call it?—a fascination, mystique, spirit; not to mention her sheer beauty and technological innovations."[29]

Not only the *Titanic* but all the great liners have vanished; an era of splendor, magnificence, and superb design has passed. "Too bad . . . I was born too late for the heyday of steamship travel," reflected James Hamilton, who described himself as "a maritime enthusiast pure and simple." James Flood, a marine architect, eloquently regretted the loss: "In these days where, in America and much of the world, it can be said that art is junk and junk is art, and when ships look like condominiums, it is refreshing to look back on an era when ships still retained that grace, that easy sheet, that long, low, lean look with beautiful counter sterns, that certain harmony with the sea over which they travelled that in this age of aluminum is totally absent." Celebrating and preserving the memory of the great liners, to which Titanic International explicitly dedicated itself, are the aesthetic equivalent to remembering the heroism of the *Titanic*'s passengers and crew. Buffs value technical information for its own sake, but their research and writing fall within a broader quest for beauty, goodness, and truth.[30]

What buffs write about offers a glimpse of their nostalgic tendencies. How they write reveals more. The Titanic is rarely just a ship; it—or "she," according to nautical convention—is the "ill-starred *Titanic*," the "ill-fated liner," "the majestic and dauntless liner," or the "proud ship," "as fine as a lady could be." The iceberg, summoned up by the "merciless Gods of the deep," inflicted a "mortal wound" or a "mortal blow." The lifeboats were lowered into "the dark, fearsome sea" or the "treacherously unruffled sea." The Strauses and other heroes "wordlessly gazed into the darksome night" and "faced the inevitable, eternal silence with a calm untroubled stillness." Many "fought a gallant fight," and they did not die but "perished" or "took death" as their "portion." They were not passengers or victims or casualties but "souls" who "went to their final account." The survivors "brush[ed] the ice of death and lived." The *Carpathia*, that "great and gallant liner," raced "o'er the sea" or "made the great dash northward," "hurtling into pounding waves preparing for mercy's flight," and "gaze[d] upon destruction and death." When she was torpedoed in 1918, it was "a sad but heroic end" to a ship whose name "will forever be linked to that fateful night in April of 1912." The *Titanic* did more than merely sink; she descended or took a "death plunge" to "her watery grave," "her inevitable watery doom," or "her final resting place."[31]

This kind of language, ubiquitous in 1912, is strikingly archaic for the 1960s, 1970s, 1980s, and 1990s. And it is not confined to remembrances of the disaster itself. A THS member who died of cancer "at the tender age of 16" was not only "Steven" or "Steve" but "Young Broadbent." In the 1965 and 1974 debates over salvage Frank Cronican made his position clear in the title of his essay, "No Man Shall Wrest Her Free." A student weighed in on the salvage issue when he joined the THS by announcing that one of his "greatest ambitions" was "to see the great lady on her ocean bed" or "resurrected out of her endless sleep." Buffs don't always write in this language, but they are versed in it from their exposure to 1912 accounts of the disaster. It is available to them in ways that it is not to nonbuffs. To write without self-consciousness or irony of watery graves or darksome seas or heroes who "went not unrewarded" to their deaths is to view the world from a perspective now well "over three score years in the past."[32]

Studium omnibus habendum est: "Everybody needs a hobby." Or, translated differently, "Everybody must have enthusiasm."

When the membership voted to change the name from Titanic Enthusiasts of America to the Titanic Historical Society, those in the minority felt regret. Philip Del Piano acknowledged that "enthusiasts" lent itself to misinterpretation—"we are not enthusiastic about the disaster or the loss of lives"—but TEA remained "the best name" because "we are enthusiastic about the ship."[33] I agree with Del Piano. The old name more vividly conveyed the spirit behind the organization. Enthusiasm means more than excitement and celebration; it means religious fervor, zeal, even ecstasy.

The *Titanic* disaster, we have seen, from the beginning inspired religious reflections, some of which have changed very little over the years. "The sinking of the *Titanic* has a strong message against too much trust in human materialism and worldly optimism," wrote Don Castel, a post office clerk and new THS member in 1979. James Ulmer Gandy, a THS member and "full-time Southern Baptist evangelist" from Mobile, Alabama, claimed when he joined in 1974 that he had delivered a sermon on the disaster 227 times since 1949. In some reflections God's mightiness no longer gets mentioned, but humanity's weakness remains a resonant theme. "It is important to remember the Titanic," Ruben and Jo Ann Olvera explain, "because it reminds us of how we are all vulnerable no matter who we are or what we are." Buffs commonly observe that "history repeats itself" because, as Karen Bowman puts it, "man, in general, is pretty thick-headed, & refuses to learn from past mistakes."[34]

There is a difference, however, between the religious meanings still evoked by the disaster and its newer status as an icon and a sacred text itself, the object of quasi-religious devotion. As described in buffdom's bible, *A Night to Remember*, the disaster is the story of the Fall; it is, either literally or symbolically, the moment when paradise was lost, when the innocent nineteenth century gave way to the sinful twentieth, when arcadian harmony collapsed into doubt, conflict, and disorder. "Man lost his innocence almost overnight on April 15, 1912," laments William Rauscher, whose interest in the disaster goes back to childhood and who read *A Night to Remember* as a teenager. As a story of "epic scope," THS member Melinda Capp believes, the disaster not only "delight[s] the mind" but "inspire[s] the soul." For Rauscher the *Titanic* encompasses both the Old and New Testaments, sin and salvation, Adam and Eve, Jesus and Mary: "[L]et us rejoice in what we have learned from her. She paid the ultimate price so that we may benefit. Long live our lady the *Titanic*!" Even Frank Johns, who is primarily interested in "the technical aspects of the ship," closed a letter to me with the phrase "Your friend in *Titanic*."[35] Buffdom is suffused with the language of Christianity, and the THS stands as a kind of alternative church, complete with saints, relics, and pilgrimages. (Some buffs object to those who "push this thing to the level of a religion." For Joe Carvalho the *Titanic* is a "lifetime hobby," but he distinguishes himself from "people who live" the *Titanic* "every day." There are degrees and varieties of buffdom.)[36]

Sacred rituals make THS conventions a unique amalgam of social meeting, professional conference, and religious communion. The 1977 convention, which commemorated the sixty-fifth anniversary of the disaster, began with an invocation by John Eaton, official THS historian and unofficial minister. "Heavenly Father," he prayed, "we ask Your blessing on the memory of Titanic and the brave men and women who sailed in her." Then he requested God's blessing for the society in its mission of remembering and spreading the word. Eaton also delivered the main eulogy at the *Titanic* Memorial Service. Praising the ship's musicians for their heroism, he spoke of the *Titanic* as an inspirational example of "devotion to duty" and steadfastness. "From them we can learn that, even though we may not be brave, we can choose our own time to be heroes. And our own actions, our own behavior in time of stress and disaster can inspire the actions, the decisions, of others." After the eulogy the congregation sang "Nearer, My God, to Thee." Kamuda, recalling that he and many others in attendance had first heard the hymn in the 1953 movie that put them on the path to this gathering, described "the emotion-filled voices" soaring in the Fairfield Room at the Greenwich, Connecticut, Sheraton. The hymn singing was shown that night as the conclusion to the last story on the *CBS Evening News*. To Kamuda's relief the story presented the convention respectfully.[37]

Eaton's eulogy and the singing of "Nearer, My God, to Thee" (despite the members' knowledge that the hymn was not really sung on board the ship) capture the buffs' sense of the *Titanic* as a sacred text that provides inspiration and life lessons. At the 1982 convention in Philadelphia the memorial service was conducted by the Reverend Father Francis Fitzhugh of St. Clement's Church, who invoked the disaster as a lesson about "decorum" and living "in accordance with the Natural Law God created." There remain those today, most obviously "the Bolshevik dictatorship in the Soviet Union and the various social humanist activists in our own country," he observed, "who believe and teach that man has complete control of himself, his society, and his environment with no deference to Almighty God." The *Titanic* proved them wrong. Fitzhugh mentioned how some of his parishioners made fun of his interest in the *Titanic* and reassured his listeners that "we haven't to give a reason for our presence" at the convention "to anyone." But he made clear that for him the disaster was an event of biblical proportions, as much a part of the sacred order as of secular history. Kamuda again described the singing of hymns "with not a dry eye in the place or a voice that was not choked with emotion." Many told him how moved they were by Fitzhugh's "common-sense" view of the disaster.[38] Why would people with no personal ties to what is, compared with other events of the twentieth century, a relatively minor tragedy, weep at its memory? This is enthusiasm—genuine passion and zeal—incomprehensible, perhaps, to noninitiates but not to be laughed at or treated, as Kamuda worried about the CBS coverage, in " 'tongue-in-cheek' style."

Survivors are—or were, as their numbers dwindle—more than celebrities at THS conventions; they are living saints. At the 1982 convention the burden of signing autographs became so great that the society's officers decided to put out a "little pot" to take up a collection, less as a form of compensation than as an offering to those who hold the key to the mystery. "Locked within their minds is the story of what happened out there in the North Atlantic 70 years ago," remarked Kamuda, "and everybody here wanted to hear every word they had to say." John Whitman, who ran his own Titanic Memorial Museum in Sidney, Ohio, from 1987 to 1994 (he estimated that fifty thousand people visited it), retained his sense of the survivors' mystique even after seeing one with her hair in curlers. "Before I met any of them I thought that they must be superhuman to have endured an ordeal like that." Though the curler episode made him realize that "they were just like everyone else," he continued to believe "in my heart" that they were "somewhat above the ordinary."[39]

Relics offer a similar kind of communion. Like survivors, they are revered as much for their aura as for their documentary value. Louis Gorman, the THS treasurer, called the gift of a *Titanic* life jacket to the society "probably the greatest thing to happen to this organization since its founding." Prominently displayed at the THS exhibit at the New York Harbor Festival in 1979, the life jacket was hailed by the festival's director as the "star of the show—truly super." That there is little to be learned from such an object is beside the point. At the conventions THS members file past locked glass cases containing the most precious relics: a *Titanic* steward's coins and buttons, a piece of the ship's railing, a swatch of carpet, a survivor's veil, coat buttons, and hair combs from the night of the disaster, a boarding pass, another survivor's razor, postcards sent from the ship in Queenstown, Ireland, before the transatlantic voyage. When the society decided to relocate its collection to the Philadelphia Maritime Museum, Kamuda was torn. He "longed to be . . . alone just for a few minutes" in the room at the museum, but it was filled with crowds from both the general public and the THS convention going on across town. Overcome with emotion, he "touched the glass of the case and bid my 'friends' good-bye." (Not for long, though; most of the relics have since been returned to Henry's Jewelry Store, and others have been moved to the Marine Museum in Fall River, Massachusetts.)[40]

Here is where the sacred meets the profane. For all their spiritual and sentimental value, pieces of authentic Titanica have also soared in market value. Kamuda and other buffs dislike the commercialization of the disaster, but THS officers and members work with individuals and auction houses to authenticate relics for sale. While the experts carefully distinguish between authentic and inauthentic objects, the *Commutator* regularly carries advertisements for memorabilia and sells its own line of reproductions as well as books and other merchandise. Sometimes the distinctions are blurry. The THS marketed a limited-series lithograph of the last photograph taken by a passenger who disembarked at Queenstown. "Mr. Jack Odell," the ad proclaimed, "the last living male who traveled first-class, now in his 91st year, has personally autographed each" of the reprints of a snapshot of the "ill-fated ship," taken by his aunt Kate as it steamed away into the Atlantic. Buffs could buy this "true collector's item" and "treasured *Titanic* keepsake" for $190.[41] The demand for commercial relics—the ardent desire to possess them and to connect through these objects with a mythic past—suggests the breadth and depth of *Titanic* piety. Meaning and marketability go together.

Like most pilgrimages, the *Titanic* Heritage Tours also blend the pious with the profitable. The tours originated with Michael Rudd of Travel Marketing Associates, who suggested the idea to some of the officers of the THS at the 1992 convention. The convention was scheduled to coincide with the eightieth anniversary of the disaster, the tour with the thirtieth anniversary of the founding of the THS. (The 1996 convention in Belfast, the first to be held overseas, was notable because April 14, "the date we particularly associate with," fell on a Sunday, just as it did in 1912.) In Southampton the tour group stood at the *Titanic*'s berth. "It was very emotional for many of us," Karen Kamuda reported, "and tears in one's eyes were common." The group then boarded a ferry "to reenact the route of the *Titanic*'s departure," the trip culminating in a visit from a Coast Guard rescue helicopter that lowered a guardsman carrying a greeting from the British Titanic Society. At the Hollybrook Cemetery THS and BTS members joined in a service to dedicate a memorial to *Titanic* lookout Frederick Fleet. But the highlight of the tour was the visit to the Harland & Wolff shipyard in Belfast. There Ed Kamuda experienced what he called the most remarkable moment in his long involvement with the *Titanic*: the feeling of actually standing "on the spot where she sailed from and where she was born." Congregating on hallowed ground, the tourists wept again. Tom McCluskie, a Harland & Wolff manager, "almost couldn't believe that everybody was crying," Kamuda remembers. The emotional pilgrimage ended in Halifax, Nova Scotia, where many of the disaster's victims came to rest. Promising visits to "profound places that will evoke poignant thoughts and deep emotions," a subsequent tour gave buffs the opportunity to "complete the voyage" (or at least the part before the Atlantic crossing) by duplicating the *Titanic*'s course from Southampton to Cherbourg to Queenstown.[42]

Following in the *Titanic*'s wake raises the mundane—a vacation, tourism—into the mystical. Historical fact, the concreteness of places and artifacts, becomes a means of transcendence. Martin Arnold and Katherine Faulkner, who wrote a memoir of the second *Titanic* Heritage Tour, recalled the experience of dining at the White Swan Hotel in Alnwick. The hotel's Olympic Room is an authentic reconstruction of the first-class lounge from the *Titanic*'s sister ship. "During dinner," they wrote, "surrounded by intricately carved paneling and fixtures so similar to the *Titanic*, one began to question one's senses." At the shipyard in Belfast they felt "the presence of spirits from another time and place." For buffs the *Titanic* heightens and even transforms lived experience, enabling them to escape the prosaic, to be swept up in what THS member Robert Warren calls the "air of mystery" surrounding the *Titanic*, to join a community committed to the "sacred trust" of preserving the memory of the ship and disaster.[43]

The one sacred place that the pilgrimages haven't reached—the remote site of the disaster itself—is the most sacred of all. Every April 15, starting long before buff and oceanographer Robert Ballard set out in search of the wreck, the THS joined the International Ice Patrol in dropping a wreath from a plane on the *Titanic*'s presumed "gravesite." For the sixtieth anniversary in 1972 two laminated packets were attached to the wreath. One contained a postcard of the *Titanic*. The other contained a copy of the *Titanic*'s passenger list from *A Night to Remember*, a THS brochure, and a list of all the current members, who thus communed with the ship and the dead more closely than ever before.[44] By the time the *Titanic* Heritage Tours began in 1993, the true location of the wreck was known, though at 49° 56' W, 41° 43' N, and a depth of twelve thousand feet, it remained inaccessible to tour groups.

CHAPTER 7

MISSION TO DESTINY

ⓔ DANIELLE STEEL'S 1991 novel *No Greater Love*, in which the *Titanic* figures centrally, plays upon a recurring theme in the meaning and memory of the disaster. From the moment the ship went down, there has been a nagging sense of incompleteness about the unconsummated "maiden voyage"—and a variety of attempts to bring it to a satisfactory finish. We have already encountered some of these attempts: the celebrations of chivalric self-sacrifice that gave the story a redemptive conclusion; Walter Lord's demarcation of the disaster as the end of an era, which transformed an accident at sea into a pivotal event in world history; the film *Titanic*'s depiction of the disaster as the resolution of domestic conflict; Molly Brown's reincarnation as a symbol of the American Way; *Titanic* buffs' efforts to combat uncertainty by knowing everything there is to know about the ship and its fate.

Steel takes the problem of consummation literally. The disaster deprives her heroine, Edwina Winfield, of the opportunity to lose her virginity; the unfinished voyage leaves her a

DOWN WITH THE OLD CANOE

maiden. Edwina is traveling on the *Titanic* with her fiancé, Charles Fitzgerald. Their marriage is planned for August, and good Victorians that they are, they resist their sexual urges: "There were moments, like this one, when she wondered how they would ever wait until August. But there was no question of that, even on this most romantic ship. Edwina would never have betrayed her parents' faith in her, nor would Charles, but it was going to be difficult to restrain themselves until mid-August." When the *Titanic* sinks and Charles goes down with it, Edwina's waiting is prolonged indefinitely.

For most of *No Greater Love*, Edwina occupies a curious position. Her parents, in imitation of the Strauses, die together, and she is left to care for her five brothers and sisters. In this sense Edwina remains the pure and self-sacrificing nineteenth-century woman. But she also insists on taking over her father's San Francisco newspaper, which she manages decisively and successfully. Yet even her independence is a form of self-sacrifice; she runs the paper to support her family, not to fulfill her own desires: "She had no regrets about her life, but she had given up her own life, in a sense, for these children, and now she wanted each of them to have everything, all their dreams, and everything life had to offer." Edwina finally sells the paper after one of her brothers dies in the Great War. Visiting another brother in Hollywood, she meets his partner, Sam Horowitz, a gentle, strong, kind, and wise movie mogul. After various adventures they fall in love, and he saves her from the fate of the "virgin spinster." Sam's career and the Hollywood setting are important. They represent the consumer society, with its promises of self-fulfillment, from which Edwina has been tragically cut off. Now, at long last, Sam introduces her to the pleasures of sex and consumption, and Edwina completes her journey into the twentieth century.[1]

Steel's novel is exceptional in that it views the problem of unconsummated maidenhood from a female (though certainly not a feminist) perspective.[2] In both fiction and reality—the line between the two has always been blurry in the case of the *Titanic*—the completion of the voyage has been almost exclusively a male narrative. While there was talk about salvaging the ship as early as 1912, these narratives of completion took their most resonant forms in the late 1970s and 1980s. In the wake of a resurgent feminism, the defeat in Vietnam, Watergate, the OPEC oil embargo, economic stagnation, and the Iran hostage crisis, the "decline" of the United States came to be seen in terms of gender. National "weakness," embodied in Jimmy Carter, was feminine. As the *Wall Street Journal* later put it:

> Jimmy Carter first presented himself to the nation as a masculine personality. Naval academy. Submariner. Nuclear engineer. Farmer. Loner. Tough governor. But once in office, he lost no time revealing his true feminine spirit. He wouldn't twist arms. He didn't like to threaten or rebuke. . . . And we watched how far this approach got him in the jungles of Washington and the world. So in a sense, we've already had a "woman" president: Jimmy Carter.[3]

Within this context the failure to consummate the *Titanic*'s maiden voyage stood for an imperiled masculinity. Finding and perhaps raising the ship would symbolically combat the peril by redressing an earlier "failure" and bringing a decisive conclusion to what had been left open-ended.

For Norman Hall, the protagonist in Donald A. Stanwood's *The Memory of Eva Ryker* (1978), revisiting the *Titanic* becomes a way of redeeming his own fall from manhood. As a young policeman in Honolulu just before Pearl Harbor, Norman bungled a double murder case involving *Titanic* survivors— "acted in a shameful manner," according to his superior—and was compelled to leave the force. Though he fought in World War II and achieved success as a journalist and novelist, his masculinity has remained suspect. His wife, who dresses in "no-bullshit tailored suits" à la Joan Crawford, manages his career and collaborates on some of his writing. "You know Norman," she tells his publisher. "Bitchy on an empty stomach." When Norman receives an assignment to cover a mission to locate the *Titanic*, he realizes that the solution to his personal disaster depends upon his ability to reveal the hidden truth behind the *Titanic* disaster. From writing books that he describes as "wet dreams set to prose," he is recast as the quintessential post-Watergate male hero—an investigative reporter. In effect he gets a second chance to be a policeman.[4]

Norman's detective work, which includes a bathyscaphe visit to the wreck and a narrow escape from death in a suspicious helicopter crash, reveals that an elaborate kidnapping and diamond-smuggling plot on board the *Titanic* led to a string of murders. By the end of the novel he has solved the mystery and overcome his "shameful" past by finding the killers, who, it turns out, were responsible for the double murder in Hawaii that cast his manhood into doubt in the first place. The victim of the kidnapping attempt remains uncertain about the benefits of uncovering her traumatic childhood memories. "Some things should be laid to rest," she explains to Norman. "Like the Titanic. All the hate and grief because of that ship. Bringing it to light was like indecent exposure." But the novel is Norman's story, not hers, and from his perspective "indecent exposure" is the only acceptable form of resolution. By exposing the truth behind the disaster and proving his manhood, he brings the story to a successful close.[5]

In Clive Cussler's 1976 best seller *Raise the Titanic!* salvaging the ship means reclaiming the nation's manhood rather than an individual's. Cussler embodies the feminization of American society in Dana Seagram, a marine archaeologist who spouts "bleeding-heart, liberal crap" about her husband's secret scientific work for the U.S. government, has a "fetish for Women's Lib," and refuses to give up her career to have children. Gene Seagram is involved in a project to build a high-tech defensive weapons system but needs a large supply of byzanium. When he discovers that the *Titanic* sank with a cargo of byzanium in its hold, he launches a project to find and raise the ship. Gene recruits Dirk Pitt, Cussler's spy hero; Dana's expertise is also required.[6]

To complete the project, it will be necessary for Dirk to defeat the Soviets. It will also be necessary for Dana to give up her "liberal crap" and recognize that national security is at stake. Though Gene's manhood is hopelessly lost—Dana has "frosted" his "balls" beyond repair—the nation's can be recovered through a reinvigorated Cold War. We see that Dana is beginning to come around when she humiliates a reporter for *Female Eminence Weekly* at a press conference. The reporter asks her how she can compete in "a profession dominated by egotistic male pigheads." Dana answers that she doesn't "have to go braless or spread my legs" to get her male colleagues' attention, that she prefers to compete with members of her own sex, who are well represented at the National Underwater and Marine Agency, and that the only "pigheads" she has met in her life have been among "the female of the species." She receives a standing ovation.[7]

Dirk and his team raise the *Titanic* in a flurry of gendered imagery—the ship is "a mess, like a hideous old prostitute who dwelt in dreams of better days and long-lost beauty"—and begin to tow it back to shore. The Soviets seize the ship and hold Dana hostage. As she shouts anti-Communist epithets, Dirk comes to her rescue and, with the help of the navy SEALs, saves the ship. American masculinity triumphs in the person of Dirk Pitt, the hero who defeats the Soviets and conquers the assertive woman. Dana and Dirk have torrid sex in a B deck suite on board the *Titanic*. She learns that all she needed was a real man. No longer will feminists and liberals sap the strength of the nation. Even the Senate majority leader, who threatens to expose the secret agency behind the project unless the president agrees to increase welfare spending, relents when he learns about the miraculous success of the new weapons program.[8]

Raise the Titanic! became a syndicated serial comic strip in 1977 and a big-budget Hollywood flop in 1980. Dana (Anne Archer) is a minor character in the movie version, a newspaper reporter duped by the Soviets into leaking the story about the discovery of the *Titanic*, and the weapons system that functions so magnificently in the novel remains unbuilt at the end of the film. But Dirk (Richard Jordan) still beats the Russians and finishes what he calls "the biggest job with the highest stakes anybody ever dreamt of." And the film, despite its box-office disappointment, reached a notable audience several years later. *Raise the Titanic!* was one of two movies (the other was *A Night to Remember*) that Robert Ballard and his fellow scientists watched on board the *Knorr* as they searched for the lost *Titanic* in the late summer of 1985.[9]

It is, of course, an accident of history that Ballard and his team of scientists from the Woods Hole Oceanographic Institution and the Institut Français de Recherche pour l'Exploitation de la Mer discovered the *Titanic* in 1985. It could have happened earlier, on the 1980 trip financed by Texas oilman Jack Grimm, for example; it could have happened later or not at all had Ballard's team on the *Knorr* narrowly missed the spot as a French team on *Le Suroit* had done several weeks earlier. In other words, it was not necessary that Ballard's accomplishment take place almost exactly in the middle of the Reagan presidency. But the story of the discovery is a triumphalist story from Reagan's America.

We have, by now, explored how the *Titanic*'s meanings have been made, not found, within a variety of historical contexts. The "conclusion" of the *Titanic* narrative, which was really a new narrative in the guise of a conclusion, would have been constructed differently if the events it described had taken place at another time or if the French rather than the Americans had found the wreck. (Actually it was both, but because Ballard was an American in charge of an American ship, the discovery quickly became an American achievement.) What if the abrasive Grimm rather than the mediagenic Ballard had succeeded on one of his three voyages, in 1980, 1981, or 1983? Instead Grimm's failure, recorded in a TV documentary narrated by Orson Welles and as a book called *Beyond Reach*, became the foil for Ballard's "mission to destiny." With Ballard as its hero the discovery of the *Titanic* emerged as the story of a revitalized American masculinity and a resurgent nation.[10]

Accounts of the discovery did not hesitate to cast it in terms of gender. The 1985 trip succeeded in locating the ship and taking still photographs from the unmanned submersible *Angus*, and Ballard proclaimed "an ending to the unfinished maiden voyage." But he quickly announced that he would return the following summer to explore the inside of the wreck using a joystick-operated video camera. The unmanned submersible had not been capable of genuine consummation. In July 1986, with the manned submersible *Alvin* and their "proud little robot soldier" *Jason Jr.*, the explorers succeeded, as news reports repeatedly pointed out, in "penetrating" the ship.[11]

Yet Ballard sounded like a disappointed lover. After the 1985 visit he said that the *Titanic* was "in beautiful condition" and "gorgeous." After the consummation, however, he revealed that the ship was "not a pretty sight." "Though still impressive in her dimensions," he wrote in *National Geographic*, "she is no longer the graceful lady that sank a mere five days into her maiden voyage, in 1912, after striking an iceberg. Her beauty has faded." The burden of fame raised still more doubts. "It's sort of like I just married someone——," Ballard remarked to an interviewer, "and is this something I want to be married to? It seemed nice at the time—you know, she was cute, she was nice and all that sort of thing—but now I'm married to her and wondering if I made a mistake. And I can't just walk away from this one. She won't let me." Consummation had its costs; finding the lost maiden saddled the hero with a shrew. "There is no divorcing the *Titanic*," he complained. "Ever." The beautiful virgin had changed into an old battleax. (Charles Haas of the Titanic Historical Society offered a more romantic metaphor and seemed less disappointed after seeing the videotapes of the wreck at Ballard's *National Geographic* press conference. "It was like meeting an old girlfriend with whom you corresponded for many, many years and this was our first face-to-face meeting," he said. "It was a very special feeling.")[12]

This narrative made clear that the task of historical resolution belonged to men. The public learned that at the end of the first trip "the team celebrated in the bunk room known as Boy's Town." Ballard's accounts of the voyages described a homosocial world in which the prevailing style was a kind of macho sentimentalism. At the "moment of triumph," members of the crew broke into "shrieks" and "war whoops." Ballard himself "didn't yelp or shout," but in the mode of the strong but silent test pilot Chuck Yeager, whose autobiography he was reading when he was called to the control room, he "simply kept repeating in a quiet but incredulous voice, 'God damn. God damn. . . .' " Excessive celebration would have undermined the serious, somber business at hand and signaled feminine frivolity rather than masculine earnestness and reserve. The mood became reflective, and Ballard announced that he would be holding a memorial service on the *Knorr*'s fantail. "I really don't have much to say," he said, "but I thought we might just observe a few moments of silence."

Then he thanked the crew and ordered them back to work. While Ballard denied that he was trying to be theatrical—and there is no reason to doubt his sincerity or what Walter Lord called his "piety"—the memorial service did make for good theater. It allowed Ballard to offer a public benediction and showed rugged men acting out the completion of a seventy-three-year-old historical narrative. The "souls" of the *Titanic* victims had been in a kind of limbo until Ballard and his team "located" them and the ship itself could "finally rest in peace."[13]

Despite the presence of a few women crew members, it was "proud wives and children" who "streamed aboard for a hug and a kiss" when the *Knorr* came into port at Woods Hole. Crowds cheered the conquering heroes who had brought the *Titanic*'s maiden voyage to a long-awaited end. The *Knorr* received "the kind of welcome that might have greeted the Titanic had the famed luxury liner completed its maiden voyage 63 [*sic*] years ago," reported the *Los Angeles Times*. (In the movie *Raise the Titanic!* the wreck is towed past the Statue of Liberty into New York Harbor as cheering crowds line the Battery.) The press zoomed in on Ballard, "eager for a word with or a glimpse of the hero who had snatched back from the sea, symbolically if not in fact, what had seemed lost to it forever." Male heroism had avenged a loss. The bold intervention of resolute men had transformed a tragedy into a triumph. "*Titanic*," proclaimed the narrator (Martin Sheen) of a 1986 documentary about the second voyage: "No longer lost. No longer legend. There are people aboard the great ship once again, after seventy-four dark and silent years."[14]

Fixing history was a standard trope in the mid-1980s; the impulse to alter the past pervaded American culture, from movies to presidential policy. Susan Jeffords has shown how the *Rambo* films enacted a rejection of the "weakness" of the Carter years and a correction of history through the "hardened body of John Rambo" (Sylvester Stallone). In *Rambo: First*

Blood, Part 2, released in the same year as the discovery of the *Titanic*, Rambo returns to Vietnam and wins the war not only by overpowering the Soviets and the Vietnamese but by refusing to let Congress and the bureaucrats allow another defeat. The invasion of Grenada, the bombing of Libya, and, under George Bush, the invasion of Panama and the Gulf War all were presented as victories over the "Vietnam Syndrome"—real interventions overseas that were also symbolic interventions to repair history. On the domestic side the *Back to the Future* films employed high technology to intervene directly in the past. The first *Back to the Future*, also a box-office hit in 1985, sends Marty McFly (Michael J. Fox) in a souped-up DeLorean to 1955, where he alters history to fix his dysfunctional family. Through Marty's manipulations his father turns out to be a strong and respected breadwinner rather than a wimp and a failure. Significantly, Marty leapfrogs over the 1960s, the period when domestic and international weakness allegedly set in, to a better time of a strong nation, economic prosperity, and traditional gender roles.[15] Though these interventions took a variety of forms, they shared the assumption that somehow the past had to be set straight in order to move ahead. Putting the disturbing events of history to rest, either by changing them or giving them happy endings, cleared the way to reaffirm progress.

The discovery of the *Titanic*, Robert Ballard explained, was simultaneously an "epilogue" and a "prologue." He meant that while the discovery ended the unfinished maiden voyage, it also opened "a new era in exploration."[16] Though Ballard had a specific goal in mind—the exploration of the oceans—his transformation of the *Titanic* from a symbol of failure into an affirmation of progress had broader implications. Ballard fashioned himself and others fashioned him as a hero who overcame limits, who made progress possible by resisting constraints—in other words, a *frontier* hero. In political terms the arrival of the rugged westerner Ronald Reagan heralded decisiveness, action, and growth after the indecision, passivity, and stagnation of the 1970s. Ballard's biography offered another version of this myth. Articles and interviews told Americans that the "lean, hard-driving" discoverer of the *Titanic* was a "high-tech cowboy" (or a "submarine cowboy"), born in Wichita, Kansas, "where his paternal grandfather, a U.S. marshal, was killed in a gunfight." His father had punched cows in Montana, and he was a distant relative of Bat Masterson: "My family came from England in the seventeen hundreds. By the eighteen hundreds they were in Kansas, and they kept going west. I'm the first Ballard to have come back. But I really didn't; I just went underwater. Why the heck am I here on Cape Cod? It's because of Woods Hole. Woods Hole doesn't belong here. It belongs in California. It's wide open, a frontier town—oceanography is a frontier." Woods Hole does not strike most visitors as "wide open," but Ballard's frontier was symbolic rather than geographical. His achievement fitted beautifully into the rhetoric and iconography of the mid-1980s, when the nation, led by a man who conflated cowboy, star, and president, rejected all talk of limits.[17]

Interviews and biographies also publicized Ballard's military pedigree. After punching cows in Montana, his father became a test flight engineer. No wonder the son was immersed in Chuck Yeager's autobiography at the moment of the *Titanic*'s discovery; his father, like Yeager, "was a guy behind the 'right stuff.' " Ballard spent his early childhood at Muroc (later Edwards) Air Base in the Mojave Desert. His father eventually headed the Minuteman missile program for North American Aviation. Ballard's career in oceanography began in earnest when the navy assigned him as a young ensign to be its liaison officer at Wood's Hole. (Dirk Pitt, the hero of *Raise the Ti-*

tanic!, is also a former navy officer.) To round out the pedigree, Ballard's brother, a theoretical physicist, was working at the time of the discovery on artificial intelligence for the Strategic Defense Initiative (SDI)—Ronald Reagan's dream of a new military/technological frontier in space.[18]

The "cowboy" label made clear that Ballard was to be seen as a *male* hero. By calling himself "an explorer wrapped up in scientific garb," Ballard cast himself as an actor rather than an observer. "I don't want to be known as a scientist," he told an interviewer; he wanted "Explorer" chiseled into his tombstone. He described his team as "the modern equivalent of Jason's mythological Argonauts who would help me in my quest to find the Golden Fleece—the *Titanic*." (The *Argo* was one of his submersibles, and we have already encountered *Jason Jr.*, the extension of the explorer's body. The Argonauts theme was a play on Senator William Proxmire's Golden Fleece Awards, given to ridiculous government expenditures. The joke in this case, Ballard implied, was on the meddlesome senator.) "In Ballard," said the *Reader's Digest*, "there is something of the astronaut, Jules Verne and Lewis and Clark wrapped into one."[19]

The narrative of exploration and discovery signaled the return of the frontier spirit—individualism, adventure, expansiveness. Reaganomics associated this spirit with unfettered capitalism, and here too Ballard served as a symbol. The cowboy hero was also an entrepreneur who parlayed exploration into profit. Ballard detected a paradox between his self-proclaimed economic conservatism and his penchant for risk taking. "As for us taking chances," he told an interviewer, "I'm about as conservative as Genghis Khan." But the paradox was more apparent than real. Reagan-style economic conservatism retained nothing of the older conservative opposition to capitalism; in its emphasis on limitless growth it was not conservative at all. Ballard's "entrepreneurial style," as a reporter summarized it, harmonized the good of society with self-aggrandizement. Woods Hole represented the ideal political economy—"a blend of cloistered academe and competitive free enterprise" where the scientist assumed the role of "independent entrepreneur." The Oceanographic Institution, with what Ballard described as its "weak and loosely defined central government existing primarily to serve a group of strong individual 'states,' " resembled Reagan's model for the new federalism.[20]

Cut loose from oppressive bureaucracy, the entrepreneur was free to compete and win. "We're in competition for access to American minds and purse strings," Ballard said of his rivalry with the space program. The progress of ocean science depended upon Ballard's talents for self-promotion and commercial exploitation. As a contemporary account put it, "With a near-monopoly over the only saleable booty from the wrecked liner—his descriptions and thousands of pictures—Ballard is in a position to profit in financial terms and less tangible ways. The selling of the *Titanic* is also the selling of Robert Ballard." Marketing the discovery through articles in *National Geographic*, a *National Geographic* video introduced during the 1986 Christmas season and then broadcast on Ted Turner's superstation TBS, coffee table and children's books (which together sold more than two million copies), and a lecture tour that brought in close to ten thousand dollars per speech, Ballard immediately transformed himself and the discovery into entertainment commodities.[21]

While there is no reason to suggest that Ballard was primarily motivated by personal profit, his success story played up the providential harmony between his own fortunes and the advancement of the nation and humanity. "I felt the magic of the lost ship would help attract funding that would enable me to make a major step forward in underwater research technology." Significantly, he also presented the benefits of that technology in terms of commodification and entertainment. By perfecting "telepresence"—the ability to see beyond the confines of the body, as in *Jason Jr.*'s exploration of the *Titanic*—Ballard hoped to give people a form of "reality" that offered even greater therapeutic benefits than movies or TV. "With telepresence," he predicted, "you won't need drugs, or *Star Wars*, or Spielberg to get your jolts. You'll get them out of reality." This was the logic of Reagan-era political economy: that everybody benefited from the energies of the liberated entrepreneur; that what mattered most of all, as Ballard said of telepresence and the discovery of the *Titanic*, was to "make people feel good"; that images *were* reality.[22]

Richard Slotkin has characterized the frontier revival of the 1980s as the "recrudescence" of "bonanza economics"—the idea that limitless wealth could be generated with virtually no social costs. Pundits discovered new frontiers everywhere, including the oceans—the "Last Earthly Frontier"—where "inexhaustible" supplies of food and energy lay waiting to be exploited. Though Ballard scoffed at the suggestion that the ocean could feed the world or supply it with raw materials, he engaged in similar rhetoric. The narrative of discovery moved from claustrophobia—men cramped in coffinlike submarines, the *Titanic* buried alive beneath the sea—to unbounded possibility. "I'm a catalyst that doesn't necessarily care whether my catalytic properties are used in science, in commercial areas, in the military, anywhere," Ballard bragged. He saw no contradiction between his environmentalist concern for the oceans as a source of life and a place of beauty and his entrepreneurial notion that they were a "practical frontier," open to commercial and military exploitation as well as scientific exploration. After the 1985 voyage he established his own company to manufacture and sell the technology that had proved its value in discovering the *Titanic*. The "likeliest customers" were oil and mining companies.[23] Ballard's assertion that the discovery might lead "anywhere" represented a triumphant faith in cost-free growth and development.

Yet Ballard and the narrative of discovery could not entirely evade troubling contradictions, like the tension between piety and progress. While they celebrated the potential uses of the technology that had found the *Titanic*, Ballard and many of his admirers wanted the wreck itself left undisturbed. Ballard spoke eloquently of the site as a memorial and vehemently opposed any salvage schemes: "There is no light at that depth, and little life can be found. It is a quiet, peaceful place and a fitting place for the remains of this greatest of sea tragedies to rest. Forever may it remain that way." Editorials echoed his plea. On the return voyage Ballard placed a plaque from the Titanic Historical Society on the *Titanic*'s stern to honor his friend and former business partner William Tantum and to designate the wreck a sacred resting place.[24]

When various groups began to develop plans to visit the site and bring up relics, the outcry grew louder. Jack Grimm announced that he would rent a submersible from the Reynolds Aluminum Company and salvage *Titanic* artifacts to recoup his two-million-dollar investment. A British naval buff tried to lure investors into a scheme to raise the wreck using inflatable bags. A Belgian engineer and entrepreneur who lived in New Orleans founded the Exploration Society of America, a travel agency that planned a seventy-fifth-anniversary party at the site of the wreck; for twenty-five thousand dollars, guests could join celebrities (the list of invitees included Glenn Ford, Jacqueline Bisset, William Shatner, and Loretta Swit) for a two-week cruise culminating in a moment of silence and trips down to the wreck in the same Reynolds Aluminum submersible that Grimm hoped to rent. Even though it has no jurisdiction over international waters, Congress, supported by Ballard's testimony, passed a bill declaring the *Titanic* a memorial and prohibiting its desecration. Sponsored by Walter

B. Jones, chairman of the House Merchant Marine and Fisheries Committee, the bill called for international cooperation to enforce the ban on desecration. President Reagan signed it into law in October 1986. In August 1987, with a French expedition under way and no international agreement, Senator Lowell Weicker pushed through a bill banning the importation of objects from the *Titanic* "for the purpose of commercial gain," but it was tabled in the House.[25]

The French, meanwhile, went about their salvage work undisturbed, and on October 28 American television viewers were treated to the dramatic opening of a *Titanic* strongbox by actor Telly Savalas in a Paris museum. The program was produced by Doug Llewelyn, master of ceremonies on *The People's Court*, whose company helped finance the French expedition. Unlike Al Capone's vault, opened in a similar stunt by Geraldo Rivera the previous year, the strongbox was not empty. Savalas, dressed in a tuxedo and black clogs, revealed a small treasure of coins, bills, and jewelry, even though the *Titanic*'s passengers had apparently claimed most of their valuables before the ship sank.[26]

In an afterword to Ballard's "Epilogue for the *Titanic*" the editor of *National Geographic* sadly reported that "Robert Ballard's hope that *Titanic* should remain undisturbed was not realized. Last July, a French expedition began to retrieve artifacts from the wreck site. Its actions were roundly criticized as grave-robbing—justifiably, for the line between curiosity and acquisitiveness seems to have been crossed." Oddly enough, nobody remarked that this exploitation of the discovery simply followed the rhetoric of entrepreneurialism to its logical conclusion—nobody, that is, but the French themselves. Robert Chappaz, head of the company that sponsored the French expedition, observed: "It's strange hearing Americans complain about doing things for profit. Usually it's the Europeans who criticize the Americans for commercial exploitation." Among conservative commentators only William F. Buckley wholeheartedly supported the salvage efforts. "I for one admire the enterprise of the consortium that is spending much of the summer retrieving from utter uselessness artifacts that, for some people, exercise an alluring historical appeal." Not all buffs, he recognized, opposed salvage; some wanted to see the artifacts on display in museums, which is where they ended up. Buckley refused to shy away from the free market when commercialism took a potentially tacky turn. He even joined the French on a submersible journey to the wreck.[27]

In Ballard, the *Titanic* buff—the leader of the memorial service, the deliverer of the THS plaque, the opponent of salvage—coexisted, sometimes uneasily, with the submarine cowboy. The buff and the cowboy represented two modes of conservatism, which also coexisted uneasily within the larger political culture. One mode yearned for the sacred and the timeless and sought to resist the depredations and devastations that accompanied "progress." The other embraced "progress," which it considered synonymous with economic growth, and sought to loosen the fetters that were supposedly holding it in check. These conservatisms merged in Reaganism and its back-to-the-future ideology.

Ballard the buff argued that he had discovered a sacred place that should forever remain free from exploitation. Ballard the cowboy crossed the "line between curiosity and acquisitiveness" as soon as he performed his first ship-to-shore interview. The narrative of discovery, with its paeans to masculinity, boundless possibility, the frontier myth, and the glories of the free market, told a Reagan-era tale of conquering limits. It was saturated with the language of acquisitiveness. A cartoon in the *Houston Post* two days after the first reports of the discovery showed Lee Iacocca, chairman of Chrysler, corporate-entrepreneurial hero, and possible presidential candidate,

towing the dripping *Titanic* ashore. An admiring passenger
in the Chrysler tow truck turns to the chairman and exclaims,
"This is some winning streak you're on, Iacocca."[28]

As a story of American ingenuity and will the discovery of the
Titanic resonated not only in terms of new frontiers and
Reagonomics but also in related terms of a revived Cold War.
While Ballard and the press treated the discovery as an act of
individual heroism, they also paid homage to the institutional
support behind the achievement. Ballard's voyages were sponsored by the U.S. Navy, which expected to reap the technological rewards of the discovery. The drama of men redeeming
themselves through high technology was the drama of the
nation redeeming itself through military strength.

We have seen how the *Titanic* figured into the culture of
the Cold War as early as the 1950s. The connections between
"finding" the *Titanic* and defeating the Soviet Union emerged
in fiction long before they took shape in reality. The 1966 pre-
miere episode of the ABC adventure series *The Time Tunnel*,
"Rendezvous with Yesterday," involved a visit from the high-
tech future to the doomed ship in 1912. Senator Leroy Clark
(Gary Merrill) threatens to investigate a top secret military
project to develop time travel. The budget-conscious Clark
appears at the eight-hundred-story Pentagon-type complex
where the research is being done and warns General Heywood
("Woody") Kirk (Whit Bissell) and electrophysicists Tony
Newman (James Darren) and Doug Phillips (Robert Colbert)
that he will cut off their funding if they don't produce results
soon. Tony, driven to save the project from the meddling
elected official, sneaks into the laboratory at night, fires up
the computers, and flings himself into the untested time tunnel. Spinning into the past, he lands on the deck of the *Titanic*
to the sounds of ragtime music. When he tries to warn Captain Smith of the imminent disaster, he is rebuffed and im-

prisoned. Doug leaps into the time tunnel to come to Tony's rescue and to bring the superior knowledge of the future to ward off catastrophe. But the captain doesn't listen until it is too late; high technology could have fixed history if only people in the past had been more enlightened. Tony and Doug are blown overboard by an explosion and then hurled back into the time tunnel by the technicians in the Pentagon control room. Though the technology isn't yet perfected—they can't be retrieved from the tunnel—the chastened senator suspends his investigation. The visit to the *Titanic* vindicates defense spending.[29]

Clive Cussler conveyed the same message in *Raise the Titanic!*, which in its film version provided entertainment and inspiration on board the *Knorr*. In reality, as in the book and movie, the discovery of the *Titanic* contributed to the struggle against the Soviets and helped make the case for increased funding for military research and development. Just after extolling the benefits of ocean exploration for the environment, Ballard observed that "[a]s long as there are global rivalries between superpowers, the seas will be of great strategic importance and deep-sea exploration will have military significance." Accounts of the discovery seized on the potential military uses of the submersible technology: retrieving lost submarines and warheads, "investigating enemy sonar arrays," and scouting out positions for American missiles. Ballard argued that the problem of concealing nuclear missiles on land could be solved by charting undersea canyons and hiding missiles there.[30]

As the label "submarine cowboy" suggests, Ballard combined the frontier hero with the military hero—a common amalgam in the culture of Reagan's America. Reaganism, as Slotkin argues, sought to achieve an economic bonanza "through the magic of supply-side economics coupled with a regeneration of the nation's spirit through more vigorous prosecution of Cold War (against Russia as 'evil empire') and savage war (against enemies like Ghadafy of Libya, Maurice Bishop of Grenada, and the Sandinista regime in Nicaragua)." Ballard's heroism struck all these chords: the regeneration of masculinity and the nation through frontier adventurism, cost-free economic expansion, and a stronger military rededicated to the struggle against the Soviets. His friend and sponsor, Reagan's secretary of the navy John Lehman, celebrated Ballard as the navy's "Bottom Gun," a play on the title of the biggest-grossing movie of 1986, *Top Gun*. In that film Lieutenant Pete ("Maverick") Mitchell (Tom Cruise), a "cowboy" navy fighter pilot, defeats the Soviets, reverses the decline of America's combat capabilities, and rescues from disgrace the memory of his father, a navy pilot who died in Vietnam. Lehman, who received thanks for his official support in the film credits, awarded Ballard a "Bottom Gun" baseball cap. Ballard himself described his exploits as "war with no one getting hurt."[31]

The discovery of the *Titanic* was thus part of the Reagan-era defense buildup—one that took place as much in the cultural realm as the material. Ballard's heroism and the successful deployment of naval technology contributed to restoring the prestige and authority of the military after its "weakening" in the 1970s. Traveling back to the future to correct a legendary technological failure reopened the road to defense-based progress and prosperity. "I find it interesting," Ballard commented, "that in one key respect the *Titanic*'s tragedy and our success in finding her are linked: technology. . . . The past and the future merged into one another two-and-a-half miles beneath the waves."[32] This theme of redemption through defense technology connected the discovery to the Reagan administration's "Star Wars" initiative and its vision of peace and security achieved through the exploration and development of militarized high-tech frontiers. The sobering narrative of tragedy and loss had been transformed into a celebratory narrative of progress and victory.

Yet no *Titanic* narrative can be completely triumphal. Lingering always is the somber awareness of accident and death. *"Jason* salutes his creator," Martin Sheen declares in the *National Geographic* documentary. "For man and machine it's a moment of eerie victory"—eerie because man and machine have successfully explored a tomb. How can we reconcile the abrupt shifts in the narrative of discovery from celebration to doubt? Or Ballard the cowboy's claims that his "remarkable accomplishment" had opened up a "new era" and Ballard the buff's recitations of the *Titanic*'s lessons about "unjustified overconfidence in technology" and the "mistake of arrogance?" How can we account for the combination of technophilia and self-criticism in Charles Pellegrino's overwrought epigraph to his account of the discovery: "This is a book about men who loved and sometimes worshiped their machines. / And God help me. / I'm one of them"? Or the editorial chorus that used the occasion of the discovery to warn yet again about the same "evergreen" lessons? Or the inevitable connections drawn between the *Titanic* and the *Challenger* space shuttle disaster, which occurred between Ballard's two voyages?[33]

The answer lies in the curiously disembodied quality of these statements about technological overconfidence. In 1912 progressives attributed the disaster to corporate malefactors or modern materialism—that is, to the actual producers or consumers of technology. The radical critique went deeper still, blaming the disaster on the excesses and inhumanity of capitalism. Whatever we may think of these critiques, they at least had the merit of grounding technology and technological hubris in the workings of society and the economy. In 1985 and 1986 commentators spoke of overconfidence as if technology were autonomous; it seemed to come into being by itself for purposes determined by its own logic. The reminders about technological hubris prompted by the discovery of the *Titanic* materialized in print as a kind of ritual or routine. Writers, especially Ballard himself, were so thoroughly versed in Titanica that the call to humility had become an almost involuntary response. "Finding the Titanic (with this technology) is almost like developing a nuclear weapon," Ballard confessed. "It's something our minds can generate, but our society can't handle. It's troubling, because the potential of this kind of technology is so immense, but will we ever be able to deal with its consequences? It seems to me this is the major struggle society is going through today—to be able to deal with what is possible." The ambivalence was undoubtedly genuine. But why, if "society" couldn't handle it, did Ballard and the navy develop and test this technology? (Around the time when the *Titanic* was discovered, seven thousand American scientists refused on ethical grounds to accept SDI funding.) Did potentially dangerous technologies hatch out of "minds" alone, Platonically, or did material and political forces come into play? Warning about the dangers of technological overconfidence while neglecting the realities of modern technology—its hierarchical organization, its corporate and military purposes—transformed the progressive jeremiad into cliché. Such a ritualized response avoided any demand for a genuine change in values away from the fetishization of consumer and military goods and toward an emphasis on public services, the quality of life, and the common good.[34]

Of all the articles written about the discovery, only a probing essay by Timothy Ferris in *Life* ventured beyond the rote invocations to explore how "blind faith in technology can kill." Ferris used the coincidence of the *Challenger* disaster, the meltdown of the Chernobyl nuclear reactor in the Ukraine, and the second Ballard expedition—all events of 1986—to awaken a democratic skepticism toward expertise and to insist that technology must be shaped by humane values rather than "by imitating machines" or "abdicating to them."[35]

The disembodiment of technology smoothed over the apparent contradiction between celebrations of progress and warnings against overconfidence. Technology was a given. It simply happened, producing and reproducing and improving on itself, occasionally with disastrous results, but "disconnected," in Neil Postman's words, from any "theory, meaning, or purpose" that might guide or control it. To cede this kind of autonomy to technology, even while warning against putting too much faith in it, was to worship and glorify it. Technophilia—whether in Ballard's exclamation to the press that he was "in love with technology" or in the photographs, diagrams, and illustrations of *Alvin* and *JJ* that adorned the pages of newspapers, magazines, and books—dominated the narrative of discovery.[36] Men will be men, said this narrative, and technology will be technology. Uttering banalities about overconfidence allowed men and technology to forge confidently ahead. As a "mission to destiny" the discovery possessed an aura of inevitability; the maiden voyage had to be completed to usher in a new era. Technological success had to redeem technological failure. The story of the *Titanic* had to have a happy ending.

REARRANGING DECK CHAIRS

e/o MANY PEOPLE, BUFFS among them, do not share professional historians' scruples about maintaining the distance between past and present, between history and lived experience. The pleasure of history, they might say, lies in the collapsing of distance; the past is meaningful not because of its pastness alone but because of its simultaneous remoteness and immediacy—its power to impart lessons, to speak to our predicaments, and, paradoxically, to find residual value and living significance in what has been "lost."

I myself am less than fully committed to the pastness of the past. In exploring the *Titanic*'s cultural currency, I have tried to show how a historical event has worked and been reworked in a series of presents—how its meanings are contingent and contextual rather than inherent or timeless. Still, I don't want to ignore the possibility that, now at least, the *Titanic* remains a part of our cultural vocabulary through sheer momentum. In the marketplace this translates into the notion that with the right amount of modification and repackaging, what has sold before will continue to sell. The *Titanic* generates interest because it generates interest. It is an icon because it is an icon. In this way a good story can prolong itself indefinitely.

The discovery of the wreck produced a deluge of Titanica. Walter Lord opened the floodgates in 1986, thirty-one years after *A Night to Remember*, with his ruminations on a variety of lingering *Titanic* issues in *The Night Lives On*: Captain Smith's disregard for the iceberg warnings sent by other ships; the possibility that the *Titanic* would have survived a head-on collision rather than a starboard scrape; the reports of gunfire on deck in the final moments; the *Californian*'s failure to respond to the *Titanic*'s distress signals; the last song; the ethics of salvage. Dozens of other new *Titanic* books followed. Robert Serling's *Something's Alive on the Titanic* (1990) placed the salvage issue at the center of a ghost story in which a 1975 mission succeeds in finding the wreck only to be wiped out by supernatural forces guarding a hidden fortune in gold against plunderers. The *Titanic*'s living dead spare Ballard because he has no intention of looting the wreck, and they even leave the French alone since they are confining their salvage operations to the debris outside the ship. Serling, author of the 1967 best seller *The President's Plane Is Missing* and brother of *The Twilight Zone*'s Rod Serling, dedicated the book to Ballard.[1]

A 1989 video game called *Search for the Titanic* let players arrange financing and purchase equipment for their own expedition. The most skillful could operate on-screen submersibles and discover the *Titanic*, in the form of a digitized picture of the wreck, for themselves. Consumers more in the mood to relax than compete could listen to Steve Cameron's New Age *Titanic Suite*, released in 1987. New York's South Street Seaport Museum invited a more substantial encounter in 1990, when it mounted the first major American exhibition on the *Titanic*. Visitors heard "a dramatic audio

diorama of the sinking ship that poignantly evoke[d] the atmosphere on board" as they looked at original design plans,
menus, life jackets, passenger tickets, newspaper clips, postcards, and wireless messages. "Titanic!" then traveled to Ful-
lerton, California, and Mystic, Connecticut.[2]

In June 1993, when I was just making the transition from
casual interest to systematic research, a tabloid headline
screamed at me across the supermarket conveyer belt: TITANIC
BABY FOUND ALIVE! I added the *Weekly World News* to my milk
and cereal, eager to learn more about the infant girl pictured
on the cover floating in the Atlantic with her pudgy arms
draped over a *Titanic* life buoy. Scientists explained that she
had passed through a time warp, much as Captain Smith had
done earlier, according to another issue. Hardly a week has
passed since without some new piece of Titanica coming to
my attention. Friends gave me books called *Make a Model Titanic* and *The Titanic* (part of the World Disasters series for
children), a facsimile of the *Boston Globe*'s front section from
April 16, 1912 (purchased, in this case, at a convenience store),
a tape of the Arts and Entertainment network's 1994 documentary on the disaster, and other assorted *Titanic* memorabilia, while I bought my father-in-law a reproduction of the
Titanic captain's bell (with which he tormented the rest of the
family on Christmas Day). My four-month-old son gave me
an excuse to buy *Polar the Titanic Bear*, a children's story written by a *Titanic* survivor for her son, whose toy bear was temporarily lost as they made their escape from the sinking ship.
The manuscript was discovered in a Long Island attic and
published, with many pictures, for the first time in 1994. (The
ubiquitous Ken Marschall and Don Lynch of the Titanic Historical Society served as advisers to the project.) In May 1995,
after viewing the giant-screen IMAX movie *Titanica*—the
storytelling is lame; the footage of the wreck is stunning—I
wandered into the gift shop at the Boston Museum of Science.

I didn't make any purchases, but I could have bought, in addition to *Polar the Titanic Bear*, the *Globe* reproduction, and the captain's bell, any number of books, video versions of *Titanica* and the 1953 *Titanic*, two model kits, and a set of Magic Rocks that grow luminously around the sunken ship.[3]

I might have bought the 1993 album by the Irish singer Kirsty MacColl in any event, since I like her music, but I was especially enticed by the title track, "Titanic Days." The song, which concerns a passionate but self-destructive relationship, hearkens back in spirit, if not intent, to Ma Rainey's "Titanic Man Blues" of 1926. Backed by Fletcher Henderson's group, Rainey borrows the melody from the Leadbelly song about Jack Johnson and the racist captain but changes "Titanic" from the ship into a two-timing lover, whom she kicks out by singing, "It's the last time, Titanic. Fare thee well." Rainey and MacColl both invoke the *Titanic* as a code for personal disaster. Rainey refuses to be dragged down. MacColl's survival is less assured, her ability to act more circumscribed, and she is left wondering if she will be saved. Playing on the old *Titanic* theme of women entrusting their lives to men, "Titanic Days" implies that the wish to be saved by a man ends up as the need to be saved from a man.[4]

A *Time* magazine article and a National Public Radio story focused on the British composer Gavin Bryars and his 1994 recording *The Sinking of the Titanic*, a chilling and evocative piece based on the Episcopal hymn "Autumn" (one of the candidates for Last Song) and punctuated with the sound of dripping water. The composition dates back to 1969, but as Bryars explains, "the discovery of the wreck by Dr. Ballard made me think again about the music." Approaching the disaster in "poetic" rather than literal terms, *The Sinking of the Titanic* tries to capture the feeling that "the music has just kept on going, forever." In the "more sound-efficient medium of water" the hymn "would descend with the ship to the ocean bed and remain there repeating itself over and over until the ship returns to the surface and the sounds re emerge [*sic*]." According to the liner notes, the 1985 discovery "renders this a possibility." Never respectful of cultural boundaries, the *Titanic* resurfaces in Bryars's piece as a fascinating mixture of "high" and "middlebrow" culture—an avant-garde recording bearing the imprimatur of Philip Glass as executive producer, featuring newspaper headlines and pictures of submersibles and *Titanic* artifacts in the album design, and written and performed by a "conceptual artist" and buff who thanks John Eaton and Charles Haas of Titanic International.[5]

In December 1995 a full-page ad designed to look like an article in *USA Today* offered collectors a rare opportunity to buy chunks of authentic *Titanic* coal for twenty-five dollars apiece. Recovered from the wreck by RMS Titanic, Inc. (the official "salvor-in-possession of the famous ship"), each piece was "presented to collectors in an ebony-finished display case with a plexiglass [*sic*] protective cover" and "a brass plaque, custom-engraved with their name, along with an individually numbered Certificate of Authenticity." According to the ad, proceeds would help finance a traveling exhibition of the other thirty-six hundred artifacts that RMS Titanic had salvaged. Buyers, meanwhile, would "own and preserve an important part of world history"—a constant reminder "that man does not control nature." CNN, CNBC, Fox, ABC, CBS, and *Time* all gave the coal sale "immediate media attention," and *USA Today*, its editorial content in sync with its advertising, reported that the "Titanic has been a global obsession almost since it sank on April 15, 1912." On April 15, 1996, ads announced the Titanic Expedition Cruise, departing in August to "witness history" as RMS Titanic tried to raise a piece of the wreck. Participants would get to view recovered artifacts, enjoy "nostalgic events," and "socialize with many of the who's who of the world." Ed Kamuda of the THS angrily denounced the schemes as proof that RMS Titanic lied when it claimed that it would not try to profit from its salvage efforts or retrieve artifacts from the wreck itself, as opposed to the debris field. "Greed and tastelessness know no bounds," he wrote.[6]

GTE Entertainment planned a November 1996 release date for a CD-ROM in which players in the role of British secret agents get to "[m]atch wits with an intriguing cast of more than 25 interactive characters while exploring the doomed vessel." A Titanic home page on the World Wide Web, run by a thirteen-year-old Australian boy, found itself in the top five percent of the most frequently visited web sites. And the disaster was also returning to an older medium: James Cameron, director of *Terminator 2* and *True Lies*, projected that his big-budget *Titanic* movie spectacular would fill theaters in the summer of 1997.[7]

It is doubtful that interest in the disaster, like the hymn in Bryars's composition, will keep on going forever, but at the moment, as my idiosyncratic survey suggests, it shows no sign of ebbing.

The surest way to know when meaning verges on extinction is to look to sportswriters, business experts, politicians, and pundits. In their hands historical and cultural references pass from the familiar to the overfamiliar, from illumination to cliché. The *Titanic* disaster has attained cultural currency not only as a marketable commodity but as a pervasive figure of speech. To use the *Titanic* as a metaphor in 1912 took work. The antisuffragist who urged his allies just to say "Titanic" recognized how the word could evoke a full-fledged narrative. He understood that the metaphor required a chain of associations to make sense: that the *Titanic* had simultaneously nothing and everything to do with women's suffrage. It served, to borrow the poet Howard Nemerov's insight, as a "compressed fable"; it insinuated that "[i]f you really want to see

something, look at something else."[8] The socialist who denounced "Our Titanic Civilization" anticipated the shock of
recognition in his readers when they saw how the *Titanic*,
which was unlike anything they had ever experienced, was
exactly like their experience of class discrimination and oppression. Walter Lord was right to claim originality for his
view of the disaster as a dividing line between then and now.
By recasting the *Titanic* as a metaphor for modern uncertainty,
he conveyed a kind of poetic (if not historical) truth that lit up
his readers' imaginations. In the 1950s there was even a freshness to the *Titanic* as a metaphor for technological hubris.

Such imaginative work is not involved when a candidate
proclaims, "I am a Republican, not a downsized Democrat. It
is not enough to just rearrange the deck chairs on the *Titanic*.
We must dramatically change the direction of the ship of state
or we'll still hit the iceberg." Politicians routinely accuse one
another of being "the captain of the *Titanic*," and the propen-
sity toward such a cliché knows no partisan boundaries. New
York Governor Mario Cuomo was fond of giving George Bush
this title—with Dan Quayle as his "cabin boy"—during the
1992 presidential race. Clinton strategist Paul Begala picked
up on the metaphor, as did Georgia Governor Zell Miller, key-
note speaker at the Democratic National Convention. The
Republican call for a renewal of the Reagan-Bush revolution,
Miller said, was "like the captain of the Titanic calling for more
icebergs." Newscaster David Brinkley speculated that Republican politicians were avoiding the convention in Houston because "they're afraid the Republican ticket is the *Titanic*."[9]

After Clinton's election Republicans seized the metaphor.
A conservative columnist, comparing Clinton with Bush on
the deficit, wrote that "[a]t least the captain of the Titanic could
say he never saw any iceberg. Mr. Clinton is standing at the
helm, iceberg in full view." At the height of the health care
debate in 1994, Senator John Chafee (R-R.I.) denounced his

colleague Jay Rockefeller (D-W.Va.) and predicted the fortunes of the Clinton health plan by labeling Rockefeller—what else?— "captain of the Titanic." Questioned about the problem of congressional gridlock, a pundit at the Heritage Foundation derisively likened the idea of giving more power to the Democratic House leadership to "promoting the captain of the Titanic after it hit the iceberg."[10]

So tired had the metaphor become that a writer for the *Orlando Sentinel Tribune*, commenting on the recent use of "rearranging deck chairs" by two Florida public officials, confessed that "I've been enjoying that Titanic line since 1967, when a comedian friend of mine used it in a New York club in regard to changing political faces in Washington. Claimed he wrote it himself. I doubt it. Nothing is original." It even crept into international affairs. Boris Yeltsin and a rival, observed a Russian expert, were embroiled in "a struggle between the captain and the first mate of the Titanic. They may determine at just what angle it goes down, but it's going down anyway"—which is to say, they were simply rearranging deck chairs. In 1986 Walter Lord noted that over the past ten years the *Titanic* had been used by political cartoonists to "depict the troubles" of Ford, Carter, and Reagan. While such things can't be quantified, deck chairs and sinking ships seemed to proliferate in the early 1990s.[11]

Not only politicians but coaches, teams, executives, and corporations drifted into the path of the floating metaphor. In 1993 the NHL's New York Islanders, the NBA's Cleveland Cavaliers, Major League Baseball's Texas Rangers, and the NFL's Washington Redskins and Houston Oilers all found themselves compared to the *Titanic*. General Motors and its presidents were particularly vulnerable; one GM president's defenders noted that "[h]e became captain after the Titanic had already hit the iceberg." Cable television mogul Ted Turner boasted that the major networks would fall victim to their own delusions; they were like "the captain of the *Titanic* telling the passengers, 'Don't worry. We've sunk 200 feet but we're going to turn the ship around.' "[12]

The *Titanic* has become a facile, all-purpose stand-in for incompetence, obliviousness, or futility. Overuse has deadened the metaphor while sanctioning its continued use as a safe linguistic practice, almost a reflex. In common speech the *Titanic* no longer jars.

Rumor has it that the three most written-about subjects of all time are Jesus, the Civil War, and the *Titanic* disaster. Perhaps this makes the reduction to cliché inevitable, and who am I, an interested party in the *Titanic* as a phenomenon of popular culture, to complain about its ubiquity? But the meanings and memories that I have explored here are anything but easy and benign. The lifelessness of the *Titanic* as a metaphor contrasts with its vitality at several moments since 1912. In its richness first as news and then as history—and in both cases as myth—the disaster has done more than trigger reflexes. It has stimulated imaginative forms of engagement with present and past and performed significant, though often not admirable, cultural work. For many people and for many reasons, the memory of the disaster has seemed worth possessing.

This book traces the life of an event of mythic stature. How tempting it is to pronounce the *Titanic*'s cultural death and give the story a neat sense of completion. The resiliency and adaptability of the event dictate otherwise. The *Titanic* disaster begs for resolution—and always resists it.

LIST OF ABBREVIATIONS

AAL   *Afro-American Ledger* (Baltimore)
AsCi   *Asheville (North Carolina) Citizen*
AC   *Atlanta Constitution*
BS   *Baltimore Sun*
BDH   *Biloxi Daily Herald*
BAH   *Birmingham Age-Herald*
BAd   *Boston Advertiser*
BA   *Boston American*
BET   *Boston Evening Transcript*
BG   *Boston Globe*
BH   *Boston Herald*
BP   *Boston Post*
BdA   *Broad Ax* (Chicago)
CO   *Charlotte Observer*
CDS   *Chicago Daily Socialist*
CD   *Chicago Defender*
CST   *Chicago Sun-Times*
CT   *Chicago Tribune*

CSM	*Christian Science Monitor*
CG	*Cleveland Gazette*
CP	*Cleveland Press*
CS	*Cronica Sovversiva* [*Subversive Chronicle*] (Lynn, Mass.)
DaPe	*Daily People* (New York)
DMN	*Dallas Morning News*
DH	*Denni Hlasatel* [*Bohemian Herald*] (Chicago)
DP	*Denver Post*
DN	*Detroit News*
DSN	*Detroit Saturday Night*
EWG	*Emporia (Kansas) Weekly Gazette*
EN	*L'Era Nuova* [*The New Era*] (Paterson, N.J.)
FI	*La Fiaccola* [*The Torch*] (Buffalo, N.Y.)
GA	*Gaelic American* (New York)
HCr	*Harvard Crimson*
HUA	Harvard University Archives
HC	*Houston Chronicle*
HP	*Houston Post*
IF	*Indianapolis Freeman*
IW	*Indianapolis World*
IrWo	*Irish World and American Industrial Liberator* (New York)
IT	*L'Italia* (Chicago)
JA	*Jewish Advocate* (Boston)
JDF	Jewish Daily *Vorwärts* [*Forward*] (New York)
LW	*Labor World* (Duluth, Minn.)
LDA	*Lawrence (Massachusetts) Daily American*
LT	*Lawrence (Massachusetts) Telegram*
LMT	*Lewiston (Idaho) Morning Tribune*
LC	Library of Congress
LAT	*Los Angeles Times*
LCJ	*Louisville Courier Journal*
MDR	*Mobile Daily Register*

MTR	Museum of Television and Radio
NOTP	*New Orleans Times-Picayune*
NYA	*New York Age*
NYC	*New York Call*
NYHT	*New York Herald Tribune*
NYT	*New York Times*
NYTr	*New York Tribune*
NYU	*New Yorkin Uutiset* [*New York News*]
OST	*Orlando Sentinel Tribune*
PEB	*Philadelphia Evening Bulletin*
PT	*Philadelphia Tribune*
PC	*Pittsburgh Courier*
PR	*Pravo* [*Justice*] (Cleveland)
RA	*Raivaaja* [*Pioneer*] (Fitchburg, Mass.)
RP	*Richmond Planet*
RoPo	*Robotnik Polski* [*Polish Worker*] (New York)
ST	*Savannah Tribune*
SLPD	*St. Louis Post-Dispatch*
SPA	*St. Paul Appeal*
SFC	*San Francisco Chronicle*
SFE	*San Francisco Examiner*
SR	*Seattle Republican*
TT	*Tampa Tribune*
TY	*Työmies* [*Worker*] (Hancock, Mich.)
USA	*USA Today*
WB	*Washington Bee*
WP	*Washington Post*
WT	*Washington Times*

NOTES

FOREWORD: NATURE JEERS AT OUR FOLLY

1. Henry Adams to Elizabeth Cameron, February 18, 1912, March 10, 1912, March 17, 1912, HA to Charles Milnes Gaskell, April 12, 1912, in *The Letters of Henry Adams,* vol. VI, *1906–1918,* ed. J. C. Levenson, Ernest Samuels, Charles Vandersee, and Viola Hopkins Winner (Cambridge: Harvard University Press, 1988), 511, 521–22, 524, 533.

2. HA to Mary Cadwalader Jones, April 15, 1912, HA to Cameron, April 16, 1912, in *Letters,* vol. VI, 534–35.

3. HA to Anne Palmer Fell, April 18, 1912, and HA to Jones, April 20, 1912, in *Letters,* vol. VI, 536–38.

4. HA to Cameron, April 21, 1912, in *Letters,* vol. VI, 538; Henry Adams, *The Education of Henry Adams* (Boston: Houghton Mifflin, 1918 [written in 1905]), 495.

5. HA to Cameron, April 21, 1912, in *Letters,* vol. VI, 538; Ernest Samuels, *Henry Adams: The Major Phase* (Cambridge: Harvard University Press, 1964), 532–34.

6. Walter Lord, interview with author, New York, October 17, 1992; John Maxtone-Graham, "It Was Sad When That Great Ship Went Down," *New York Times Book Review,* December 13, 1992, 9.

7. Walter Lord, *The Night Lives On* (New York: William Morrow, 1986), 16–17.

8. Walter Lord, *A Night to Remember* (New York: Henry Holt, 1955), 115; Wyn Craig Wade, *The Titanic: End of a Dream* (New York: Rawson, Wade, 1979), 296; Charles Pellegrino, *Her Name, Titanic: The Untold Story of the Sinking and Finding of the Unsinkable Ship* (New York: McGraw-Hill, 1988), 32.

Richard Garrett has challenged the "end of an epoch" idea in arguing that the "only epoch it can take any credit for ending is that of gross negligence to do with matters concerning safety at sea." Garrett, *Atlantic Disaster: The Titanic and Other Victims of the North Atlantic* (London: Buchan & Enright, 1986), 253–54.

9. For a summary of the anthropological concept of social dramas, see Chandra Mukerji and Michael Schudson, "Introduction: Rethinking Popular Culture," in *Rethinking Popular Culture: Contemporary Perspectives in Cultural Studies*, ed. Chandra Mukerji and Michael Schudson (Berkeley: University of California Press, 1991), 23. See also Victor Turner, "Liminality and the Performative Genres," in *Rite, Drama, Festival, Spectacle: Rehearsals toward a Theory of Cultural Performance*, ed. John J. MacAloon (Philadelphia: Institute for the Study of Human Issues, 1984), 19–41.

CHAPTER 1: APRIL 1912

1. Stephen Kern, *The Culture of Time and Space, 1880–1918* (Cambridge: Harvard University Press, 1983), 65–67.

2. According to later figures, there were eighty-nine lynchings in 1912—eighty-six with black victims. See Walter White, *Rope and Faggot: A Biography of Judge Lynch* (New York: Arno Press, 1969 [1929]), 231. The discussion that follows is based on National Association for the Advancement of Colored People, *Thirty Years of Lynching in the United States, 1889–1918* (New York: Arno Press, 1969 [1919]), 29, 21–22; W. Fitzhugh Brundage, *Lynching in the New South: Georgia and Virginia, 1880–1930* (Urbana: University of Illinois Press, 1993), 25, 276, 310 (n. 19); "Lynchings in 1912," *CT*, December 31, 1912, 22; "Surrounded in Swamp, Negro Shot by Sheriff as He Runs," *TT*, April 15, 1912, 1; "Lynched Negro Found in River," *AC*, April 27, 1912, 1; "Race Riot Feared; Troops on Guard," *AC*, April 26, 1912, 12; "Along the Color Line," *Crisis*, June 1912, 65; "2000 Persons See Negro Burned at Stake, Tyler, Tex.," *SLPD*, May 25, 1912, 1; Charles Flint Kellogg, *NAACP: A History of the National Association for the Advancement of Colored People* (Baltimore: Johns Hopkins University

Press, 1967), vol. I, 124–25; "The Conference at Chicago," *Crisis*, May 1912, 25; "The Fourth Annual Conference of the National Association for the Advancement of Colored People," *Crisis*, June 1912, 80; "Speakers Encourage and Tell of Advance," *CD*, May 4, 1912, 1–2; Graham Taylor, "Race Prejudice a Peril to Democracy," *CD*, May 18, 1912, 1, 6.

3. My description of the parade comes from *Woman's Journal*, May 11, 1912, 145–47, 152; *NYT*, May 5, 1912, pt. 1, 1–2, and pt. 9, 1–4; *NYTr*, May 5, 1912, pt. 1, 1–3; Harriot Stanton Blatch and Alma Lutz, *Challenging Years: The Memoirs of Harriot Stanton Blatch* (New York: G. P. Putnam's Sons, 1940), 179–84.

4. For this account of the San Diego free speech fight, I am drawing on Melvyn Dubofsky, *We Shall Be All: A History of the Industrial Workers of the World* (Chicago: Quadrangle, 1969), 189–97; Robert Justin Goldstein, *Political Repression in Modern America: From 1870 to the Present* (Boston: G. K. Hall, 1978), 86–87; Roger A. Bruns, *The Damndest Radical: The Life and World of Ben Reitman, Chicago's Celebrated Social Reformer, Hobo King, and Whorehouse Physician* (Urbana: University of Illinois Press, 1987), 118–32; Emma Goldman, *Living My Life* (New York: Dover, 1970 [1931]), vol. 1, 494–503.

5. The following discussion is based on U.S. Congress, *Congressional Record*, vol. 48, pt. 5, 62d Congress, 2d Session, 1912–13, 4906–17, 4966–76, 5017–33; U.S. Department of Commerce and Labor, *Statistical Abstract of the United States*, vol. 35, 1912, 102–03; Thomas J. Archdeacon, *Becoming American: An Ethnic History* (New York: Free Press, 1983), 163–64; Roger Daniels, *Coming to America: A History of Immigration and Ethnicity in American Life* (New York: HarperCollins, 1990), 276–77; Thomas J. Curran, *Xenophobia and Immigration, 1820–1930* (Boston: Twayne, 1975), 126.

6. Walter Lord provides these facts in *A Night to Remember*, pp. 171–73, while noting that there is uncertainty about the exact times of events and the number of victims.

CHAPTER 2: THE RULE OF THE SEA AND LAND

1. I choose the term "conventional" to describe an interpretive framework that affirmed existing power relations—that made sense of the disaster according to dominant conceptions of gender, class, ethnicity, and race. I also call it conventional because it was pervasive, defying clear-cut divisions between conservatives and reformers, between high culture and

low culture, between staid and sensational reporting, between sections and regions of the country. It was a collective work of interpretation (though the interpreters often claimed only to be telling the truth), constructed and reinforced in the days, weeks, and months after the wreck by people who consciously or unconsciously needed to understand and represent a shocking event in familiar and comfortable terms.

Several recent studies of historical memory have shaped my own interpretive framework. John Bodnar, *Remaking America: Public Memory, Commemoration, and Patriotism in the Twentieth Century* (Princeton: Princeton University Press, 1992), David Glassberg, *American Historical Pageantry: The Uses of Tradition in the Early Twentieth Century* (Chapel Hill: University of North Carolina Press, 1990), George Lipsitz, *Time Passages: Collective Memory and American Popular Culture* (Minneapolis: University of Minnesota Press, 1990), and David Thelen, ed., *Memory and American History* (Bloomington: University of Indiana Press, 1990) all make use of the concept of "struggles" or "contestations over meaning." In drawing the distinction between conventional and unconventional views of the *Titanic* disaster, I am guided by Bodnar's distinction between "official culture" and "vernacular culture" (see esp. pp. 13–15), though I find these terms too limiting for my discussion.

2. "Giant Titanic Goes Down," *BS*, April 16, 1912, 2; "Titanic Sinks Four Hours after Hitting Iceberg," *NYT*, April 16, 1912, 2; "Hope There May Be More Survivors," *WP*, April 16, 1912, 3; "Saved from Wreck," *CT*, April 17, 1912, 1–2; "Titanic Disaster Hits Home of the Entire Nation," *SFE*, April 17, 1912, 2; "Men on Titanic Heroes," *DP*, April 17, 1912, 1; "All Hope Abandoned for Those Who Are Not aboard the Carpathia," *BAH*, April 17, 1912, 1; "Believed Now That Californian Carries Bodies of Titanic's Victims," *BDH*, April 17, 1912, 4; "Details Intensify Titanic Tragedy," *TT*, April 17, 1912, 1; "Titanic Heroes Elected Death to Save Women," *AC*, April 17, 1912, 1.

George Bernard Shaw bluntly observed of the British press "that when news of a shipwreck arrives without particulars, and journalists immediately begin to invent particulars, they are lying." Shaw, in Michael Davie, *The Titanic: The Full Story of a Tragedy* (London: Bodley Head, 1986), 232.

3. *New York Sun*, quoted in "Newspapers Denounce Conditions Which Led to Sacrifice of Life," *WP*, April 18, 1912, 11; "Greatest of Ocean Disasters," *SLPD*, April 16, 1912, 12; "The Titanic Disaster," *CT*, April 17, 1912, 8.

4. Richard Slotkin, *The Fatal Environment: The Myth of the Frontier in*

the Age of Industrialization, 1800–1890 (Middletown, Conn.: Wesleyan University Press, 1986 [1985]), 19.

5. "Story of the Survivors," *WP*, April 19, 1912, 6.

6. "Great Men and Women Pay Tribute to Heroes of the Wreck in Messages to Denver Post," *DP*, April 21, 1912, pt. I, p. 4; Charles Hanson Towne, "The Harvest of the Sea," *Bookman*, June 1912, 358.

7. "Soror," "Tribute to Titanic Dead," *NYT*, April 17, 1912, 7.

8. Mary Reynolds Carter, "Let Women Honor Titanic Heroes," *AC*, April 21, 1912, 2B; "Women First Certainly Is the Law," *NYT*, April 17, 1912, 12; "The Law of the Sea," *Independent*, April 25, 1912, 900; "The Titanic," *Nation*, August 22, 1912, 171.

9. "Noblesse Oblige," *Collier's*, May 4, 1912, 8; E. Anthony Rotundo, *American Manhood: Transformations in Masculinity from the Revolution to the Modern Era* (New York: Basic Books, 1993), 274.

10. "An Ismay Message Now Bothers Smith," *NYT*, May 4, 1912, 3; "What Man Donned a Dress?," *SFE*, April 20, 1912, 1; "Man Wore Woman's Clothing to Gain Place in Lifeboat," *SLPD*, April 20, 1912, 2; "Man in Woman's Clothing in One of the Lifeboats," *WP*, April 20, 1912, 4; "Mates Enforce Unwritten Law," *LAT*, April 20, 1912, 3; U.S. Congress, Senate, *Hearings of a Subcommittee of the Senate Commerce Committee Pursuant to S. Res. 283 Directing the Committee on Commerce to Investigate the Causes Leading to the Wreck of the White Star Liner "Titanic,"* 62d Congress, 2d Session, 1912, Doc. No. 726 (#6167), 1020; Logan Marshall, *Sinking of the Titanic and Great Sea Disasters* (Ann Arbor: University Microfilms, 1980 [1912]), 77–78; "Resented Hint of Cowardice," *BS*, April 22, 1912, 1.

11. Archibald Gracie, *Titanic* (Toronto: NC Press Limited, 1986 [first published in 1913 as *The Truth about the Titanic*]), 64–76; "As Soldiers Should," *LDA*, April 24, 1912, 4; "Oscar," *The Titanic Tragedy* (Brooklyn: J. M. Moncada, 1912), 38. See also, for example, the testimony of Charles Herbert Lightoller, Arthur C. Peuchen, Andrew Cunningham, Henry Samuel Etches, William Burke, Hugh Woolner, J. Bruce Ismay, C. E. Henry Stengel, Archibald Gracie, and Dickinson Bishop, *Senate Hearings*, 91–92, 336, 794–95, 817, 822, 887–88, 960, 972, 993–95, 1002-3.

12. Julian Barnes, *A History of the World in 10¹/₂ Chapters* (New York: Vintage, 1990 [1989]), 173–75.

13. For an overview of these developments, see Peter G. Filene, *Him/Her/Self: Sex Roles in Modern America*, 2d ed. (Baltimore: Johns Hopkins University Press, 1986), esp. pt. I.

In a compelling article—one of the few to treat the *Titanic* as a cultural text—Ann E. Larabee argues that the media pay attention to the disaster at times "when traditional masculinity has been under reconstruction." In the 1910s, with the emergence of the New Woman, and in the post-Vietnam period of second-wave feminism, the *Titanic* "provided a symbolic framework for a politically-useful revival of traditional male roles." Larabee's discussion centers on the *Titanic* as a symbol of "technological man's desire for a dead, artificial, ultimately male world, where no real women are present." See Ann E. Larabee, "The American Hero and His Mechanical Bride: Gender Myths of the *Titanic* Disaster," *American Studies* 31, 1 (Spring 1990), 5–23, esp. 5–6.

14. Editorial, *NOTP*, April 20, 1912, 8; Mrs. Maxwell, "Danger Brings Out Simple Primitive Truths of Woman's Relation to Man," *CP*, April 17, 1912, 9.

On this theme of dominant cultures representing themselves as "universal and 'given,' " see Dick Hebdige, *Subculture: The Meaning of Style* (London: Routledge, 1979), 9, and Stephen Toulmin, *Cosmopolis: The Hidden Agenda of Modernity* (Chicago: University of Chicago Press, 1990), 193–94.

15. A. C. Messerlr [*sic*], letter, *BS*, April 24, 1912, 6; "Women's Best Protection," *BS*, April 19, 1912, 6; "Mere Man," letter, *BS*, April 22, 1912, 6; Clark McAdams, "Enough Said," *SLPD*, April 22, 1912, 10. McAdams's poem is also printed in Larabee, "The American Hero and His Mechanical Bride," 15–16.

16. "No Subject for the Inexperienced," *NYT*, April 18, 1912, 12; "Only Poets Should Write Verse," *NYT*, April 30, 1912, 10; "Recent Poetry," *Current Literature*, June 1912, 713.

17. Bryan, quoted in "Hold Memorial for the Titanic," *CT*, April 22, 1912, 2; Parks, quoted in "The Lesson That Came from the Sea—What It Means to the Suffrage Cause," *The Woman's Protest*, May 1912, 8; "The Age of Chivalry," *TT*, April 22, 1912, 6; Annie Nathan Meyer, quoted in Blatch and Lutz, *Challenging Years*, 180–81.

18. *New York Herald*, quoted in "The Lesson That Came from the Sea," 8–9; "The Lesson That Came from the Sea," 8; W. C. Rickster, "A Man's View," *SLPD*, April 26, 1912, 14.

19. Aileen S. Kraditor, *The Ideas of the Woman Suffrage Movement, 1890–1920* (New York: Anchor, 1971 [1965]), 16; William L. O'Neill, *Divorce in the Progressive Era* (New Haven: Yale University Press, 1967), 58; Filene, *Him/Her/Self*, 42. The best book on divorce in this period is Elaine Tyler May, *Great Expectations: Marriage and Divorce in Post-Victorian America* (Chicago: University of Chicago Press, 1980).

20. "745 Saw Titanic Sink With 1,595, Her Band Playing," *NYT,* April 19, 1912, 1; "The Nobility of Self-Sacrifice," *NOTP,* April 26, 1912, 8; J. H. McKenzie, *The Titanic Disaster Poem* (Guthrie, Okla.: Co-Operative Pub. Co., 1912), 7; "Faithful unto Death," *NYT,* April 20, 1912, 14.

21. "Priest Preaches on Straus' Death," *NOTP,* April 29, 1912, 5; "1,350,000 Divorces in U.S. Last Year," *DP,* April 20, 1912, 5; Adolf Guttmacher, "The Ideal Home," *BS,* May 19, 1912, 6; Louis White, "Memorial to Mrs. Straus", *BS,* April 22, 1912, 11; Frances Wayne, "Women Must Explain Why They Abandoned Mates in Death," *DP,* April 18, 1912, 5. See also Larabee, "The American Hero and His Mechanical Bride," 15.

22. Natalie F. Hammond, "Plan Titanic Memorial," *WP,* April 29, 1912, 6; "Women's Fund Growing Fast," *NYT,* May 4, 1912, 3; "Senators Aid Women's Plan," *NYT,* May 6, 1912, 4; "To Men Who Died for Women," *NYT,* April 29, 1912, 3; "Woman's Titanic Memorial," *The Keystone* (South Carolina Federation of Women's Clubs), November 1912, 3; "Georgia Women Will Help in the Titanic Memorial," *AC,* May 18, 1912, 6.

23. "Artist Aids Titanic Fund," *NYT,* May 31, 1912, 6; "In Memory of Titanic Heroes," *NYT,* June 16, 1912, pt. 5, p. 10; "A Plea to Army Women," *NYT,* June 10, 1912, 15; "Fete for Titanic Fund," *NYT,* August 5, 1912, 12; "Pageant Typifying the Sea," *NYT,* November 7, 1912, 13; "Titanic Memorial Benefit," *NYT,* December 1, 1912, pt. 3, p. 5; "Women Raise $10,000 by Titanic Benefit," *NYT,* December 7, 1912, 15; "Splendid Prospects for Titanic Benefit," *NYT,* December 4, 1912, 9; *The Programme: An Open-Air Benefit Performance for the Woman's "Titanic" Memorial* (Gloucester, Mass.: n.p.,1912).

On pageantry in this period, see Glassberg, *American Historical Pageantry,* esp. chaps. 1 and 2. Glassberg observes competing impulses at work in the pageantry movement. The *Titanic* pageant strikes me as the organizers' attempt "to reinforce their particular definition of civic identity, social order, and the moral principles they associated with the past—to preserve Anglo-Saxon supremacy in public life" rather as "an elaborate ritual of democratic participation." See Glassberg, p. 64.

24. "A Woman's Memorial to Men," *SFE,* May 23, 1912, 24; "Mrs. H. P. Whitney Wins," *NYT,* January 8, 1914, 5. The memorial took much longer to complete than the organizers anticipated. It was finally unveiled, in modified form, in 1931. See Rustie Brown, *The Titanic, the Psychic and the Sea* (Lomita, Calif.: Blue Harbor Press, 1981), 113n.

25. Lawrence Beesley, E. I. Taylor, and D. H. Bishop, quoted in "Survivors' Tales from the Titanic," *NYT,* April 19, 1912, 3–4; Lawrence Beesley, *The Loss of the SS. Titanic: Its Story and Its Lessons* (Boston:

Houghton Mifflin, 1912), 75; "Mrs. J. J. Astor Tells How None Realized Danger," *SFE*, April 21, 1912, 2; "745 Saw Titanic Sink with 1,595, Her Band Playing," *NYT*, April 19, 1912, 2.

26. The early figures appear in Wade, *Titanic: End of a Dream*, 61. Walter Lord provides the official House of Commons figures in the revised edition of *A Night to Remember*, p. 128. According to these official figures, 63 percent of the first-cabin passengers survived, compared with 42 percent of the second cabin and 25 percent of the steerage.

27. See, for example, "Titanic Disaster Hits Home of the Entire Nation," *SFE*, April 17, 1912, 2; "Heroic Acts on Titanic Never Surpassed in World's Annals," *DP*, April 17, 1912, 2; "Saved from Wreck," *CT*, April 17, 1912, 1; "Waters of Atlantic Sound Requiem over Thousand Departed Souls," *AsCi*, April 17, 1912, 1; "Thousands Now Abandon All Hope for Loved Relatives on Titanic," *CO*, April 17, 1912, 1; "Why Many May Not Hope That Loved Ones' Lives Are Spared," *WP*, April 18, 1912, 12. Again, note the dates.

28. Elbert Hubbard, "The Titanic," *DP*, May 27, 1912, 5; Hans Gimm and Franz Hoffman, "When the Great Titanic Went Down" (Washington: H. Kirkus Dugdale, 1913) and John Hargreaves, "The Loss of the Titanic" (n.c.: John Hargreaves, 1912), Music Division, LC; *Philadelphia North American*, quoted in "The Loss of the Titanic: A Poll of the Press," *Outlook*, May 4, 1912, 22b.

The remarkable collection of *Titanic* sheet music at the Library of Congress is largely the work of Solomon Goodman, a retired postal worker from Long Island. He also compiled a handwritten list of copyrighted songs. See Solomon Goodman, *Titanic Disaster Music: A Listing by Copyright Registration Number, and Showing Names of Authors, Composers, Copyright Proprietors and Publishers, and Dates of Copyright Registration*, Copy No. 13, August 1985, American Folklife Center, LC.

29. Mrs. Churchill Candee, "God's Noblemen Aid Women and Children," *SFE*, April 20, 1912, 4; "Lying Message 'Titanic Safe' Was Signed by 'White Star Line,' " *DP*, April 20, 1912, 1; "Guggenheim, Dying, Sent Wife Message," *NYT*, April 20, 1912, 9.

30. "Col. Astor a Hero, Declare Titanic Survivors," *SLPD*, April 19, 1912, 10; "Col. Astor Put Wife in Boat, Turned and Died Like a Hero," *BS*, April 19, 1912, 12; "These Wealthy Men Went to Brave Deaths," and "Giving Place to Last Woman, John J. Astor Went to Death," *AC*, April 20, 1912, 7–8; Daisy Minahan, "Bravery of Noble Men on Titanic Saved Women," *LAT*, April 21, 1912, pt. I, p. 1; McKenzie, *Titanic Disaster*, 5–6; J. W. Willis and M. C. Hanford, "A Hero Went Down with the Monarch

of the Sea" (Washington: H. Kirkus Dugdale, 1912), American Folklife Center, LC; Owen Lynch and William H. Farrell, "The Titanic Is Doomed and Sinking" (New York: Mozart Music Library, 1912), Music Division, LC; "Greatest Astor of Them All," *DP*, April 19, 1912, 4.

31. "Heroes Lay Down Their Lives That Others May Live," *BS*, April 19, 1912, 2; Rev. Dr. Leighton Parks, quoted in "Religious Views of the 'Titanic,' " *Literary Digest*, May 4, 1912, 938; Frances Wayne, "Men of Brains and Millions Sacrificed for Lowly Women," *DP*, April 16, 1912, 18; Dr. Burdette, quoted in "Whole City Unites in Sorrow and Sympathy," *LAT*, April 22, 1912, pt. II, p. 3; "The Comparative Value of Lives," *BS*, April 20, 1912, 6.

32. Edwin Ginn, "The 'Titanic' Disaster and Peace," *Independent*, June 13, 1912, 1319; Albert S. J. Owens, quoted in "Baltimoreans Praise Heroism of Men on Titanic," *BS*, April 20, 1912, 9; Rev. Johnston Meyers, quoted in "Hold Memorial for the Titanic," *CT*, April 22, 1912, 2; "As to Special Privilege," *LAT*, April 21, 1912, pt. II, p. 4.

33. "The Law of the Sea," *Independent*, April 25, 1912, 901; Wayne, "Men of Brains," 18; "The Tragedy of the Titanic," *Outlook*, April 27, 1912, 876; Bentztown Bard, "Down to a Common Grave," *BS*, April 19, 1912, 6; Rev. Frank Brunner, quoted in "Hold Memorial for the Titanic," *CT*, April 22, 1912, 2; Rev. Dr. Ruben Parker, quoted in "Speed Mania Denounced in Sermons on the Titanic Disaster," *BS*, April 22, 1912, 12; "Women in Hysterics," *WP*, April 16, 1912, 2; "Giant Titanic Goes Down," *BS*, April 16, 1912, 2; "Women in Silk and Rags Together Await News— Patricians Weep in Peasants' Arms," *DP*, April 17, 1912, 4; "Wealth and Poverty United Through One Sorrow—All Classes Rub Elbows in Dense Crush as Liner Comes Up Harbor," *SFE*, April 19, 1912, 3.

An editorial in the *Biloxi Daily Herald* suggests how these interpretations drew on established meanings. The *Herald* reprinted an old piece entitled "The Democracy of Death" from the *Memphis Commercial-Appeal* and pointed out how "appropriate and timey [*sic*] it reads now" in light of the *Titanic* tragedy. "The Democracy of Death," *BDH*, May 1, 1912, 4.

34. "A Succinct Story of the Sinking of the Great Ship Titanic," *BS*, May 5, 1912, pt. 4, p. 8; Horace Greeley, *The Wreck of the Titanic: A Poem* (Brooklyn: Donald Sinclair, 1913), 30; Dodge, quoted in "Officer Shot 2 Frenzied Men," *SLPD*, April 19, 1912, 6; A. Dick, quoted in "Some Men Shot on the Titanic," *AC*, April 19, 1912, 7; Slater, quoted in "Pathetic Scenes of Parting Told," *MDR*, April 19, 1912, 6; Washington Sherman and Hazel Fern Sherman, "The Titanic's Doom" (Greenville, Ill.: Wash-

ington Sherman, 1912), Music Division, LC; "The Drift of the Testimony," *NYT*, April 20, 1912, 14.

35. "The Drift of the Testimony," *NYT*, April 20, 1912, 14; Alex. McD. Stoddart, "Telling the Tale of the 'Titanic,' " *Independent*, May 2, 1912, 953.

36. "The Anglo-Saxon Ideal," *Temperance Educational Quarterly*, July 1912, 9; "The Tragedy of the 'Titanic' and Its Lesson," *American Review of Reviews*, May 1912, 549; Jay Henry Mowbray, *Sinking of the "Titanic": Most Appalling Ocean Horror* (Philadelphia: National Publishing Co., 1912), iv; "Titanic Stories a Tribute to Anglo-Saxon Manhood," *BS*, April 20, 1912, 2; "Women and Children First," *BS*, April 17, 1912, 6; Mrs. Francis T. Redwood and Mrs. Donald R. Hooker, quoted in "Baltimoreans Praise Heroism of Men on Titanic," *BS*, April 20, 1912, 9; "Safe at Home," *LCJ*, April 21, 1912, 6; Gracie, *Titanic*, 34; Brand Whitlock, "The Titanic," *Collier's*, May 4, 1912, 7; "Remembering Marconi," *AC*, April 19, 1912, 8.

37. Shaw and Conan Doyle, quoted in Michael Davie, *Titanic: The Death and Life of a Legend* (New York: Knopf, 1987), 230. The full exchange, which originally appeared in the *Daily News and Leader*, is reprinted as an appendix in the British version of Davie's book, *Titanic: The Full Story*, 229–34.

38. "Col. Astor Died a Hero," *DP*, April 19, 1912, 8; Lowe, quoted in Gracie, *Titanic*, 156; *Senate Hearings*, 417, 1100; "Heroes Met Mob," *BS*, April 21, 1912, 2.

39. *Senate Hearings*, 406–08, 613, 247, 823.

Bederman writes, " 'Civilization' *naturalized* white male power by linking male dominance and white supremacy to human evolutionary development. Harnessing manliness to white supremacy, and celebrating both as essential to human progress, 'civilization' temporarily revitalized middle-class Victorian manliness." Gail Bederman, " 'Civilization,' the Decline of Middle-Class Manliness, and Ida B. Wells's Antilynching Campaign (1892–94)," *Radical History Review* 52 (Winter 1992), 5–30, esp. 9 (emphasis hers). See also Gail Bederman, *Manliness & Civilization: A Cultural History of Gender and Race in the United States, 1880–1917* (Chicago: University of Chicago Press, 1995), esp. chap. 1.

40. Harold Bride, "Thrilling Story By Titanic's Surviving Wireless Man," *NYT*, April 19, 1912, 1; "Hero's Lifebelt Stolen," *BS*, April 19, 1912, 11; "Colonel Astor Died a Hero," *DP*, April 19, 1912, 8; Marshall, *Sinking of the Titanic*, 55–56.

One version of the story blamed "a party of fear-crazed first-cabin passengers" for the assault on Phillips—a very rare mention of panic outside the steerage. See "Fought Phillips for Lifebelt," *BS*, April 19, 1912, 10. Walter Lord describes the stoker "gently unfastening Phillips' lifejacket." In the ensuing struggle Bride held the stoker and Phillips knocked him unconscious. See Lord, *Night to Remember*, 94–95, 113.

41. "Butt an Honor to His Uniform," *DP*, April 19, 1912, 4; "Titanic Plot to Flee Balked by Senators," *SFE*, April 20, 1912, 1; "Titanic Horror Told by Survivors," *SFE*, April 19, 1912, 1; "Butt Died a Hero," *WP*, April 20, 1912, 5; "Graphic Stories Are Told of the Heroism of Major A. W. Butt," *BAH*, April 20, 1912, 1; "Maj. Archie Butt Hero of Disaster," *CO*, April 19, 1912, 1; "Example for Generation Set by Acts of Heroism," *LAT*, April 20, 1912, pt. I, p. 2; "Butt Trod Doomed Decks with Courage That Was Inspiration," *TT*, April 20, 1912, 1; Taft, quoted in "Butt's Heroism Prevented Panic," *CT*, April 20, 1912, 4; "High Speed Wrecked the Liner Titanic," *BS*, April 19, 1912, 1; "Hit Berg at 21-Knot Speed," *NYTr*, April 19, 1912, 1; Elbert Hubbard, "The Titanic," *DP*, May 27, 1912, 5; "The Memorial to 'Archie' Butt," *AC*, May 20, 1912, 4; "Taft's Tribute to Butt," *NYT*, April 16, 1914, 4.

See Joel Williamson, *The Crucible of Race: Black/White Relations in the American South Since Emancipation* (New York: Oxford University Press, 1984), for a discussion of the connections among race, class, and gender in the New South.

42. "Story of Awful Night Told by the Survivors," *LAT*, April 19, 1912, pt. I, p. 1; Rev. Dr. Alfred Mortimer, quoted in "Lauds Titanic's Dead Heroes," *PEB*, April 26, 1912, 1.

43. "The Tragedy of the Titanic—A Complete Story," *NYT*, April 28, 1912, pt. 6, p. 2; "How Heroes of Titanic Went Bravely to Their Deaths," *SFE*, April 21, 1912, 3. See also "The Tragedy Revealed," *Nation*, April 25, 1912, 404.

44. "Heroines on Titanic," *WP*, April 21, 1912, 12; "Women Were Heroic," *BS*, April 20, 1912, 10; "Women Revealed as Heroines by Wreck," *NYT*, April 20, 1912, 4; "Why Wonder at Woman's Heroism?," *AC*, April 24, 1912, 6.

45. "An Admirer of the Times," "Memorial to Titanic Heroines," *NYT*, May 7, 1912, 10; Harriet Monroe, "A Requiem," *CT*, April 21, 1912, 4.

46. Andrews, quoted in "Heroines on Titanic," *WP*, April 21, 1912, 12; "The Children of the Titanic," *SLPD*, May 19, 1912, 5; Charlotte Collyer, "How I Was Saved from the Titanic," *CT*, May 26, 1912, magazine sect., 4; "The Engineers," *NYT*, April 29, 1912, 10; "Survivors Agree on Heroic Deeds," *CT*, April 20, 1912, 3; "Heroism and Nationality," *WP*, April 25, 1912, 6.

47. "A Tragedy of Errors," *Hearst's*, June 1912, 2497; "The Victorious Human Spirit," *Outlook*, May 4, 1912, 12; "Real Heroism," *CO*, April 29, 1912, 4; "Heroes and Heroines," *CSM*, April 29, 1912, 16; Annie Leakin Sioussat, letter, *BS*, May 9, 1912, 6; "The 'Titanic' Memorial Arch in Washington," *Pan American Union*, August 1912, 276.

48. "Racial Glorification," *LT*, April 24, 1912, 6; Lawrence Beesley, "Titanic's Loss due to Faulty System," *NYT*, April 29, 1912, 12; "Rich Share Horror but on Poor Rests Heaviest Burdens," *CP*, April 19, 1912, 9; "In the Interpreter's House," *American*, July 1912, 382–83.

Chapter 3: Mammon

1. C. H. Parkhurst, *My Forty Years in New York* (New York: Macmillan, 1923), 113. My discussion of Parkhurst draws on ideas from Susan Curtis, *A Consuming Faith: The Social Gospel and Modern American Culture* (Baltimore: Johns Hopkins University Press, 1991), T. J. Jackson Lears, *No Place of Grace: Antimodernism and the Transformation of American Culture, 1880–1920* (New York: Pantheon, 1981), and Miles Orvell, *The Real Thing: Imitation and Authenticity in American Culture, 1880–1940* (Chapel Hill: University of North Carolina Press, 1989). On Parkhurst, see also Lary May, *Screening Out the Past: The Birth of Mass Culture and the Motion Picture Industry* (New York: Oxford University Press, 1980), 43, 47, 54, 60–61.

2. Parkhurst, *Forty Years*, 18.

3. Parkhurst, *Forty Years*, 13, 10–11, 18 (emphasis his); Rotundo, *American Manhood*, 232, 248–51.

4. Parkhurst, *Forty Years*, 114.

5. Quoted in "Religious Views of the 'Titanic,' " *Literary Digest*, May 4, 1912, 939.

6. Parkhurst, *Forty Years*, 85, 78, 69. Charles H. Parkhurst, *A Brief History of the Madison Square Presbyterian Church and Its Activities* (New York: Irving Press, 1906), 14 and passim. On advertising's ideal of the human body as a machine, see Thomas J. Schlereth, *Victorian America: Transformations in Everyday Life, 1876–1915* (New York: HarperCollins, 1991), 165–66.

7. Lord, *Night Lives On*, chap. 11.

8. "All Due to Greed, Says Parkhurst," *NYT*, April 22, 1912, 4.

9. See, for example, Bernard Bailyn, *The Origins of American Politics* (New York: Vintage, 1968), esp. chap. 1; Bailyn, *The Ideological Origins of*

the American Revolution (Cambridge: Harvard University Press, 1967), esp. chap. 2; Gordon S. Wood, *The Creation of the American Republic, 1776–1787* (New York: Norton, 1972 [1969]), esp. pt. 1; Drew R. McCoy, *The Elusive Republic: Political Economy in Jeffersonian America* (New York: Norton, 1980); David E. Shi, *The Simple Life: Plain Living and High Thinking in American Culture* (New York: Oxford University Press, 1985); Michael Barton, "The Victorian Jeremiad: Critics of Accumulation and Display," and Jackson Lears, "Beyond Veblen: Rethinking Consumer Culture in America," in *Consuming Visions: Accumulation and Display of Goods in America, 1880–1920*, ed. Simon J. Bronner (New York: Norton, 1989), 55–71 and 73–97, esp. 55 and 82.

10. "In the 1910s," William Leach points out, "confusion over the difference between luxuries and necessaries (and their relative moral stature) still existed. . . . By the 1920s, luxury seems to have lost for many people much of its negative meaning." William Leach, *Land of Desire: Merchants, Power, and the Rise of a New American Culture* (New York: Pantheon, 1993), 295.

11. "All Due to Greed, Says Parkhurst," 4; Cardinal Gibbons, quoted in "Homage to a Hero," *WP*, April 22, 1912, 2; O'May, quoted in "Hold Memorial for the Titanic," *CT*, April 22, 1912, 2; Stires, quoted in "Dead of the Titanic Honored in Church," *NYT*, April 14, 1913, 5.

12. Rev. J. R. Jones, Rev. Dr. Alfred R. Hussey, and Rev. Dr. J. Wynne Jones, quoted in "Speed Mania Denounced in Sermons on the Titanic Disaster," *BS*, April 22, 1912, 10; "Homage to a Hero," *WP*, April 22, 1912, 2; "The Wreck of the Titanic," *Baptist and Reflector*, April 25, 1912, 8; Fred Clare Baldwin, "Who Was to Blame? Lines on the Loss of the Steamship Titanic with Sixteen Hundred Souls on Board," *Christian Advocate*, April 25, 1912, 573.

See also Sacvan Bercovitch, *The American Jeremiad* (Madison: University of Wisconsin Press, 1978), esp. chap. 1.

13. "Titanic Chivalry," *Religious Telescope*, April 24, 1912, 4; "The Loss of the Titanic," *Pittsburgh Christian Advocate*, April 25, 1912, 3.

For a discussion of liberal versus conservative Protestantism in this period, see William R. Hutchison, *The Modernist Impulse in American Protestantism* (Durham: Duke University Press, 1992), esp. chaps. 5–6. The standard accounts of the Social Gospel are Charles Howard Hopkins, *The Rise of the Social Gospel in American Protestantism, 1865–1915* (New Haven: Yale University Press, 1940) and Henry F. May, *Protestant Churches and Industrial America* (New York: Harper & Brothers, 1949), 170–262.

14. George A. Campbell, "The Sinking of the Titanic," *Christian Cen-*

tury, April 25, 1912, 3; "The Titanic Disaster," *Christian Socialist*, April 25, 1912, 5; *Bible Society Record*, May 1912, n.p.

15. "The Titanic," *Religious Telescope*, April 24, 1912, 8 (reprinted from the *Dayton Daily News*); Campbell, "Sinking of the Titanic," 3; "The Wreck of the Titanic," *Congregationalist and Christian World*, April 27, 1912, 573; "The Tragedy," *Herald and Presbyter*, May 1, 1912, 26 (originally in the *Advance*).

16. "Oscar," *Titanic Tragedy*, 50–51, 13.

17. George A. Campbell, "The Fatal Delusion," *Christian Century*, May 9, 1912, 3.

18. "Judgment of God on Astor Says Pastor Who Denounced Marriage," *DP*, April 18, 1912, 4; "The Attack on Astor," *WP*, May 14, 1912, 6; *The Richmond Ecclesiastical Trial* (Philadelphia: n.p., 1917), 2, 27.

19. "The Unspeakable Disaster," *Baptist Courier*, April 25, 1912, 4; "Ranting against the Most High," *Lutheran Herald*, May 9, 1912, 434–35; Wheeler, quoted in "Ranting," 435; Price Alexander Crow, "The Titanic Disaster," *Western Christian Advocate*, May 1, 1912, 13.

20. Henry F. May, "The Religion of the Republic," in *Ideas, Faiths, and Feelings: Essays on American Intellectual and Religious History* (New York: Oxford University Press, 1983), esp. 176–78; editorial, *Christian Advocate*, April 18, 1912, 529; "Safety Sacrificed for Luxury, Ship's Architect Asserts," *SLPD*, April 17, 1912, 3; "The Titanic Disaster," *EWG*, April 25, 1912, 1; "Degenerate Luxuries," *NYT*, April 18, 1912, 6; "Luxury Blamed for Wreck by Engineer," *NYT*, April 17, 1912, 8; *Omaha Bee*, quoted in "The Loss of the Titanic: A Poll of the Press," *Outlook*, May 4, 1912, 21; J.M.H., "The Lesson of the Titanic," *Nation*, May 16, 1912, 492; "A Delusion-Smashing Disaster," *SLPD*, April 18, 1912, 14; "The Titanic Investigation," *American Review of Reviews*, June 1912, 666; Marshall Everett, ed., *Wreck and Sinking of the Titanic: The Ocean's Greatest Disaster* (n.c.: L. H. Walter, 1912), 24, 26; Rayner, quoted in "Titanic Verdict Is Negligence," *NYT*, May 29, 1912, 3.

21. "The Loss of the Titanic," *Pittsburgh Christian Advocate*, April 25, 1912, 3.

22. Wade, *Titanic: End of a Dream*, 279–85.

23. "Realities and Mockeries," *Independent*, April 25, 1912, 904; Sydney Reid, "The 'Titanic' Disaster," *Independent*, May 2, 1912, 940; "Collective Carelessness," *Lutheran Standard*, May 4, 1912, 286; Baldwin, "Who Was to Blame?," 573.

24. Dr. Frederick W. Millar, quoted in "Hold Memorial for Titanic," *CT*, April 22, 1912, 2; "One Picture That Will Stay in the Public Mind,"

SFE, April 22, 1912, 20; "Cheers vs. Hisses," *SFE*, May 22, 1912, 22; "As a 'Skulking Coward' Bruce Ismay Is Described by Rev. H. Stiles Bradley," *AC*, April 23, 1912, 4; "J. Bruce Ismay—Remember the Name—the Benedict Arnold of the Sea," *DP*, April 18, 1912, 1; "Ismay Crowded into Lifeboat Leaving Women and Babes to Die," *DP*, April 19, 1912, 1; Lee, quoted in "Whole City Unites in Sorrow and Sympathy," *LAT*, April 22, 1912; Walt Mason, "Ismay," *EWG*, April 25, 1912, 3; "Ismay to Change Name," *SLPD*, April 30, 1912, 1; "Disgusted with Cowardly Ismay Two Towns Will Change Name," *DP*, May 2, 1912, 1.

25. "The Lost and the Saved," *WP*, April 18, 1912, 6; comment above banner, *DP*, April 21, 1912, 1. On the different models of daily newspapers in this period and their readerships, see Michael Schudson, *Discovering the News: A Social History of American Newspapers* (New York: Basic Books, 1978), 91–120.

26. Louis F. Post, "The Lesson of the 'Titanic,' " excerpted in *Crisis*, June 1912, 72. See also, for example, *Tile Layers' and Helpers' Journal*, May 1912, 11–13, and *Plumbers', Gas and Steam Fitters' Journal*, June 1912, 35–36. The essay originally appeared in the *Chicago Public*.

27. Crow, "Titanic Disaster," 13.

28. The transition from character to personality and the emergence of a consumer culture are discussed in Warren I. Susman, " 'Personality' and the Making of Twentieth-Century Culture," in *Culture as History: The Transformation of American Society in the Twentieth Century* (New York: Pantheon, 1984), 271–85, esp. 274–77; T. J. Jackson Lears, "From Salvation to Self-Realization: Advertising and the Therapeutic Roots of the Consumer Culture, 1880–1930," in *The Culture of Consumption: Critical Essays in American History, 1880-1980*, ed. Richard Wightman Fox and T. J. Jackson Lears (New York: Pantheon, 1983), 3–38.

29. Lord, *Night to Remember*, 109-10; Lord, interview with author, October 17, 1992.

30. Attempts to mediate between the cultures of character and personality are the subject of several of Susman's essays in *Culture as History*. In addition, see Joan Shelley Rubin, *The Making of Middlebrow Culture* (Chapel Hill: University of North Carolina Press, 1992) and Roland Marchand, *Advertising the American Dream: Making Way for Modernity, 1920–1940* (Berkeley: University of California Press, 1985).

31. William Inglis, "Greatest of Sea Tragedies," *Harper's Weekly*, April 20, 1912, 30. For a discussion of the martial ideal and the strenuous life, see Lears, *No Place of Grace*, 98–139, and Rotundo, *American Manhood*, 232–39.

32. Thomas H. Mulvey, "Just Whisper the Message" (New York: Mulvey Publishing Co., 1912), American Folklife Center, LC; Gail Bederman, " 'The Women Have Had Charge of the Church Work Long Enough': The Men and Religion Forward Movement of 1911–1912 and the Masculinization of Middle-Class Protestantism," *American Quarterly* 41, 3 (September 1989), 432–65, esp. 435; Gracie, *Titanic*, 75–76, 43.

33. Dr. Manning, quoted in "Many Creeds Pray for Titanic Dead," *NYT*, April 22, 1912, 4; "The Memorial Services," *NYT*, April 22, 1912, 10; Rev. Edward S. Reaves, "Lessons from the Tragedy of the Sea," *Baptist Courier*, May 2, 1912, 1; R.C.H., "Christian Heroism," *Baptist Courier*, May 2, 1912, 10; "Wreck of the Titanic," 8; "Two Civilizations," *Lutheran Herald*, April 25, 1912, 392; "Heroes and Heroines," *CSM*, April 29, 1912, 16; Harding, quoted in "Homage to a Hero," *WP*, April 22, 1912, 2.

Homages to Christian heroism were not confined to Protestants. John Cardinal Farley of New York similarly fused lessons about human arrogance and "truly Christian" bravery and chivalry. Farley, quoted in "Death Sat upon the Bow of the Titanic," *Pilot*, April 27, 1912, 1.

34. Rev. Dunbar H. Ogden, quoted in "Atlanta Honors Victims of Sea," *AC*, April 22, 1912, 3.

35. Birckhead, quoted in "Memorial Services for Titanic's Dead," *NYT*, April 29, 1912, 5; Katharine Lee Bates, "The Titanic," *Current Literature*, June 1912, 714; Katharine Lee Bates, "America the Beautiful," in *America the Beautiful and Other Poems* (New York: Thomas Y. Crowell, 1911), 3; "When the Titanic Sank," *Western Christian Advocate*, April 24, 1912, 2.

36. "Sense of Horror Remains," 568; editorial, *Mennonite*, April 25, 1912, 4; "Loss of the Titanic," 3; Everett, *Wreck and Sinking*, 4; H. Rea Woodman, *In Memoriam: The Titanic Disaster* (Poughkeepsie: A. V. Haight, 1913), pt. II, sec. XXI.

37. "Titanic Chivalry," 4; "Men," *DN*, April 24, 1912, 4; Thomas H. Herndon, "The Titanic," *WP*, April 25, 1912, 2.

38. [Edward T. Devine], "In the Shadow of Death," *Survey*, April 27, 1912, 154; "Heroism in Disaster," *American Friend*, Fourth Month 25, 1912, 1; "The Re-Emphasis of Religion," *Congregationalist and Christian World*, May 4, 1912, 609.

39. W. B. Glisson, "The Titanic" (Rutherford, Tenn.: W. B. Glisson, 1914), Music Division, LC; Frank Durwood Adams, "S.O.S.—Save Our Souls," *Christian Socialist,* 3; "The Last Call!," *Baptist Record*, April 25, 1912, 4; "Save Our Souls," *Herald and Presbyter*, April 17, 1912, 3; "Loss of the Titanic," 3.

Susan Curtis provocatively argues that the Social Gospel, "which began in opposition" to corporate capitalism and consumer culture, "eventually mirrored and affirmed important dimensions of the emerging culture," while William Leach contends that mainstream Protestantism (and Judaism and Catholicism) "generally turned away from any duty to confront critically the new pecuniary culture and economy." However true this may have been in the long run, ministers and religious writers were still highly ambivalent about modernity in 1912. See Curtis, *Consuming Faith*, xii and passim, and Leach, *Land of Desire*, chap. 7, esp. 220.

40. Speech of Isidor Rayner, May 28, 1912, U.S. Congress, Senate, *Report of the Committee on Commerce Pursuant to S. Res. 283 Directing the Committee on Commerce to Investigate the Causes Leading to the Wreck of the White Star Liner "Titanic"*, 62d Congress, 2d Session, Report No. 806 (#6127), 91–92.

41. The Bentztown Bard, "Redeemed!," *BS*, April 18, 1912, 6; "Thank God for Archie Butt," *Harper's Weekly*, May 4, 1912, 5.

42. McCready, quoted in "Pastors Pay Tribute to Heroism of Victims of Titanic Disaster, *LCJ*, April 22, 1912, 10; Christopher Lasch, "The Moral and Intellectual Rehabilitation of the Ruling Class," in *The World of Nations: Reflections on American History, Politics, and Culture* (New York: Knopf, 1973), 80–99.

INTERWORD: A NOBLE STRUCTURE OF
ENDURING STONE

1. For earlier descriptions of the library, see William C. Lane, "The Widener Memorial," *Harvard Alumni Bulletin*, June 16, 1915, 672; *The Harvard Library and the Harry Elkins Widener Memorial Library Building* (Cambridge: Harvard University Press, 1921), n.p.; "The Widener Memorial Library of Harvard University," *Scientific Monthly*, January 1916, 101–04.

2. William Bentinck-Smith, *Building a Great Library: The Coolidge Years at Harvard* (Cambridge: Harvard University Library, 1976), 7, 55; "Please Give Harvard a Library," *BA*, May 21, 1911(?), clipping in HUA.

3. "Harvard's 'Titanic' Victims," *HCr*, April 22, 1912, 1; Bentinck-Smith, *Building*, 50, 53; "Proposed New Building for the Library," *Harvard Alumni Bulletin*, October 11, 1911, 20–23. On Beaux Arts monumentality, see William H. Jordy, *American Buildings and Their Architects:*

Progressive and Academic Ideals at the Turn of the Century (Garden City, N.Y.: Doubleday, 1972), esp. 349, 356, 362, 366.

4. Bentinck-Smith, *Building*, 55–57; Wayne Andrews, "Horace Trumbauer," *Dictionary of American Biography* (New York: Scribner's, 1958), vol. XXII, supp. 2, 668; Alfred Branam, Jr., *Newport's Favorite Architects* (Newport: Classical America, 1976), n.p.; James T. Maher, *The Twilight of Splendor: Chronicles of the Age of American Palaces* (Boston: Little, Brown, 1975), 44–51; William Bentinck-Smith, *". . . a memorial to my dear son": Some Reflections on 65 Years of the Harry Elkins Widener Memorial Library* (Cambridge: Harvard College Library, 1980), 16.

5. Eleanor Elkins Widener to A. Lawrence Lowell, [August 1912], and Lowell to Charles A. Coolidge, October 3, 1912, quoted in Bentinck-Smith, *Building*, 65–66, 67–68; *Dial*, September 1, 1912, clipping in HUA; "Harvard's New Library: The Widener Memorial," *BET*, September 5, 1912, sec. 2, p. 1; "A New Library Building for Harvard," *Outlook*, September 21, 1912, 96–97; F. Lauriston Bullard, "The Widener Memorial Library for Harvard," *Harper's Weekly*, October 5, 1912, 14; "Gore Hall Will Be Replaced—New Library Generous Gift of Mrs. Widener in Memory of Son," *HCr*, September 20, 1912, 1; "Harvard's New Library—Memorial to Titanic Victim Presented by Mrs. George D. Widener to House Valuable Collection of Books Left by Her Son, Harry Elkins Widener," *NYT*, September 22, 1912, sec. 6, p. 14; "News for Bibliophiles," *Nation*, September 12, 1912, 230–31.

6. Bentinck-Smith, *Building*, 79, 70, 83, 91; "Widener Library Work Is Started," *BAd*, February 12, 1913, clipping in HUA; "Beginning of New Library," *HCr*, February 12, 1913, 1; Alfred Claghorn Potter to A. C. Coolidge, February 14, 1913, Coolidge to Potter, May 29, 1913, "A. C. Coolidge—Remarks at the Laying of the Cornerstone of the New Library," Coolidge to Robert F. Herrick, January 25, 1915, in Bentinck-Smith, *Building*, 80, 81–82, 91; "Harvard's New Library—Phi Beta Kappa Day," *BET*, June 16, 1913, 3; "For Widener Memorial—Cornerstone Laid by Mother of Titanic Victim," *NYT*, June 17, 1913, 10; "Library's Cornerstone Laid," *HCr*, June 17, 1913, 1; "Library Workmen on Strike," *HCr*, November 12, 1913, "Widener Library Strike," *BET*, November 12, 1913, 5; "$2,000,000 Widener Memorial Library Is Being Hastened to Completion," *BP*, December 4, 1913, clipping in HUA.

7. Thorstein Veblen, *The Theory of the Leisure Class* (New York: Penguin, 1979 [1899]), 75; "The Loss of a Young Booklover," *Literary Digest*, June 15, 1912, 1254; "Harvard to Get Harry Widener's Famous Library," *NYT*, June 2, 1912, 7; Florence Milner, "The Harry Elkins

Widener Memorial Library at Harvard," *DSN*, October 30, 1915, clipping in HUA.

8. "Loss of a Young Booklover," 1254.

9. Veblen, *Theory*, 94; "Harvard to Get," 7; "Widener Books at Harvard—Anniversary Week," *BET*, May 23, 1912, 1; Frederick A. King, "The Complete Collector in Two Parts. Part II. The Poor Collector and His Problems," *Bookman*, February 1913, 616; "The First Adequate Account of the Splendid Structure to Be Built at Harvard in Memory of the Young Man Who Went Down on the Titanic," *BH*, September 8, 1912, clipping in HUA; A. Edward Newton, "A Word in Memory," *Atlantic*, September 1918, 352–53.

10. "Opinion and Comment," *Harvard Alumni Bulletin*, September 2, 1912, 2; Daniel Hugh Verder, "Two Sonnets by Daniel Hugh Verder to Harry Elkins Widener" (n.p., 1915), in HUA.

11. Henry Cabot Lodge, "The Meaning of a Great Library," *Harvard Graduates Magazine*, September 1915, 31–32, 33, 38; Lowell, quoted in "Dedication of the Library," *Harvard Graduates Magazine*, 82; "Widener Is Dedicated," *BET*, June 24, 1915, 2; "Harvard's Largest Class Graduated," *NYT*, June 25, 1915, 11.

CHAPTER 4: UNKNOWN AND UNSUNG

1. Alma White, *The Titanic Tragedy—God Speaking to the Nations* (Bound Brook, N.J.: Pentecostal Union, 1912), Preface [n.p.], 124, 125, 142, 147, 199, 137 (emphasis hers). For a discussion of her life and career, see Susie Cunningham Stanley, *Feminist Pillar of Fire: The Life of Alma White* (Cleveland: Pilgrim Press, 1993). On the Pentecostal Union (Pillar of Fire), see Robert Mapes Anderson, *Vision of the Disinherited: The Making of American Pentecostalism* (New York: Oxford University Press, 1979), 36, 63, 141, 147, 149.

2. The Dixon Brothers, "Down with the Old Canoe," *Smoky Mountain Ballads*, RCA Victor LPV-507; "Dixon, Dorsey," in *The Encyclopedia of Folk, Country & Western Music*, 2d ed., ed. Irwin Stambler and Gerlun Landon (New York: St. Martin's Press, 1983), 191–92. Other versions of the ballad were more conventional, with verses celebrating the first-cabin heroes and suggesting that they were prepared to meet God. See, for example, Cowboy Loye and Just Plain John, *Old Time Ballads and Cowboy Songs*, 43–44, and D. K. Wilgus, *Doc Hopkins*, photocopies in "Titanic" folder 5, American Folklife Center, LC.

3. Eleanor Flexner, *Century of Struggle: The Woman's Rights Movement in the United States*, rev. ed. (Cambridge: Harvard University Press, 1975), 256, 263–68.

4. Kraditor, *Ideas of the Woman Suffrage Movement*, 38–39, 51, 52 (emphasis hers); Nancy F. Cott, *The Grounding of Modern Feminism* (New Haven: Yale University Press, 1987), 29–30; Alan Dawley, *Struggles for Justice: Social Responsibility and the Liberal State* (Cambridge: Harvard University Press, 1991), 96.

5. Mrs. William M. Ellicott, quoted in "Women First, She Says," *BS*, April 18, 1912, 11.

6. Emma Goldman, "Suffrage Dealt Blow by Women of Titanic," *DP*, April 21, 1912, sec. 1, p. 8.

7. Frances Wayne, "Titanic Disaster Furnishes No Proof That Women Are Unfit for Suffrage," *DP*, April 22, 1912, 6; Helen Grenfell, Ben B. Lindsey, and John T. Barnett, quoted in Wayne, "Titanic Disaster Furnishes No Proof," 6.

8. Cott, *Grounding of Modern Feminism*, 3–5.

9. Rheta Childe Dorr, " 'Women and Children First,' " *Woman's Journal*, May 4, 1912, 141; Alice Stone Blackwell, "The Lesson of the Titanic," *Woman's Journal*, April 27, 1912, 132; Milholland, quoted in "Women First Barbarous," *NYTr*, April 19, 1912, 16. See also Larabee, "The American Hero and His Mechanical Bride," 15–18.

10. Alice Stone Blackwell, "Suffrage and Life-Saving," *Woman's Journal*, April 27, 1912, 132; "Masculine Chivalry," *Progressive Woman*, May 1912, 8.

11. Agnes E. Ryan, "Lives against Lives," *Woman's Journal*, April 27, 1912, 136; Blackwell, "Suffrage and Life-Saving," 132; Mary McDowell, "The New Chivalry and Industrial Life," *Life and Labor*, July 1913, 196, 198. McDowell's article was originally given as a speech at a WTUL meeting in St. Louis on June 2, 1912.

12. "Masculine Chivalry," 8; Charlotte Perkins Gilman, "The Saving of Women in Disaster," *Forerunner*, May 1912, 140. See also Charlotte Perkins Gilman, *Women and Economics: A Study of the Economic Relation between Men and Women as a Factor in Social Evolution* (New York: Harper & Row, 1966 [1898]), 62 and passim.

Gail Bederman makes a convincing case that Gilman's racism was fundamental to her feminism. Bederman, *Manliness and Civilization*, chap. 4.

13. "A Woman," letter, *BS*, April 22, 1912, 6; Grace Guyton Kempter, letter, *BS*, April 25, 1912, 6; "Daughter of Eve," letter, *BS*, May 1, 1912, 6; Emma Maddox Funck, letter, *BS*, April 26, 1912, 6.

14. Henry Louis Gates, Jr., *Colored People: A Memoir* (New York: Knopf, 1994), 92–93; Henry Louis Gates, Jr., "Sudden Def," *The New Yorker*, June 19, 1995, 37.

15. The phrase was the title of an editorial in the *St. Louis Post-Dispatch*, May 4, 1912, 4.

16. "Titanic Disaster Hits Home of the Entire Nation," *SFE*, April 17, 1912, 2. Wyn Craig Wade notes the black press's lack of attention to the disaster in *Titanic: End of a Dream*, 294. The *Cleveland Gazette, Richmond Planet, Savannah Tribune, St. Paul Appeal*, and *Washington Bee* printed some of the standard wire service material.

17. "The Lesson of the Titanic," *IF*, April 27, 1912, 4; "The Awakening," 4; "The Horror of the Sea," *IW*, April 27, 1912, 4.

18. "The Awakening," 4; Mary D. Turner, "Bethel A.M.E. Church," *PC*, April 27, 1912, 6; Mrs. Mattye E. Anderson, "The Titanic," *CD*, April 20, 1912, 4; Lucian B. Watkins, "O Sea! A Dirge; the Tragedy of the Titanic, Memorable of 1912," *RP*, May 25, 1912, 4.

19. "Belshazzar's Feast," *RP*, April 20, 1912, 4; "A Very Sad Affair with an Important Lesson," *AAL*, April 20, 1912, 4. See also, for example, "Sermon on the Titanic Disaster," *AAL*, May 18, 1912, 2.

20. Carl Sandburg, *The American Songbag* (New York: Harcourt, Brace, 1927), 254–56; Samuel B. Charters, *The Country Blues* (London: Michael Joseph, 1959), 62–63; Newman I. White, *American Negro Folk-Songs* (Cambridge: Harvard University Press, 1928), 347–48; Harold Courlander, *Negro Folk Music, U.S.A.* (New York: Columbia University Press, 1963), 76–77; John A. Lomax and Alan Lomax, *Our Singing Country: A Second Volume of American Ballads and Folk Songs* (New York: Macmillan, 1941), 26–27.

Dos Passos was simultaneously entranced and appalled by the sight he described as four "black shiny coons amid the pinkish faces and khaki of the soldiers crowded round" to hear the song. John Dos Passos, diary, November 4, [1918], in *The Fourteenth Chronicle: Letters and Diaries of John Dos Passos*, ed. Townsend Ludington (Boston: Gambit, 1973), 228–29.

21. "The Horror of the Sea," 4; "Afro-American Cullings," *PC*, June 7, 1912, 8.

22. Editorial, *SPA*, April 20, 1912, 2.

The information about the Laroche family is from Olivier Mendez, "The last French Lady, Mademoiselle Louise Laroche, A *Titanic* Survivor," *Titanic Commutator* 19, 2 (August–October 1995), 40–47.

23. "Editorial Notes," *NYA*, April 25, 1912, 4; "Current Notes," *ST*, May 25, 1912, 3; editorial, *PT*, April 27, 1912, 4.

24. *Louisville News*, quoted in *CD*, May 4, 1912, 4; editorial, *CD*, May 4, 1912, 4; *Solid Rock Herald*, quoted in "Afro-American Press on Titanic Disaster," *BA*, May 4, 1912, 2; editorial, *PC*, April 27, 1912, 4.

25. White, *American Negro Folk-Songs*, 348–49; Charles Wolfe and Kip Lornell, *The Life and Legend of Leadbelly* (New York: HarperCollins, 1992), 44–45; Jerry Silverman, *Folk Blues* (New York: Macmillan, 1968), 149–50; Courlander, *Negro Folk Music*, 77–78; Lawrence W. Levine, *Black Culture and Black Consciousness: Afro-American Folk Thought from Slavery to Freedom* (New York: Oxford University Press, 1977), 258.

26. Bruce Jackson, "The *Titanic* Toast," in *Veins of Humor*, Harvard English Studies 3, ed. Harry Levin (Cambridge: Harvard University Press, 1972), 205–23; Roger D. Abrahams, *Deep Down in the Jungle: Negro Narrative Folklore from the Streets of Philadelphia*, rev. ed. (Chicago: Aldine, 1970), 120–29; Levine, *Black Culture and Black Consciousness*, 428–29.

27. Robert L. Dorman, *Revolt of the Provinces: The Regionalist Movement in America, 1920–1945* (Chapel Hill: University of North Carolina Press, 1993), esp. chaps. 3–4; Lawrence W. Levine, "The Folklore of Industrial Society: Popular Culture and Its Audiences," *American Historical Review* 97, 5 (December 1992), 1369–99, esp. 1376.

28. Levine, "The Folklore of Industrial Society," 1377 and passim; Alan Lomax, *The Land Where the Blues Began* (New York: Pantheon, 1993), 48–54.

29. The process at work in the African American folk songs and toasts was the vernacular strategy of "Signifyin(g)," which Gates defines as "a metaphor for textual revision"—the playing of language games—often "aimed at demystifying a subject." Henry Louis Gates, Jr., *The Signifying Monkey: A Theory of Afro-American Literary Criticism* (New York: Oxford University Press, 1988), 88, 57, 52.

In writing only about the content of the *Titanic* toasts, I am doing exactly what Gates warns against in his discussion of Signifyin(g): ignoring its broader definition as "a game of language, independent of reaction to white racism or even to collective black wish-fulfillment vis-à-vis white racism" (70). My excuse is that I am writing a cultural history of the *Titanic* disaster, not a work of literary criticism or theory.

30. Ira Kipnis, *The American Socialist Movement, 1897–1912* (New York: Monthly Review Press, 1952), 335, 366–69; Melvyn Dubofsky, *We Shall Be All,* chap. 10, esp. 253; James Weinstein, *The Decline of Socialism in America, 1912–1925*, 2d ed. (New Brunswick: Rutgers University Press, 1984), 93–103; Dawley, *Struggles for Justice*, 136.

31. "The Great Catastrophe," *American Federation of Labor Weekly*

News Letter, April 20, 1912, n.p.; "The Titanic Disaster—to Prevent Recurrence," *American Federationist*, July 1912, 545–48; "The Titanic Disaster," *Weekly Bulletin of the Clothing Trades*, April 26, 1912, 4; editorial, *Glass Worker*, May 1912, 12; editorial, *Mixer and Server*, May 1912, 46; "The Titanic Sea Horror Should Be a Lesson to the World," *Journal of the Switchmen's Union of North America*, May 1912, 287; editorial, *Coopers International Journal*, May 1912, 8; "What Shall the Harvest Be?," *Coast Seaman's Journal*, April 24, 1912, 6; "Furnseth's Warning," *Shoe Workers' Journal*, June 1912, 11–12; "Remember!," *Railway Carmen's Journal*, June 1912, 413; editorial, *Car Worker*, July 1912, 45–46; "Senator Smith's 'Titanic' Speech," *Paper Makers' Journal*, June 1912, 4; "Another Sacrifice to the God of Speed," *Steam Shovel and Dredge*, May 1912, 403; La Follette, quoted in Belle Case La Follette and Fola La Follette, *Robert M. La Follette, June 14, 1855–June 18, 1925* (New York: Macmillan, 1953), vol. I, 528. The Seamen's Act was signed by Woodrow Wilson in March 1915.

32. "It Was Necessary to Kill Fifteen Hundred at a Time to Get Action," *Railroad Trainman*, June 1912, 535–36; Norm Cohen, *Long Steel Rail: The Railroad in American Folksong* (Urbana: University of Illinois Press, 1981), 171; "Mika Alheuttaa Titanic-Onnet-Tomuudessa Valtavan Huomion [Why All the Attention Directed to the Titanic Disaster?]," *RA*, April 18, 1912, 7; Adams, "S.O.S.—Save Our Souls," 2; George Emery, "Thoughts on the Titanic Disaster," *Metal Polishers, Buffers, Platers, Brass and Silver Workers Union of North America Journal*, May 1912, 6; editorial, *Official Magazine of the International Brotherhood of Teamsters, Chauffeurs, Stablemen and Helpers of America*, May 1912, 10; "Man Is as Chaff before the Breath of God," *Blacksmiths Journal*, May 1912, 41.

Most of the foreign-language press I cite can be found in the collections of the Immigration History Research Center at the University of Minnesota.

33. "At Work, with First Chance of Death," *American Federationist*, June 1912, 470; "First-Class Scabs," *United Mine Workers Journal*, May 2, 1912, 4.

34. George A. Hill, "The Titanic," *Advance Advocate*, June 1912, 458; "Titanic Disaster," *Railway Conductor*, May 1912, 391; "Aftermath," *Locomotive Firemen and Enginemen's Magazine*, June 1912, 838; William Havenstrite, "A Tragedy Glorified," *Elevator Constructor*, May 1912, 13; Thomas E. Burke, "Comment on Current Topics," *Plumbers', Gas and Steam Fitters' Journal*, May 1912, 27; "Sublime!," *International Musician*, May 1912, 6; "The Flesh and the Spirit," *LW*, April 27, 1912, 4; "The Titanic Disaster," *Journal of the International Brotherhood of Boiler Makers, Iron Ship Builders*

and Helpers of America, June 1912, 468; James E. Kinsella, "The Conquered Titan," *Union Postal Clerk*, July 1912, 11-12; "The Sinking of the Titanic," *Locomotive Engineers' Monthly Journal*, May 1912, 493–94.

35. Gilman, "The Saving of Women," 140; Morris Rosenfeld, "The People without Names Who Perished on the Ship 'Titanic,' " *JDF*, April 17, 1912, 4; "The Titanic Tragedy," *Appeal to Reason*, May 4, 1912, 4. A dissenting account, which appeared in the *Asheville Citizen*, observed that "the ever-present law of the submerged tenth decrees that no lists be made of steerage passengers, and, except in the households where death has laid its hand, the names of the Titanic's steerage passengers will never be known." "The Loss of the Titanic," *AsCi*, April 17, 1912, 4.

An African American popular song made a similar point:

> *The rich folks with their millions had to go down,*
> *Such as Astor, Mister Straub [sic] and Guggenheim,*
> *The poor folks on the vessel were not mentioned,*
> *We'll know them at the end of future time.*

William Jackson and Charles Wright, "The End of the Titanic in the Sea" (Medina, N.Y.: Krompart Publishing Co., 1912), American Folklife Center, LC.

36. "A Popular Scapegoat," *NYC*, April 23, 1912, 6; "L'Immane Disastro del 'Titanic' (The Great 'Titanic' Disaster)," *EN*, April 27, 1912, 1; Mother Jones, "Speech at a Public Meeting on the Steps of the Capitol, Charleston, West Virginia, 15 August 1912," in *The Speeches and Writings of Mother Jones*, ed. Edward Steel (Pittsburgh: University of Pittsburgh Press, 1988), 93–94.

37. " 'There Are Others,' " *Miners Magazine*, May 2, 1912, 6; "The Proletariat," "The Floating Cemetery: A Conversation among the Drowned Ones of the 'Titanic,' " *JDF*, April 28, 1912, 4.

38. "Flowers of British Chivalry," *GA*, May 18, 1912, 4; Robert Ellis Thompson, "The Titanic Disaster," *IrWo*, April 27, 1912, 5; "British Blundering," *GA*, May 25, 1912, 2.

39. "La Catastrofe del 'Titanic' Descritta dai Naufraghi Salvati (The 'Titanic' Catastrophe Described by Shipwreck Survivors)," *IT*, April 27, 1912, 7.

40. "A Quality of Courage," *JA*, April 26, 1912, 8; "A Fight for Freedom," *JA*, May 10, 1912, 8. The sheet music for Solomon Small's Yiddish song "The Titanic Disaster," for example, featured an illustration of the

Strauses hovering in an embrace above the sinking ship, about to be crowned by an angel. Solomon Small (Smulewitz) and H. A. Russotto, "The Titanic Disaster" (New York: Hebrew Publishing Co., 1912), Music Division, LC.

41. " 'Titanicin' Suomalaiset Maikustajat (Finnish Passengers on the 'Titanic')," *NYU*, April 20, 1912, 1; "Češi Na 'Titanic'? (Were There Czechs on the 'Titanic'?)," *DH*, April 17, 1912, 1; "Irish Victims on Titanic," *IrWo*, May 11, 1912, 7; "Lista Completa dei Naufraghi Italiani (Complete List of Shipwrecked Italians)," *IT*, May 4, 1912, 1; "Many Jews Were Passengers on Ill-Fated S.S. Titanic," *JA*, April 19, 1912, 1.

42. "Titanic Passengers in Steerage Brave," *NYC*, April 25, 1912, 2 (emphasis its); "Titanic Tragedy," 4; "Virtus," "Titanic—La Stampa— Eroismo dei Ricchi (The Titanic—The Press—The Heroism of the Rich)," *FI*, May 4, 1912, 1.

43. "Preventable Deaths of Workers," *Progressive Woman*, September 1912, 2; M. L. Clawson, "Fair Play," *IW*, May 18, 1912, 1.

44. Editorial, *Miners Magazine*, May 9, 1912, 6; "Titanic Tragedy," 4; "Our 'Titanic' Civilization," *Masses*, June 1912, 3; Charles Edward Russell, "Murdered for Capitalism," *Coming Nation*, April 27, 1912, 3; "A Titanic Demonstration," *DaPe*, April 18, 1912, 2.

45. Berger, quoted in "Rich Men Not Only Heroes in Shipwreck," *CP*, April 24, 1912, 11; John M. Work, "The Greater Tragedy," *NYC*, May 4, 1912, 6 (also printed in *Bridgemen's Magazine*, May 1912, 343–44); Szczypawka, "Z Tygodniowych Refleksji (From the Weekly Reflections)," *Bicz Bozy (God's Whip)*, April 28, 1912, 4.

46. "Titanicin Haaksirikko Ja Kapitalismi (The Titanic Disaster and Capitalism)," *TY*, April 21, 1912, 2; A. M. Simons, "Died That Dividends Might Grow," *Coming Nation*, April 27, 1912, 16; "Titanic Tragedy," 4; "News and Views," *Solidarity*, May 4, 1912, 2; "A Popular Scapegoat," 6; Russell, "Murdered for Capitalism," 4; Charles Edward Russell, "Inside of the Titanic Case," *Coming Nation*, May 4, 1912, 3; "Futile Questioning," *NYC*, April 22, 1912, 6.

47. "Lessons from the Titanic Disaster," *Ladies' Garment Worker*, May 1912, 14; "Titanic Tragedy," 4; "Our 'Titanic' Civilization," esp. 3; editorial, *PR*, April 30, 1912, 2; "Capitalistic Hurry-Up and the Titanic Disaster," *JDF*, April 18, 1912, 4.

48. "Our 'Titanic' Civilization," 3; "News and Views," *Solidarity*, April 27, 1912, 2; "Titanic Tragedy," 4.

49. "Titanic Tragedy," 4 (emphasis its); Charles Edward Russell, "Realities," *Coming Nation*, May 4, 1912, 4.

50. Charles Edward Russell, "Human Nature," *Coming Nation*, May 4, 1912, 4; Victor A. Olander, "The Titanic," *Life and Labor*, June 1912, 180; "Human Nature as Evinced in the 'Titanic' Disaster," *JDF*, April 20, 1912, 4; Jozef Sawicki, "Z Powodu Wypadku Z Okretem Titanic (On the Occasion of the Titanic Disaster)," *RoPo*, April 25, 1912, 4; Goldman, quoted in "Suffrage Dealt Blow," *DP*, April 21, 1912, sec. 1, p. 8.

CHAPTER 5: A NIGHT TO REMEMBER

1. *Who Was Who in America* (Chicago: A. N. Marquis, 1943), vol. I, 211–12; Howard M. Chapin, *The Titanic Disaster* (Providence: E. A. Johnson, 1913); Howard M. Chapin, "Bibliotheca Titanic: List of Books Relating to the Loss of S.S. Titanic," *Americana Collector*, January 1926, 144–48.

2. See, for example, "Titanic's 1,517 Dead, Lost 11 Years Ago, to Be Honored Today on Sea and Land," *NYT*, April 15, 1923, 1; "Titanic Anniversary to Be Observed," *NYT*, April 4, 1926, pt. IX, p. 16; "Titanic Was Sunk Just 15 Years Ago," *NYT*, April 10, 1927, pt. IX, p. 6; "Loss of Titanic on April 15, 1912," *NYT*, April 10, 1932, pt. XI, p. 11; "Memorial Service at Titanic Tower," *NYT*, April 16, 1932, 33; "Honor Titanic Dead Where Liner Sank," *NYT*, April 15, 1937, 25; "At the Titanic Memorial Services Here," *NYT*, April 16, 1937, 5; "Monument to the Titanic," *NYT*, April 14, 1952, 18; "Titanic Sank 40 Years Ago Today; Patrols Now Chart Iceberg Perils," *NYT*, April 14, 1952, 39.

3. "New Monuments to Rise in Washington," *New York Times Magazine*, September 23, 1928, 4; "Unveil Memorial to Titanic's Heroes," *NYT*, May 27, 1931, 29; Clara Bird Kopp, "The New Titanic Memorial," *National Republic*, May 1932, 7, 41; Barbara Melosh, *Engendering Culture: Manhood and Womanhood in New Deal Public Art and Theater* (Washington: Smithsonian, 1991), 1.

4. J. Gresham Machen, *Christianity and Liberalism* (Grand Rapids, Mich.: Wm. B. Eerdmans, 1946 [1923]), 126–27.

5. Henry Brenner, *Titanic's Knell: A Satire on Speed* (St. Meinrad, Ind.: The Raven, 1932), 19, 44, and passim.

6. Carlton Stowers, *The Unsinkable Titanic Thompson* (Toronto: PaperJacks, 1988 [1982]), 64, 1–2.

7. Wilson Mizner, "You're Dead!" in *Stories for Men*, ed. Charles Grayson (Boston: Little, Brown, 1936), 391–407.

8. James Card, "When Newsreels Stood Still: A Little-Known Ancestor of the Nightly News Comes to Light," *American Heritage*, Febru-

ary–March 1985, 48–53; Frank Thompson, "Lost at Sea," *Film Comment*, May–June 1994, 2, 7. As Thompson's title suggests, *Saved from the Titanic* is lost. The Travelers advertisement is on the back cover of the *Survey*, May 4, 1912.

9. For a full discussion of the Selznick episode, see Eric Schaefer, "The Sinking of David O. Selznick's 'Titanic,'" *Library Chronicle of the University of Texas at Austin* 36 (1986), 57–73. At one point Selznick bought the rights to Hanson W. Baldwin's "R.M.S. Titanic," which appeared in *Harper's* in January 1934—one of the very few narrative treatments of the disaster to appear between 1913 and 1955. For a brief survey of the *Titanic's* film career, see Harry M. Geduld, "Nearer My Wreck to Thee," *Humanist*, July–August 1987, 45.

10. Geduld, "Nearer My Wreck," 45; Robert Prechtl, *Titanic*, trans. Erna McArthur (New York: E. P. Dutton, 1940), 56, 333, 331.

Prechtl's *Titanic* sounded a Germanic version of the redemption theme. At the end of the novel Astor gives up his place in a lifeboat to a "miserable Polish woman" and her "dropsical" child, "two human mites among a million other swarming human mites." Prechtl's Astor is a kind of Nietzschean Superman, misdirecting his extraordinary will toward purely material ends until, at last, he achieves his full spiritual stature.

11. Lord, interview with author, October 17, 1992; "Walter Lord: Man behind the Book," *Titanic Commutator* 3, 28 (Winter 1980), 8.

12. *Publishers Weekly*, August 27, 1955, 1–2; Lord, interview with author; Gene Fowler, "The Unsinkable Mrs. Brown," *Coronet*, October 1949, 116–21; Lady Duff Gordon, "I Was Saved from the Titanic," *Coronet*, June 1951, 94–97; Robert Schwartz, "The Sea Tragedy That Shocked the World," *Cosmopolitan*, March 1953, 102; "Survivors Watch the 'Titanic' Go Down Again," *Life*, May 18, 1953, 91–96; Bud Greenspan, "Deaf to Disaster," *Coronet*, May 1953, 31; Jack Weeks, "Titanic," *Holiday*, June 1953, 91–94; Walter Lord, "A Night to Remember," *Ladies' Home Journal*, November 1955, 62–63, 125–62; Walter Lord, "Maiden Voyage," *American Heritage*, December 1955, 46–53, 103–05; Walter Lord, "A Night to Remember," *Reader's Digest*, January 1956, 43–48, 156–72; *Book-of-the-Month Club News*, June 1956, 12; Walter Lord, "Twenty-five Years Ago," and Edward S. Kamuda, "*A Night to Remember* in Retrospect," *Titanic Commutator* 3, 28 (Winter 1980), 9, 13, 6; "That 'Titanic' TV Triumph," *Variety*, April 4, 1956, 23; "Kraft Theatre Show Will Always Be a Night to Remember for Walter Lord," *Variety*, April 25, 1956, 27.

The sales figures are from *Publishers Weekly*, January 7–June 11, 1956.

13. Quoted in Kamuda, "*A Night to Remember* in Retrospect," 3; Lord, *Night to Remember*, 13, 167; Lord, interview with author.

14. Alex McNeil, *Total Television: A Comprehensive Guide to Programming from 1948 to the Present*, 3d ed. (New York: Penguin, 1991), 848.

15. Lord, *Night to Remember*, 21.

16. Ibid., 158, 177, 65, 68, 71–72, 96.

17. Ibid., 177, 166.

18. Ibid., 166, 112, 109, 114–15; Lord, interview with author.

19. See Paul Fussell, *The Great War and Modern Memory* (New York: Oxford University Press, 1975), esp. 312–13, and David M. Kennedy, *Over Here: The First World War and American Society* (New York: Oxford University Press, 1980), 214.

For two contemporary complaints about literary modernism's attainment of middle-class respectability, see Dwight Macdonald, "Masscult and Midcult" (1960), in *Against the American Grain* (New York: Random House, 1962), 3–75, and Lionel Trilling, "On the Teaching of Modern Literature" (1961), in *Beyond Culture: Essays on Literature and Learning* (New York: Viking, 1965), 3–30.

20. Lord, *Night to Remember*, 113; Lord, interview with author; Elaine Tyler May, *Homeward Bound: American Families in the Cold War Era* (New York: Basic Books, 1988), 24 and passim. Michael Kammen uses the phrase "nostalgic modernism" in a different context in *Mystic Chords of Memory: The Transformation of Tradition in American Culture* (New York: Knopf, 1991), 300.

21. Walter Lord, *The Good Years: From 1900 to the First World War* (New York: Bantam, 1962 [1960]), viii.

22. Orville Prescott, "Books of the Times," *NYT*, November 22, 1955, 33; William Hogan, "A Reconstruction of the Titanic Story," *SFC*, November 25, 1955, 19; Burke Wilkinson, "The Nightmare of April 14, 1912," *New York Times Book Review*, November 20, 1955, 3; John M. Connole, "A Night to Remember," *America*, December 10, 1955, 310; "The Fabric of Disaster," *Newsweek*, December 12, 1955, 126; Richard Blakesley, "A Night of Gallantry, Devotion, Death," *Chicago Tribune Book Review*, November 20, 1955, 1; "Down to the Sea," *Christian Century*, January 4, 1956, 19.

23. John K. Hutchens, "Book Review," *NYHT*, November 23, 1955, 17.

24. Fred Davis, *Yearning for Yesterday: A Sociology of Nostalgia* (New York: Free Press, 1979), 49.

25. Wilkinson, "Nightmare of April 14," 3; "Down to the Sea," 19. See also Katherine Gauss Jackson, "Books in Brief," *Harper's*, January

1956, 92, "Briefly Noted," *The New Yorker*, December 3, 1955, 213, and Harriet Forbes Burdick, "A Night to Remember," *Library Journal*, October 15, 1955, 2235.

26. Davis, *Yearning for Yesterday*, 45; "Down to the Sea," 19.

27. "Disaster of the Century," *Time*, February 13, 1956, 98.

28. Anthony F. C. Wallace, *Human Behavior in Extreme Situations: A Survey of the Literature and Suggestions for Further Research* (Washington: National Academy of Sciences-National Research Council, 1956), 2–4; Paul Boyer, *By the Bomb's Early Light: American Thought and Culture at the Dawn of the Atomic Age* (New York: Pantheon, 1985), chap. 15.

29. Philip Wylie, "When Disaster Strikes," *Bulletin of the Atomic Scientists*, December 1956, 376–77; Boyer, *By the Bomb's Early Light*, 323–24. Wylie himself was a strong advocate of civil defense and served as a consultant to the Federal Civil Defense Administration. See May, *Homeward Bound*, 97.

Some of the work on disasters was, and is, quite compelling. There was nothing inherently insidious about exploring how people responded to disasters and suggesting strategies for helping them cope, even if the impetus for much of the undertaking was the federal government's attempt to manage the nuclear threat. But what is troubling about even such a thoughtful and humane study as Martha Wolfenstein's *Disaster: A Psychological Essay* (Glencoe, Ill.: Free Press, 1957) is that in attempting to construct a morphology of responses, it collapsed the distinctions between kinds of disasters.

30. "A Night to Remember," *Kraft Television Theatre*, March 28, 1956, dir. George Roy Hill, MTR; George Roy Hill and John Whedon, "A Night to Remember," in *The Writers Guild of America Presents the Prize Plays of Television and Radio, 1956* (New York: Random House, 1957), 81–118, esp. 112, 118; Jack Gould, "TV: Last Hours of Titanic," *NYT*, March 29, 1956, 55; "Tele Follow-Up Comment," *Variety*, April 4, 1956, 29.

31. *A Night to Remember*, prod. William MacQuitty, dir. Roy Baker, J. Arthur Rank Organization, 1958, videocassette; Bosley Crowther, "Screen: Sinking of Titanic," *NYT*, December 17, 1958, 2; Walter Lord, "Candid Reflections on 'A Night to Remember,' " and "Advertising A NIGHT TO REMEMBER in the U.S.," *Titanic Commutator* 2, 7 (September 1975), n.p.

32. "Night to Remember," *Kraft Television Theatre*; Hill and Whedon, "Night to Remember," 106, 110. On the changing ideology of domesticity—the shift from "sacrifice" to "satisfaction"—see May, *Great Expectations*, chap. 3, and May, *Screening Out the Past*, chap. 5. On the connections between the bomb and domesticity, see May, *Homeward Bound*, chap. 4.

My point here is not that these gender messages reflected a uniform reality or even a seamless ideology. Historians have begun to explore the diversity of women's experiences and to mount challenges to the domestic stereotypes of the 1950s. Despite the ideal of middle-class domesticity, women continued to work outside the home. By the middle of the decade they had matched the unprecedented employment levels of World War II, and the number of married women engaged in paid labor grew by more than 40 percent between 1950 and 1960. In other words, representations of "traditional" families and gender roles, such as those in 1950s Titanica (and, more dramatically, in situation comedies like *Leave It to Beaver*, *Ozzie and Harriet*, and *The Donna Reed Show*), performed a new kind of cultural work. Popular culture sent mixed messages, but much of it tried to idealize and normalize particular modes of behavior and belief precisely because these modes were not universal in Cold War America.

The essays in Joanne Meyerowitz, ed., *Not June Cleaver: Women and Gender in Postwar America, 1945–1960* (Philadelphia: Temple University Press, 1994) vividly convey the complexity of women's lives in this period. The statistics on women's paid labor come from the essay by Susan M. Hartmann, "Women's Employment and the Domestic Ideal in the Early Cold War Years," 86.

33. *Titanic*, prod. Charles Brackett, dir. Jean Negulesco, Twentieth Century-Fox, 1953, videocassette; "The Screen in Review," *NYT*, May 28, 1953, 27; "New Films," *Newsweek*, May 18, 1953, 108; Hollis Alpert, "Mr. Belvedere Strikes Again," *Saturday Review*, May 16, 1953, 30; "Titanic," *Variety*, April 15, 1953, 6. The film made "May's Big 10" and the "June Golden Dozen" in *Variety*, June 3, 1953, 4, and July 1, 1953, 4.

For a discussion of how films have more directly reflected—or deflected—nuclear anxiety, see Mick Broderick, "From Atoms to Apocalypse: Film and the Nuclear Issue," in Broderick, *Nuclear Movies: A Critical Analysis and Filmography of International Feature Length Films Dealing with Experimentation, Aliens, Terrorism, Holocaust and Other Disaster Scenarios, 1914–1989* (Jefferson, N.C.: MacFarland, 1991), 1–52. Broderick quotes the psychologist J. E. Mack on the subject of the more recent appeal of disaster films: "The great interest in the last few years in disaster films about air crashes, earthquakes, tidal waves, and fires in tall buildings, grows out of an unconscious need to displace the larger terror contained in the threat of nuclear disaster and annihilation to a smaller, more finite, comprehendable and manageable catastrophe" (p. 36).

34. Christopher Durang, "Titanic," in *Christopher Durang Explains It All for You: Six Plays by Christopher Durang* (New York: Avon, 1983), 61–97.

35. Lord, *Night to Remember*, 107, 112. On the ideology of consensus, see Robert Booth Fowler, *Believing Skeptics: American Political Intellectuals, 1945–1964* (Westport, Conn.: Greenwood Press, 1978), and Stephen J. Whitfield, *The Culture of the Cold War* (Baltimore: Johns Hopkins University Press, 1991), chap. 3.

36. Weeks, "Titanic," 91–94; Richard O'Connor, *Down to Eternity* (New York: Fawcett, 1956), 119, 150–51, back cover, 23, 190.

37. Boyer, *By the Bomb's Early Light*, 299–300, 302.

38. Fowler, "Unsinkable Mrs. Brown," 116–21.

39. George Lipsitz, *Rainbow at Midnight: Labor and Culture in the 1940s* (Urbana: University of Illinois Press, 1994), chap. 11, esp. 261. I encountered the advertisement on the back cover of *Commonweal*, December 9, 1955.

40. Meredith Willson and Richard Morris, *The Unsinkable Molly Brown* (New York: G. P. Putnam's Sons, 1961), 171, 158, 117, 172, 180; Gerald Bordman, *American Musical Theatre: A Chronicle*, 2d ed. (New York: Oxford University Press, 1992), 618; Gerald Mast, *Can't Help Singin': The American Musical on Stage and Screen* (Woodstock, N.Y.: Overlook Press, 1987), 294; Stanley Green, *Broadway Musicals: Show by Show*, 3d ed. (Milwaukee: Hal Leonard, 1990), 191; Stanley Green, *Hollywood Musicals: Year by Year* (Milwaukee: Hal Leonard, 1990), 229.

41. Robert Cantwell, "When We Were Good: Class and Culture in the Folk Revival," in *Transforming Tradition: Folk Music Revivals Examined*, ed. Neil V. Rosenberg (Urbana: University of Illinois Press, 1993), 35–60; Wolfe and Lornell, *Leadbelly*, 252; Rev. Gary Davis and Pink Anderson, *Gospel, Blues and Street Songs*, Riverside OBCCD-524-2; *Smoky Mountain Ballads*, RCA Victor LPV-507; "Dixon, Dorsey," in Stambler and Landon, *Encyclopedia of Folk*, 192; Mance Lipscomb, *Texas Songster Volume 2: You Got to Reap What You Sow*, Arhoolie CD 398; Glen Alyn, *I Say Me for a Parable: The Oral Autobiography of Mance Lipscomb, Texas Bluesman* (New York: Norton, 1993), 219–23. On the *Titanic* toasts as part of the white "discovery" of black culture in the 1950s, see W. T. Lhamon, Jr., *Deliberate Speed: The Origins of a Cultural Style in the American 1950s* (Washington: Smithsonian, 1990), 38–40.

42. William McKeen, *Bob Dylan: A Bio-Bibliography* (Westport, Conn.: Greenwood Press, 1993), 8–11; Wilfred Mellers, *A Darker Shade of Pale: A Backdrop to Bob Dylan* (New York: Oxford University Press, 1985), 118, 142; Bob Dylan, *Highway 61 Revisited*, Columbia CK09189; Tim Riley, *Hard Rain: A Dylan Commentary* (New York: Knopf, 1992), 122–24; Robert Shelton, *No Direction Home: The Life and Music of Bob Dylan* (New

York: Beech Tree Books, 1986), 282–83; Dave Harker, *One for the Money: Politics and Popular Song* (London: Hutchinson, 1980), 136–42.

CHAPTER 6: ENTHUSIASTS

1. Chris Reidy, "Titanic's Unsinkable Memory," *BG*, April 10, 1992, 26; "R.M.S. *Titanic* Remembered," Titanic Historical Society brochure.

2. Edward S. Kamuda, interview with author, Indian Orchard, Massachusetts, June 9, 1994; Joseph Carvalho, telephone interview with author, April 6, 1995; "*Titanic* Enthusiasts at Meeting," *Marconigram* 1, 1 (October 1963), n.p.; Edward S. Kamuda, "A Truly *Titanic* Convention," *Titanic Commutator* 6, 1 (Spring 1982), 27; Edward C. Burks, "Titanic Survivors Recall the 'Night to Remember,' " *NYT*, September 10, 1973, 39; Kevin L. Goldman, "Survivors Recall the Titanic," *NYT*, April 24, 1977, sec. 23, p. 6; Reidy, "Titanic's Unsinkable Memory," 21.

The full run of the *Marconigram* and the *Titanic Commutator* is available on microfilm at the New York Public Library.

3. My statistics are based on the listings that appeared in the *Commutator* from the June 1966 issue, which included the names of all the members at that time, through the Spring 1985 issue. The listings were discontinued with the surge of new members after the wreck's discovery.

4. I should note that the later listings indicate a larger proportion of women among new members, but they remain greatly outnumbered by men.

5. Kamuda, interview with author.

6. Dru Schillow to author, March 15, 1995. Ellipsis is his.

7. Kamuda, interview with author; Goldman, "Survivors Recall the Titanic," 7; R. Michael Little, quoted in "Welcome Aboard, Mates!," *Titanic Commutator* 2, 13 (Supplement, Spring 1977), n.p.

8. Don Lynch, "The Life and Art of Ken Marschall," *Titanic Commutator* 12, 2 (1988), 4

9. "The Men on the 'Bridge,' " *Titanic Commutator* 2, 4 (December 1974), n.p.

10. John A. Waterhouse, quoted in "Welcome Aboard, Mates!," *Titanic Commutator* 2, 19 (Supplement, Fall 1978), n.p.; Jack Finney, *From Time to Time* (New York: Simon & Schuster, 1995), 256, 150, 140, 270, 58.

11. Steve Rasmussen to author, March 21, 1995; Charles Haas, quoted in Allen Pusey, "Legend of Titanic Still Looms Larger Than Life," *DMN*, September 8, 1985, 10A; George Behe to author, February 7, 1995.

12. Bruce A. Trinque to author, March 19, 1995; Charles Haas, telephone interview with author, March 7, 1995; Joseph M. Ryan, "Sea Poste," *Titanic Commutator* 2, 22 (Supplement, Summer 1979), n.p. Trinque is an engineer and semiprofessional military historian.

13. Kenneth W. Bilbo, quoted in "Welcome Aboard, Mates!," *Titanic Commutator* 7, 2 (Supplement, Summer 1983), n.p.; W.F. Moshier, quoted in "Welcome Aboard, Mates!," *Titanic Commutator* 2, 15 (Supplement, Fall 1977), n.p.; Chad Audinet to author, March 16, 1995; Geoffery Evers to author, March 30, 1995.

14. Karen Kamuda, " 'Women and Children First': The Legacy of the *Birkenhead* and the *Titanic*," *Titanic Commutator* 17, 4 (February–April 1994), 10. See also Linda Lichter, "The Lost Luxuries of Ladyhood," *National Review*, October 18, 1993, 58–60, "Chivalry Went Down with the Titanic," *Wall Street Journal*, April 21, 1993, A14, and "What Ever Happened to Chivalry?," *Reader's Digest*, November, 1993, 187–88.

15. Ronald J. Klubnik, quoted in "Welcome Aboard, Mates!," *Titanic Commutator* 2, 21 (Supplement, Spring 1979), n.p.; Robin Wehrlin to author, May 10, 1995.

16. John Nolan, quoted in "Welcome Aboard, Mates!," *Titanic Commutator* 1, 41 (Supplement, Dec. 1973), n.p.; Michael J. Temons, quoted in "Welcome Aboard, Mates!," *Titanic Commutator* 9, 1 (Supplement, Spring 1985), n.p.; Sheri Calvert to author, March 29, 1995; Robert D. Ballard, "Introduction," in Don Lynch and Ken Marschall, *Titanic: An Illustrated History* (New York: Hyperion, 1992), 13.

For a fascinating discussion of Civil War reenactors—a discussion that touches on many themes of this chapter—see Jim Cullen, *The Civil War in Popular Culture: A Reusable Past* (Washington: Smithsonian, 1995), chap. 6.

17. David B. Peterson and Edward P. Levin, quoted in "Welcome Aboard, Mates!," *Titanic Commutator* 2, 13 (Supplement, Spring 1977), n.p.; Fred L. Miller, Jr., quoted in "Welcome Aboard, Mates!," *Titanic Commutator* 2, 15 (Supplement, Fall 1977), n.p.; Joe MacInnis, "Hooked on the Titanic," *HP*, September 9, 1985, 16A.

Sachs began modestly with a cake and period-costume affair to commemorate the sixtieth anniversary. The sixty-fifth-anniversary event was more elaborate, a twenty-dollar-per-person dinner-dance on board the *Queen Mary* at which the food and wine ran out early and the air conditioning broke down. Subsequent affairs have apparently gone more smoothly. See Charles Ira Sachs, "1912–72: The 60th Year," *Titanic Commutator* 1, 35 (June 1972), n.p., and Gregg Hunter's article about the unfortunate sixty-fifth celebration from the *Glendale News-Press/Burbank Daily Review-Star*, reprinted in *Titanic Commutator* 2, 14 (Summer 1977), n.p.

18. Kamuda, "A *Night to Remember* in Retrospect," 3.

19. Kamuda, interview with author; Lord, *Night to Remember*, 9; John P. Eaton and Charles A. Haas, *Titanic: Triumph and Tragedy*, 2d ed. (Somerset, England: Patrick Stephens, 1994), 9.

20. George Behe, *Titanic: Psychic Forewarnings of a Tragedy* (Wellingborough, England: Aquarian Press, 1989 [1988]), 13, 162 (emphasis his); Vaughan, quoted in Brown, *Titanic, Psychic, Sea*, 4 (emphasis his); H. Wayne Summerlin, "The Big Clock," *Titanic Commutator* 5, 2 (Fall 1981), 23. For a skeptical discussion, see Martin Gardner, ed., *The Wreck of the Titanic Foretold?* (Buffalo: Prometheus, 1986).

21. Brown, *Titanic, Psychic, Sea*, 140.

22. John P. Eaton, telephone interview with author, April 18, 1995; Jay R. Browne to author, April 25, 1995; Darwin Rizzetto to author, March 19, 1995 and July 23, 1995. Mr. Rizzetto was kind enough to send me copies of his reports, dated August 20, 1994, and July 21, 1995.

23. John Eaton, quoted in Bob Drogin, "There Is No 300-Foot Gash, Titanic Explorer Concludes after Last Dives," *LAT*, July 27, 1986, 14.

David Riesman discussed hobbies as a search for competence and autonomy—"inner-directed" versus "other-directed character"—in a modern America dominated by corporations and consumer capitalism. See David Riesman with Nathan Glazer and Reuel Denney, *The Lonely Crowd: A Study of the Changing American Character*, abr. ed. (New Haven: Yale University Press, 1961), esp. 292–97.

24. Behe to author, February 7, 1995.

25. Stuart A. MacDonald, "Preserving the *Good* Name of the *Titanic*!," *Titanic Commutator* 1, 12 (June 1966), 6; Kamuda, quoted in Reidy, "Titanic's Unsinkable Memory," 21.

26. Tarn Charles Stephanos to author, March 16, 1995; Kenneth B. Westover, quoted in "Welcome Aboard, Mates!," *Titanic Commutator* 2, 2 (June 1974), 27.

In his ethnography of television fans Henry Jenkins writes that "one of the most often heard comments from new fans is their surprise in discovering how many people share their fascination with a particular series, their pleasure in discovering that they are not 'alone,' " their sense of "participating in a larger social and cultural community." Henry Jenkins, *Textual Poachers: Television Fans & Participatory Culture* (New York: Routledge, 1992), 22–23.

27. Haas, interview with author; Eaton, interview with author.
28. "About the Author," *Titanic Commutator* 2, 12 (December 1976), 13; introduction to survivors' issue, *Titanic Commutator* 2, 21 (Spring 1979), 3.
29. Haas, interview with author; Robert J. McCooley, quoted in "Welcome Aboard, Mates!," *Titanic Commutator* 2, 18 (Supplement, Summer 1978), n.p.; Donato Natiello, Jr., quoted in "Welcome Aboard, Mates!," *Titanic Commutator* 2, 21 (Supplement, Spring 1979), n.p.; Randall W. Arnett, quoted in "Welcome Aboard, Mates!," *Titanic Commutator* 2, 22 (Supplement, Summer 1979), n.p.; Richard W. Fluharty, quoted in "Welcome Aboard, Mates!," *Titanic Commutator* 6, 1 (Supplement, Spring 1982), n.p.
30. James L. Hamilton to author, May 2, 1995; James A. Flood, quoted in "Welcome Aboard, Mates!," *Titanic Commutator* 2, 13 (Supplement, Spring 1977), n.p.; "An Invitation to Join a Unique Group . . . Titanic International," Titanic International brochure.
31. These phrases come primarily, though not exclusively, from poems written by THS members and published in the *Commutator*. Edward S. Kamuda, "Reflections of a Disaster," *Titanic Commutator* 1, 9 (June 1965), n.p., and 2, 1 (April 1974), n.p.; Henry Lapa, Jr., "Falling Titan," "The Sin of Complacency," and "The Mortal Saviors," *Titanic Commutator* 2, 1 (April 1974), n.p.; W. Roland Herzel, "*Olympic* and *Titanic*—How Different?," *Titanic Commutator* 2, 2 (June 1974), 18; Terry J. Kessler, "Sea Poste," *Titanic Commutator* 2, 2 (June 1974), 21–22; "Foreword," *Titanic Commutator* 2, 9 (April 1976), n.p.; Samuel F. Mordecai, "Mrs. Strauss [*sic*]—Sunk on the *Titanic*," *Titanic Commutator* 2, 12 (December 1976), 23; William L. Rabenstein, "The First and Last Voyage of the *Titanic*" and "Till Death Do Us Part," *Titanic Commutator* 2, 13 (April 1977), 9–11, 17; John W. Ziemann, quoted in "Welcome Aboard, Mates!," *Titanic Commutator* 2, 14 (Supplement, Summer 1977), n.p.; Joseph Ward, "The *Titanic*," *Titanic Commutator* 2, 19 (Fall 1978), 30; Joseph G. Gallant, "The *Titanic*," *Titanic Commutator* 2, 21 (Spring 1979), 25; Joseph G. Gallant, "*Carpathia*," *Titanic Commutator* 2, 24 (Winter 1979), 14; Laurence V. Lomax, "An Item of Interest," *Titanic Commutator* 1, 32 (September 1971), n.p.; Robert F. Dedmon to author, March 22, 1995.
32. "Acknowledgements [*sic*]," *Titanic Commutator* 2, 9 (April 1976), n.p.; Frank Cronican, "No Man Shall Wrest Her Free," *Titanic Commutator* 1, 9 (June 1965), n.p., and 2, 1 (April 1974), n.p.; Carlos E. Ruiz, quoted in "Welcome Aboard, Mates!," *Titanic Commutator* 2, 13 (Supplement, Spring 1977), n.p.; Rabenstein, "First and Last Voyage" and "Till Death," 11, 17.

33. Philip Del Piano, quoted in *Titanic Commutator* 2, 1 (April 1974), n.p.

34. Don Castel, quoted in "Welcome Aboard, Mates!," *Titanic Commutator* 2, 23 (Supplement, Fall 1979), n.p.; James Ulmer Gandy, quoted in "Welcome Aboard, Mates!," *Titanic Commutator* 2, 4 (December 1974), n.p.; Ruben and Jo Ann Olvera to author, May 12, 1995; Susan Richardson to author, April 19, 1995; Karen M. Bowman to author, March 18, 1995.

35. Melinda M. Capp to author, March 20, 1995; William Rauscher to author, March 31, 1995; Frank D. Johns, Jr., to author, March 30, 1995.

36. Carvalho, interview with author.

37. Eaton, quoted in Edward S. Kamuda, "The T.H.S. Banquet" and "Sunday, 17 April 1977," *Titanic Commutator* 2, 14 (Summer 1977), 23, 33–34; Kamuda, "Sunday, 17 April," 34, 36–37.

38. Rev. Father Francis C. Fitzhugh, "A Remembrance of the *Titanic*," and Kamuda, "Truly *Titanic* Convention," 29–33, 27–28.

39. Kamuda, "Truly *Titanic* Convention," 26; Whitman, quoted in Karen S. Edwards, "A Great Ship," *Americana*, December 1989, 64.

40. [Edward S. Kamuda], "G. J. Rencher: Eyewitness to History on *Carpathia*," *Titanic Commutator* 2, 22 (Summer 1979), 18; Edward S. Kamuda, "Convention '77: From Blueprints to Launching," *Titanic Commutator* 2, 14 (Summer 1977), 6; Kamuda, "Truly *Titanic* Convention," 25.

41. Kamuda, interview with author; Lord, interview with author; "The Chance of a Lifetime . . . Own a Rare Piece of *Titanic* History!!," THS circular, 1994.

42. "The Titanic Historical Society, Inc. Convention '96," *Titanic Commutator* 19, 1 (Supplement, May–July 1995), 1; Karen Kamuda, "Our *Titanic* Heritage Tour," *Titanic Commutator*, Special Edition (1993), esp. 7; Edward S. Kamuda, interview with author; "*Titanic* Heritage Tour III," advertisement, *Titanic Commutator* 18, 3 (Supplement, November 1994–January 1995), 1.

43. Martin Arnold and Katherine Faulkner, "*Titanic* Heritage Tour II: The Sequel," *Titanic Commutator* 18, 3 (November 1994–January 1995), 32, 34; Robert B. Warren, Jr., to author, April 3, 1995.

44. "*Titanic*'s 60th . . . We Didn't Forget," *Titanic Commutator* 1, 35 (June 1972), n.p.

CHAPTER 7: MISSION TO DESTINY

1. Danielle Steel, *No Greater Love* (New York: Dell, 1991), 21, 265, and passim. Hildegard Hoeller has explored how Steel's fiction links love

and consumption by combining nineteenth-century sentimental genre conventions and advertising techniques. Hildegard Hoeller, "The Triumph of Danielle Steel's Post-Modern Sentimentality" (unpublished ms.) and "Designer Selves: Tom Wolfe's *The Bonfire of the Vanities* and Danielle Steel's *Crossings*," *Names* 42, 1 (March 1994), 1–11.

NBC broadcast a TV movie version of *No Greater Love* on New Year's Day, 1996.

2. *No Greater Love* is not, technically speaking, a romance, but it does meet some of the expectations that Janice Radway has identified for romance readers, especially "the fairy-tale union of the hero and heroine" as "the symbolic fulfillment of a woman's desire to realize her most basic female self *in relation* with another." Like the ideal romance, *No Greater Love* ends with a "perfect marriage." Janice A. Radway, *Reading the Romance: Women, Patriarchy, and Popular Literature* (Chapel Hill: University of North Carolina Press, 1991 [1984]), chap. 4, esp. 155, 149.

3. Quoted in Susan Jeffords, *Hard Bodies: Hollywood Masculinity in the Reagan Era* (New Brunswick: Rutgers University Press, 1994), 10.

4. Donald A. Stanwood, *The Memory of Eva Ryker* (New York: Coward, McCann & Geoghegan, 1978), 25, 27.

5. Ibid., 345 and passim.

6. Clive Cussler, *Raise the Titanic!* (New York: Viking Press, 1976), 20, 29.

7. Ibid., 160–61.

8. Ibid., 197, 240–65, 280–81, 297.

9. *Raise the Titanic!*, prod. William Frye, dir. Jerry Jameson, ITC, 1980, videocassette; "The Unsinkable Titanic," *Reader's Digest*, April 1986, 230; Edward Oxford, "Titanic: Pyramid in the Sea," *American History Illustrated*, April 1986, 35; Robert D. Ballard with Rick Archbold, *The Discovery of the Titanic* (New York: Warner Books, 1987), 68.

10. Bruce Smith and Alton Slagle, "The Magnetic *Titanic*: An Unsinkable Story," *Oceans*, July 1981, 4; William Hoffman and Jack Grimm, *Beyond Reach: The Search for the Titanic* (New York: Beaufort Books, 1982). "Mission to Destiny" is the title of one of Charles Pellegrino's chapters about Ballard's exploits in *Her Name, Titanic*.

11. Oxford, "Titanic," 33; William J. Broad, "Wreckage of Titanic Reported Discovered 12,000 Feet Down," *NYT*, September 3, 1985, A1; Richard Homan, "U.S.-French Team Finds Wreckage of Titanic," *WP*, September 3, 1985, A19; Joe MacInnis, " 'We Found It!'—A Report from the Men Who Located the Titanic," *HP*, September 3, 1985, 1A; Natalie Angier, "After 73 Years, a *Titanic* Find," *Time*, September 16, 1985, 69;

Richard Saltus, "High-Tech Robot Explores Titanic," *BG*, July 16, 1986, 8; "Expedition Views Titanic for Last Time," *WP*, July 25, 1986, A6; Bob Drogin, "Titanic Camera Finds Beauty Is a Joy Forever," *LAT*, July 17, 1986; pt. I, p. 1; Robert D. Ballard, *Exploring the Titanic* (New York: Scholastic, 1988), 48; Walter Sullivan, "Titanic Receives a Full Inspection," *NYT*, July 17, 1986, A17. See also Larabee, "The American Hero and His Mechanical Bride," 20.

12. William D. Marbach, "The Sea Gives Up a Secret," *Newsweek*, September 16, 1985, 44; Robert D. Ballard, "A Long Last Look at *Titanic*," *National Geographic*, December 1986, 702; Pellegrino, *Her Name, Titanic*, 133, 234; Bob Drogin, "Explorer Gives a Video Tour of Titanic," *LAT*, July 31, 1986, pt. I, p. 12.

13. Doris G. Kinney, "Titanic: After 73 Years the Great Ship Is Found—and Photographed—Two Miles Deep in the Atlantic," *Life*, January 1986, 70; Robert D. Ballard in association with Jean-Louis Michel, "How We Found the *Titanic*," *National Geographic*, December 1985, 707; Ballard, *Discovery*, 82–84; Ballard, *Exploring*, 33–34; Lord, *Night Lives On*, 239; Gregory Katz, "Titanic: To Raise or Not?," *USA*, September 4, 1985, 1A; "Titanic Expedition Returns to Port," *HP*, July 29, 1986, 14A.

14. Ballard, *Discovery*, 100; Bob Drogin, "Ship That Found Wreck of the Titanic Returns Home," *LAT*, September 10, 1985, pt. I, p. 8; *Raise the Titanic!*, videocassette; Frederic Golden, "A Man with Titanic Vision," *Discover*, January 1987, 52; *Secrets of the Titanic*, prod. Nicolas Noxon, dir. Graham Hurley and Robert D. Ballard, National Geographic, 1986, videocassette.

15. Jeffords, *Hard Bodies*, 34–38, 68–71; Richard Slotkin, *Gunfighter Nation: The Myth of the Frontier in Twentieth-Century America* (New York: HarperCollins, 1992), 649; Garry Wills, *Reagan's America*, rev. ed.(New York: Penguin, 1988), 422–23. See also Susan Jeffords, *The Remasculinization of America: Gender and the Vietnam War* (Bloomington: Indiana University Press, 1989), esp. 168–69.

16. Oxford, "Titanic," 33.

17. Jane P. Tompkins, *West of Everything: The Inner Life of Westerns* (New York: Oxford University Press, 1992); Wills, *Reagan's America*, 2–3; Golden, "Man with Titanic Vision," 53; Ballard, *Discovery*, 31; Oxford, "Titanic," 33; Pellegrino, *Her Name, Titanic*, 56; "Interview: Robert Ballard," *Omni*, July 1986, 66; Slotkin, *Gunfighter Nation*, 644.

18. "Interview: Robert Ballard," 66; Golden, "Man with Titanic Vision," 53; "Robert Ballard: Undersea Explorer Who Found *Titanic*," *U.S. News & World Report*, September 23, 1985, 9; Erik Eckholm, "Robert

Ballard: Explorer of the Sea," *NYT*, September 10, 1985, C3; Pellegrino, *Her Name, Titanic*, 56–59. See also Paul Ciotti, "Ralph White's Titanic Adventure," *Los Angeles Times Magazine*, October 27, 1985, 15–17, 56, for a puff piece about the heavily armed ex-marine who served as photographer on the *Knorr*.

19. Kinney, "Titanic," 72; Golden, "Man with Titanic Vision," 52; "Interview: Robert Ballard," 81; Ballard, *Discovery*, 54; "Unsinkable Titanic," 226. A profile of Ballard by Doug Garr in the April 1992 *Reader's Digest* was titled "The Real Captain Nemo." In 1995 Ballard published his autobiography, *Explorations: My Quest for Adventure and Discovery under the Sea* (New York: Hyperion, 1995).

20. "Interview: Robert Ballard," 64; Richard Saltus, "Titanic Explorer Loves the Limelight," *BG*, July 27, 1986, 71; Ballard, *Discovery*, 32–33.

21. "Interview: Robert Ballard," 64; Saltus, "Titanic Explorer," 71; Alex Beam, "Selling the Titanic: It's Full Speed Ahead," *Business Week*, December 1, 1986, 56; Joy Waldron Murphy, "The Search for the *Titanic* Is Over but Now a Rush for the 'Gold' Has Begun," *Smithsonian*, August 1986, 59; Reidy, "Titanic's Unsinkable Memory," 26; "Robert Ballard: Undersea Explorer," 9.

22. Ballard, *Discovery*, 31; Golden, "Man with Titanic Vision," 62; "Interview: Robert Ballard," 79. On the dissolution of "the boundary between life and image" in the Reagan era, see Michael Paul Rogin, "Ronald Reagan, the Movie," in *Ronald Reagan, the Movie and Other Episodes in Political Demonology* (Berkeley: University of California Press, 1987), 1–43, esp. 42.

23. Slotkin, *Gunfighter Nation*, 647; "Interview: Robert Ballard," 81; William J. Broad, "Finder of Titanic Aims to Capitalize," *NYT*, September 11, 1985, D26; "Robert Ballard: Undersea Explorer," 9; Golden, "Man with Titanic Vision," 62.

24. Ellie McGrath, "Haunting Images of Disaster," *Time*, September 23, 1985, 58; "Respecting the Titanic," *WP*, September 15, 1985, D6; "Voyage of Discovery," *LAT*, August 1, 1986, pt. 2, p. 4; Stewart Powell, "Journey through the Portholes of a Gilded Past," *U.S. News & World Report*, July 28, 1986, 8; Marcia Satterthwaite Wertime, "Sounding the Depths: An Encounter with the Titanic," *Archaeology*, January–February 1987, 88; "Where the Titanic Belongs," *NYT*, February 21, 1987, 26; Ballard, *Discovery*, 156–58; Ballard, *Exploring*, 60; Jamie Murphy, "Down into the Deep," *Time*, August 11, 1986, 54.

25. Murphy, "Search for *Titanic* Is Over," 66–67; Paul Lewis, "French Expedition to Start Diving for Treasures on Titanic Today," *NYT*, July 23,

1987, A1; Michael D. Lemonick, "Tempest over the *Titanic*," *Time*, August 3, 1987, 56; Eaton and Haas, *Titanic: Triumph and Tragedy*, 308–11.

26. Steven Greenhouse, "French Will Raise Titanic Strongbox," *NYT*, August 14, 1987, A32; Michael D. Lemonick, "Treasures Reclaimed from the Deep," *Time*, November 2, 1987, 70–72; Mark Kemp, "We All Loot in a Yellow Submarine," *Discover*, January 1988, 62–63; Eaton and Haas, *Titanic: Triumph and Tragedy*, 310.

27. Editor's note in Ballard, "Epilogue for the *Titanic*," *National Geographic*, October 1987, 459; Steven Greenhouse, "Official Plans Museum for Artifacts of Titanic," *NYT*, August 22, 1987, 8; William F. Buckley, "Excavating the *Titanic*," *National Review*, September 25, 1987, 65; William F. Buckley, "Down to the Titanic," *National Review*, October 9, 1987, 71; William F. Buckley, "Down to the Great Ship," *New York Times Magazine*, October 18, 1987, 40–41, 70, 77–79, 93.

28. James Margulies, "This Is Some Winning Streak You're On, Iacocca," *HP*, September 5, 1985, 1B.

29. "Rendezvous with Yesterday," *The Time Tunnel*, ABC-TV, September 9, 1966, dir. Irwin Allen, MTR.

30. Ballard, *Discovery*, 211; William J. Broad, "Titanic Wreck Was Surprise Yield Of Underwater Tests for Military," *NYT*, September 8, 1985, 1, 36; "A Titanic Coup for Science," *U.S. News & World Report*, September 16, 1985, 11; Constance Holden, "Americans and French Find the *Titanic*," *Science*, September 27, 1985, 1368; Walter Sullivan, "Deep Seeing," *Oceans*, January 1986, 19–23; Murphy, "Search for Titanic Over," 65–66; Powell, "Journey through the Portholes," 8.

31. Slotkin, *Gunfighter Nation*, 645; Murphy, "Down into the Deep," 49; Ballard, *Discovery*, 101; Jack Kelley, "Finding Ocean-Liner Just a Sideline for Geologist," *USA*, September 12, 1985, 2A; *Top Gun*, prod. Don Simpson and Jerry Bruckheimer, dir. Tony Scott, Paramount, 1986, videocassette; "Interview: Robert Ballard," 80. Lehman apparently missed *Top Gun*'s not-very-subtle homoeroticism.

32. Ballard, *Discovery*, 195.

33. *Secrets of the Titanic*, videocassette; Pellegrino, *Her Name, Titanic*, xx, 134–41, and passim; Ballard, *Discovery*, 210, 213; "The Titanic Lesson," *NYT*, September 4, 1985, A26; "The Titanic Legend," *CT*, September 5, 1985, 22; "Titanic," *CSM*, September 6, 1985, 17; "A Night Long Remembered," *LAT*, September 8, 1985, pt. 4, p. 4; "Respecting the Titanic," D6. Pellegrino and Ballard both made direct references to the *Challenger* explosion in their books, as did a number of newspaper and magazine articles.

34. Jerry Gladman, "Ballard Fighting Titanic Depression," *HP*, September 12, 1985, 16A. The parentheses appear in the original. See Thomas P. Hughes, *American Genesis: A Century of Invention and Technological Enthusiasm, 1870–1970* (New York: Viking, 1989), chap. 9, esp. 471, for a historically informed critique of modern technological systems. Neil Postman discusses the dangerous myth of technological autonomy in *Technopoly: The Surrender of Culture to Technology* (New York: Vintage, 1993 [1992]), esp. 70, 114, 142.

35. Timothy Ferris, "The Year the Warning Lights Flashed On," *Life*, January 1987, 67–68.

36. Postman, *Technopoly*, 70; Ken Ringle, "Discoverer Reveals Titanic's Secrets," *WP*, September 12, 1985, A33. Leo Marx describes this attitude as a "distinctive form of American fatalism"—preferring "fatalism" to "determinism" because it better conveys the political resignation of such a world view. He notes in particular the fatalistic tendencies in the work of such critics of technology as Lewis Mumford and Jacques Ellul and in the pastoralism of the New Left and the 1960s' counterculture. Leo Marx, "Literary Culture and the Fatalistic View of Technology" (1978), in *The Pilot and the Passenger: Essays on Literature, Technology, and Culture in the United States* (New York: Oxford University Press, 1978), 179–207.

AFTERWORD: REARRANGING DECK CHAIRS

1. Lord, *Night Lives On*; Robert Serling, *Something's Alive on the Titanic* (New York: St. Martin's, 1990).

2. Neil Randall, "Search for the Titanic," *Compute!*, December 1989, 110–11; Kathleen Madden, "The Legend of the *Titanic*," *USA Today* (periodical), September 1990, 78–81.

3. Rex Wolfe, "Titanic Baby Found Alive!," *Weekly World News*, June 22, 1993, 4–5; David Woodroffe and Fiona Macdonald, *Make a Model Titanic* (Bristol, England: Parragon, 1993 [1989]); Tom Stacey, *The Titanic* (San Diego: Lucent Books, 1989); Daisy Corning Stone Spedden, *Polar the Titanic Bear* (Boston: Little, Brown, 1994).

4. Kirsty MacColl, *Titanic Days*, IRS 7243 8 27214 20; Ma Rainey, "Titanic Man Blues," *Riverside History of Classic Jazz*, Riverside 3RBCD-005-2.

5. Gavin Bryars, *The Sinking of the Titanic*, Point Music 446-061-2; Michael Walsh, "Raising the Titanic," *Time*, March 13, 1995, 110.

6. Don Nagle, "Rare Coal from Titanic in Limited Availability for $25," *USA*, December 5, 1995, 7D; "Announcing the Titanic Expedition Cruise,"

BG, April 15, 1996, 76; Edward S. Kamuda, "The Selling of the *Titanic*," *Titanic Commutator* 19, 4 (Supplement, February–April 1996), 11.

7. "Titanic: Adventure Out of Time," GTE Entertainment promotional flyer; http://gil.ispwichcity.qld.gov.au/~dalgarry/main.html; Michael Fleming, "Buzz," *Variety*, December 11–17, 1954, 4.

8. Howard Nemerov, "On Metaphor," in *New & Selected Essays* (Carbondale: Southern Illinois University Press, 1985), 125, 114.

9. Larry Eastland, "Turnabout: Teaching Right Values Isn't Homophobia," *LMT*, February 27, 1994, 2F; Cuomo, on *Larry King Live*, Cable News Network, CNN Transcripts, July 12, 1992; Begala, quoted in "Economic Figures: More Bad News for Bush," *The Hotline*, American Political Network, September 8, 1992; Miller, quoted in Andrew Mollison, "Politics in Brief," *AC*, August 13, 1992, 14A; Brinkley, on "World News Tonight with Peter Jennings," ABC News, August 19, 1992. These citations—and most of those that follow, as well as scores more that I don't mention—are the result of a NEXIS search under the commands "Find Titanic w/5 captain" and "Find Titanic w/5 deck chairs."

10. Richard Sull, "Clinton Just Doesn't Get It on the Deficit," *DMN*, March 3, 1993, 11C; Chafee, quoted in Edwin Chen, "Senators on TV Show Spar over Health Care," *BG*, May 23, 1994, 1; David Mason, quoted in J. Jennings Moss, "House Considers Reform to Break Gridlock," *WT*, December 8, 1992, A3.

11. Allen Rose, "Quotes with Flair Are Rare, So They Deserve Repeating," *OST*, January 2, 1993, B1; Bob Adams, "Going to Pieces?," *SLPD*, March 28, 1993, 1B; Lord, *Night Lives On*, 15.

12. Robin Finn, "Islanders Should Be Ecstatic, Right? Try Irate Instead," *NYT*, April 30, 1993, sec. B, p. 9; Bud Shaw, "Paging Mr. Somebody . . . Cleveland's Calling," *CST*, May 16, 1993, 5; Larry Powell, "Rangers a Reason for Putting Up with This Summer's Heat," *DMN*, July 15, 1993, 26A; Dan Daly, "Finally, a Win Team Can Enjoy," *WT*, January 4, 1993, D1; Terry Blount, "The Oilers," *HC*, September 28, 1993, Sports, 1; John Greenwald, "What Went Wrong?," *Time*, November 9, 1992, 42; Turner, quoted in Larry Reibstein, "The Revenge of the 'Nets,' " *Newsweek*, May 16, 1994, 44.

ACKNOWLEDGMENTS

MANY TIMES OVER the last few years, I have found myself almost overcome by metaphor. What did it mean that I was writing a book about a sinking ship? I don't think that my choice of subjects was in any sense autobiographical, but at several points I came face-to-face with the vagaries of the shrinking academic job market and the larger absurdities of the so-called Third Wave economy. In other words, I was on the verge of unemployment.

At a moment when I felt particularly isolated and uncertain about whether to turn my research on the *Titanic* into a book, Lyde Cullen Sizer asked me to join a writing group she was starting for historians and literary critics at Harvard. The members of that group—Tom Augst, Kim Hamilton, Hildegard Hoeller, Joseph Lease, John McGreevy, Jeff Melnick, Dan Morris, Allison Pingree, and especially Jim Cullen, Ruth Feldstein, Lyde Sizer, and Vince Tompkins—encouraged me at every step of the writing process. Their support made this a book; their comments and suggestions made it a better book.

In 1994–95 I had the good fortune to be a fellow at the Charles Warren Center for Studies in American History at Harvard. Aside from an office with a very big window, this gave me an uninterrupted year of writing and the opportunity to draw inspiration from five ideal colleagues: Stephen Alter, Mia Bay, Allen Guelzo (a seasoned *Titanic* hand himself), Laura Kalman, and Stephen Nissenbaum. They and Susan Hunt, the Warren Center's administrator, helped make for a rare experience. Donald Fleming, who ran our colloquium, withheld any suspicions he may have harbored about one of his former students slumming in the field of popular culture; he has championed this project from its early stages.

John L. Thomas also expressed enthusiasm from the outset and read the manuscript with his usual gusto. Kit Boss, Mark Kramer, and Richard Marius brought their enviable literary gifts to bear on the manuscript too and reassured me that what I had written would make sense to readers who are not professional cultural historians.

David Guralnik and Bruce Venarde were extraordinarily generous in translating Yiddish and Italian materials. Timo Riippa, Nora Hamplova, and Ursula Klingenberg made it possible for me to include Finnish, Czech, and Polish materials as well. Maureen Rybnik provided valuable assistance at the beginning of my research. Eleanor Sparagana, Michael Prokopow, Lou Masur, Greg Herman, Jim Samalis, Tom Siegel, Jerry Sweeney, Brett Flehinger, and Henry Sapoznik brought sources to my attention that I might otherwise have missed. Stephen Sylvester and Robert Zinck of Harvard Photographic Services went out of their way to supply me with the clearest possible illustrations.

Ledlie and John Woolsey introduced me to Walter Lord, and Mary Woolsey and Mark Peterson accompanied me on the first of two delightful visits to Walter's home. Other *Titanic* experts shared their insights in person, by phone, or by letter: Edward Kamuda, George Behe, Joseph Carvalho, Charles Haas, John Eaton, and the many members of the Titanic Historical Society who took the time to respond to my ad in the *Titanic Commutator*.

When I started to look for a publisher, Jonathan Groff put me in touch with his brother David, who introduced me to my agent, Michele Rubin. Michele genially guided me through the often baffling world of trade publishing and brought the book to my editor, Alane Salierno Mason. Alane skillfully weeded out my academic excesses—I take full responsibility for any that remain—and marshaled the book to completion.

As easy as it might be to imagine mixed messages in the dedication of a book about the *Titanic* disaster, Jean Kolling, Jacob Biel, and Claire and Morton Biel know that the only message here is love and gratitude.

INDEX

Acuff, Roy, 118, 172
Adams, Henry, 3–6, 8, 155
Advertising Council, 168, 171,
    173
African Americans, 10–12, 50–
    51, 52, 106, 107–18, 132,
    147, 177, 183
Afro-American Ledger, 110
Allums, Ernest, 10
Alvin, 209, 225
American, 57

American Federation of Labor
    (AFL), 118–19, 120
American Heritage, 150
American Press Association, 148
"America the Beautiful," 14, 79
Amerika, 175
Amherst College, 60
anarchists, 130
Anderson, Mattye E., 109–10
Anderson, Pink, 171
Andrews, Cornelia, 55

Andrews, Thomas, 162
Anglo-Saxon race, 47–50, 52, 56, 57, 78, 106, 124
Angus, 209
Anthony, Susan B., 14
anthropology, 106
Apollo 11 spaceflight, 179
Appeal to Reason, 122, 130
Archer, Anne, 208
Argo, 214
Arline, Samuel, 10–11
Armstrong, Neil, 179
Arnold, Martin, 202
Arnold, Matthew, 94
Asian Americans, 177
Astor, John Jacob:
  anecdotes about, 25, 41, 112, 116, 123
  corpse of, 10
  divorce of, 68–69, 73
  funeral of, 12
  heroism of, 25, 38, 39, 40, 41–42, 44, 46, 47, 57, 68, 72, 80, 87, 98, 125, 149, 156, 166
Astor, Madeleine, 27, 38
astrology, 187
Atlanta Constitution, 11, 48, 52
Atlantic, 149
atomic age, 157, 158, 159–60, 162, 167, 173
Audinet, Chad, 182–83
"Autumn," 63, 153, 161, 229–30

Back to the Future films, 212
Bacon, Francis, 93
Baldwin, Fred Clare, 65
Ballard, Robert, 185, 202, 208–25, 227, 229
Baltimore Sun, 30, 43, 83, 107
Bantam Books, 151

Baptist and Reflector, 77–78
Baptist Courier, 69
Barnes, Julian, 28–29
Bates, Katharine Lee, 79
Bederman, Gail, 49, 76–77
Beesley, Lawrence, 28, 57
Begala, Paul, 232
Behe, George, 181, 186–87, 190
Beiderhase, Josephine, 12–13
Belford, Walter, 175
Bentztown Bard, 45, 82–83
Berger, Victor, 127
Beyond Reach (Hoffman and Grimm), 209
Bible, 65, 97, 197
Bible Society Record, 66
"Bibliotheca Titanic" (Chapin), 144
Bilbo, Kenneth, 182
Bill of Rights, 16
Birckhead, Hugh, 79
Bishop, D. H., 38
Bishop, Jim, 152
Blacksmiths Journal, 120
Blackwell, Alice Stone, 13, 103–4, 105, 106
Blackwell, Antoinette Brown, 13
Blatch, Harriot Stanton, 13
Bontemps, Arna, 147
book collecting, 87, 88–89, 91–93
Book of Negro Folklore (Hughes and Bontemps), 147
Book-of-the-Month Club, 150
Borah, William E., 20
Boston American, 87–88
Boston Globe, 228, 229
Boston Herald, 93
Boston Museum of Science, 228–29
Bowman, Karen, 196

Boyer, Paul, 160
"Bread and Roses" strike, 56, 118
Brenner, Henry, 146
Bride, Harold, 50–51
Brinkley, David, 232
British Titanic Society (BTS), 201
Brown, D. Russell, 143
Brown, John, 57
Brown, "Leadville Johnny," 168
Brown, Margaret Tobin "Molly,"
    53–54, 168–71, 172, 173,
    203
Brown, Rabbit, 111
Brown, Rustie, 187, 188
Brown Alumni Monthly, 143
Browne, Jay, 188
Brown University, 143
Bryan, William Jennings, 35
Bryan, W. S. Plumer, 31
Bryars, Gavin, 229–30, 231
Bryce, Lord, 78
Buckley, Daniel, 27
Buckley, William F., 219
Bulletin of the Atomic Scientists,
    159
Burke, Billie, 36
Bush, George, 212, 232
Butt, Archibald W., 25, 39, 40, 41,
    44, 46, 47, 51–52, 57, 73, 80,
    98, 116, 121, 123, 125, 156,
    166, 180
Butt Memorial Bridge, 52

Cahan, Abraham, 131
Californian, 6, 152, 153, 154, 160,
    185, 191, 193, 227
Calvert, Sheri, 184, 185
Cameron, Elizabeth, 3
Cameron, James, 231
Cameron, Steve, 227

Candee, Helen, 40–41
capitalism, 63–64, 75, 81, 82, 122,
    123, 127–30, 214, 223
Capone, Al, 218
Capp, Melinda, 197
Carnegie, Andrew, 35, 88
Carpathia, 21, 23, 47, 50, 86, 143,
    146, 153, 154, 161, 166, 195
Carter, Jimmy, 205, 211, 233
Carvalho, Joseph, 175, 197
Casilio, Frank, 180
Castel, Don, 196
CBS Evening News, 198, 199
Chafee, John, 232–33
Challenger space shuttle disaster,
    223, 224
Chapin, Hope, 143, 144
Chapin, Howard Millar, 143–44,
    173
Chappaz, Robert, 218–19
character, 75–76, 78, 80
Chernobyl meltdown, 224
Chicago Defender, 109, 113–14
Chicago Tribune, 54
chivalry, 25–26, 51, 54, 83–84,
    101, 103–6, 108, 112, 116,
    121, 130, 155
Christian Century, 66, 68, 156–57,
    158
Christianity, 59–84, 109, 145–46
Christian Science Monitor, 56, 78
Christian Socialist, 66
civilization, 3–6, 49–50, 95,
    108–9, 129, 232
Civil War, 176, 184, 234
Clark, Champ, 25, 35
Cleveland, Grover, 35
Clinton, Bill, 232, 233
coal strike, British, 3–4
Cohan, George M., 36

Cold War, 156, 162, 167, 169, 171, 173, 207, 220, 221–22
Collier's, 26
Columbus, Christopher, 146
Congregationalist and Christian World, 81
consumer society, 75, 76, 163, 204
consumption, conspicuous, 63–71, 78, 84, 91, 95, 126–27, 164, 204
Coolidge, Archibald Cary, 87, 89, 90–91
Coronet, 150, 168
corporate capitalism, 63–64, 81, 82
corporate liberalism, 169
Cosmopolitan, 150
cowardice, 27, 45–47, 49–50, 78, 132, 156
Cronican, Frank, 195
Cronkite, Walter, 151
Crow, Price Alexander, 74–75
Cruise, Tom, 222
Cuomo, Mario, 232
Current Literature, 31, 69
Cussler, Clive, 206–8, 211, 213–14, 221

Daily People, 127
Daughter of Eve, 107
Davis, Daniel, 10, 11–12
Davis, Fred, 157
Day Christ Died, The (Bishop), 152
Day Lincoln Was Shot, The (Bishop), 152
Day of Infamy (Lord), 152
Debs, Eugene V., 118
Declaration of Independence, 100
Declaration of Rights and Sentiments, 100

Del Piano, Philip, 196
democracy, 45, 74, 95, 120, 130, 224–25
Denver Post, 72, 73
Depression, 144
"Desolation Row" (Dylan), 172–73
Devine, Edward T., 81
Dewey, George, 40
Dewey, John, 14
Dial, 90
Dillingham, William P., 18–19
disaster research, 158–60
divorce, 29, 33, 68–69, 73, 164
Dixon, Dorsey, 98, 171
Dixon, Howard, 98
Dixon Brothers, 98, 100
Dodge, Washington, 46
Dorr, Rheta Childe, 103, 106
Dos Passos, John, 111
"Down to a Common Grave" (Bentztown Bard), 45
Down to Eternity (O'Connor), 166–67, 168
"Down with the Old Canoe" (Dixon Brothers), 98–100, 171
Doyle, Arthur Conan, 48–49
Du Bois, W. E. B., 12
Dupont, E. A., 149
Durang, Christopher, 164–65
Dylan, Bob, 171, 172–73

Eaton, John, 186, 188, 189, 191, 192, 197–98, 230
Edd, G. W., 10
Education of Henry Adams, The (Adams), 5
Edwardian era, 7, 166–67, 178, 179

Elkins, William, 90
Entex *Titanic* model kit, 176, 177
"Epilogue for the *Titanic*"
   (Ballard), 218
Episcopal Church, 69, 77
Equal Rights Amendment, 97
Etheridge, Henry, 10, 11
Everett, Marshall, 70
Evers, Geoffrey, 183
existentialism, 156–57
Exploration Society of America,
   217

"Fabric of Disaster, The," 156
"Fair Play" (Clawson), 126
fame, 75–76, 79
family values, 60, 145, 157, 164
Fanck, Arnold, 149
Faulkner, Katherine, 202
femininity, 60, 76, 77, 106, 205–8
feminism, 29, 36, 52, 102–3, 105–
   7, 118, 125, 132, 169, 178,
   205, 207–8
Ferris, Timothy, 224–25
Finney, Jack, 180–81
Fitzhugh, Francis, 198–99
Fleet, Frederick, 151, 175, 201
Flood, James, 194
"Flowers and the Sea, The," 36
Ford, Gerald, 233
Fowler, Gene, 168, 169
Fox, Michael J., 212
Frankfurt, 7
Frederick, Henry, 144
Free Speech League, 15, 18
Friedman, William S., 34
From Time to Time (Finney),
   180–81
fundamentalist Christianity, 145–
   46

Futility (Robertson), 186

Gandy, James Ulmer, 196
Gates, Henry Louis, Jr., 107–8
Gates, Henry Louis, Sr., 115
Gayle, Philip, 11
Geduld, Harry, 149
gender roles, 23–42, 101, 102, 107,
   157, 162–63, 178, 183, 205,
   207–8, 209
General Motors, 233
Germany, Imperial, 7
Gibbons, Robert, 179
Gibson, Charles Dana, 35–36
Gibson, Dorothy, 148
Gilman, Charlotte Perkins, 106,
   121–22
Ginn, Edwin, 44
Glass, Philip, 230
Glisson, W. B., 81
"God Moves in a Mysterious
   Way, His Wonders to
   Perform," 109
"God Moves on the Water," 111–
   12, 171
God's Whip, 127
Goebbels, Joseph, 149
Goldman, Emma, 17–18, 101–2,
   107, 131
Gompers, Samuel, 35
Good Years, The (Lord), 156
Gorman, Louis, 199
Gracie, Archibald, 28, 47, 77, 161
Great Migration, 147
"Great Titanic, The," 111, 117–
   18
greed, 65–66, 70, 71, 72, 95, 127
Grimes, Tammy, 170
Grimm, Jack, 208, 209, 217
GTE Entertainment, 231

Guggenheim, Benjamin, 25, 38–39, 40, 41, 46, 47, 48, 124, 125
Guttmacher, Adolf, 34

Haas, Charles, 181, 182, 186, 189, 190, 191, 192, 210, 230
Haffer, Charles, 117
Hamilton, James, 194
Hammond, Natalie F., 35, 36
Harding, Alfred, 78
Harland & Wolff shipyards, 148, 193, 201
Harper's, 76
Harriman, E. H., 35
Harris, Henry B., 25, 39, 46, 47, 124
Harvard University, 85–95
Hay, John, 35
Hays, Charles M., 25, 40, 46
Hearst, William Randolph, 35
Hearst newspapers, 72, 87
Hearst's, 56
Hemingway, Ernest, 155
Henderson, Fletcher, 229
Henry Holt, 150
Henry's Jewelry Store, 174, 200
Heritage Foundation, 233
"Heroes and Heroines of the Titanic Disaster" (Warchol), 193
"Hero Went Down with the Monarch of the Sea, A" (Willis and Hanford), 41–42
Hill, George Roy, 151, 160
"hillbilly" music, 118
Hinton-Fell-Elliott, 148
History of the World in 10 ½ Chapters, A (Barnes), 28–29

Hitchcock, Alfred, 148
Holiday, 150, 166
Hollywood, 148–49
Hoover, Herbert, 144, 145
Houghton Mifflin, 28
Houston Post, 219
Hubbard, Elbert, 39–40, 52
Hughes, Howard, 148
Hughes, Langston, 147
hydrogen bomb, 160
hydrophobia, 132
hymns, 63, 78, 81, 82, 109, 111, 120, 121, 144, 145, 153, 161, 162, 165, 198, 229–30

Iacocca, Lee, 219–20
"I Ain't Down Yet" (Willson), 170
immigration, 10, 18–21, 43, 52, 57, 124, 125
imperialism, 48
Independent, 44–45, 71
Indianapolis Freeman, 108
Indianapolis World, 109
Industrial Workers of the World (IWW) (Wobblies), 15–18, 56, 118, 128, 129
Institut Français de Recherche pour l'Exploitation de la Mer, 208
International Brotherhood of Maintenance of Way Employes, 120
International Ice Patrol, 144, 202
International Negro Conference, 108
International Seamen's Union, 119
Irish Americans, 124
Ismay, J. Bruce, 72–74, 128
Italian Americans, 124

Jason Jr., 209, 214, 216, 223, 225
Jefferson, Blind Lemon, 114
Jeffords, Susan, 211
Jewish Advocate, 124
Jewish Daily Forward, 123–24, 129
Jews, 34, 48, 124
Johanssen, Karl, 52
Johns, Frank, 197
Johnson, Blind Willie, 117, 171
Johnson, Carrie, 11
Johnson, Jack, 114–15, 229
Jones, Mother, 122–23
Jones, Walter B., 217–18
Jordan, Richard, 208
"Just Whisper the Message" (Mulvey), 76
J. Walter Thompson, 150

Kamuda, Edward, 174, 175, 176, 178, 179, 180, 186, 191, 198–99, 201, 230–31
Kamuda, Karen, 175, 183, 201
Kent, Edward Austin, 193
Kern, Stephen, 9, 152
Kinsella, James E., 121
Klein, Wilhelm, 57
Klubnik, Ronald, 184
Knorr, 208, 210, 211, 221
Kraditor, Aileen, 33
Kraft Foods, 151, 163
Ku Klux Klan, 97

labor movement, 10, 15–18, 44, 91, 118–32
Ladies' Garment Worker, 128
Ladies' Home Journal, 150
La Follette, Robert M., 119
Lasch, Christopher, 84
Latin race, 47, 49

Leadbelly (Huddie Ledbetter), 114–15, 117, 171, 172, 229
Lee, Baker P., 72–73
Lehman, John, 222
"leisure class," 64, 84, 91, 92, 93–94
Levin, Edward, 185
Levine, Lawrence, 115, 117
Lichter, Linda, 183
Life, 150, 224
Lightoller, Charles, 144, 153, 161
Lindbergh, Anne Morrow, 150
Lindsey, Ben, 102
Lipscomb, Mance, 171
Lipsitz, George, 169
literacy test, 20–21
Literary Digest, 91, 92
Llewelyn, Doug, 218
Locomotive Engineers' Monthly Journal, 121
Lodge, Henry Cabot, 94–95
Logan, John, 10–11
Lomax, Alan, 98, 147
Lord, Stanley, 185
Lord, Walter, 6, 7, 8, 149–63, 168, 171, 173, 175, 178, 179, 182, 183–84, 186, 187, 196, 197, 202, 203, 211, 227, 232, 233
Los Angeles Times, 16, 44, 211
Loss of the S.S. Titanic, The (Beesley), 28
"Lost and the Saved, The," 73
"Lost Luxuries of Ladyhood, The" (Lichter), 183
Louisville Courier-Journal, 47
Louisville News, 113
Lowe, Harold, 49
Lowell, A. Lawrence, 88, 89
Luce, Robert, 144

luxury, 58, 61–62, 64–71, 84, 126–27

Lynch, Don, 6, 179, 185, 192–93, 228

Lynch, Owen, 42

lynchings, 10–12, 108

Lynn, Loretta, 118

McCluskie, Tom, 201

MacColl, Kirsty, 229

McCready, R. L., 84

MacDonald, Stuart, 190–91

Machen, J. Gresham, 145

McIntosh, C. M., 10

Mackay-Bennett, 10

McKenzie, J. H., 34

McNamara brothers, 44

Madison Square Presbyterian Church, 59

Magazine Publishers of America, 168

manliness, 49–50, 60, 75–84, 128–29

Marconi, Guglielmo, 176

Marconigram, 176

marriage, 33–34, 102, 106, 164

Marschall, Ken, 6, 17–79, 185, 228

Marshall, Logan, 50–51, 190

Maryland Equal Suffrage League, 101

Maryland Federation of Women's Clubs, 56

Mason, Walt, 73

Masses, 126–27, 129

Masterson, Bat, 213

materialism, 58, 61–71, 78, 84, 91, 95, 126–27, 164, 181, 204, 223

matriarchy, 106

Matthison, Edith Wynne, 36

Maxtone-Graham, John, 6

May, Elaine Tyler, 155–56

May, Henry F., 70

Mechanics Illustrated, 175

Melosh, Barbara, 145

Memory of Eva Ryker, The (Stanwood), 205–6

Men and Religion Forward Movement (M&RFM), 77

"Men on the Bridge, The," 179

Mikolasek, Joseph, 17

Milholland, Inez, 104

Miller, Fred, 185

Miller, Zell, 234

Millet, Francis D., 39, 47, 87

Mizner, Wilson, 146–47

modernity, 7, 8, 57, 58, 60–62, 63, 69, 82, 83–84, 95, 161–62, 223

Monroe, Harriet, 54–55

Moore, Clarence, 39

morality, 60, 75–84, 93–95, 145, 157, 164, 182–84, 185, 186

More, Kenneth, 161

Morgan, J. P., 88, 127–28

Morris, Richard, 170

Moshier, W. F., 182

Mott, Lucretia, 14

mountaineering, 62

Mulvey, Thomas H., 76, 77

Munsters, The, 190

"muscular Christianity," 60–62, 76–77

Narsani, Nadji, 57

National American Woman Suffrage Association (NAWSA), 14, 100, 103

National Association for the Advancement of Colored

People (NAACP), 10, 11, 12, 108
National Association Opposed to Woman Suffrage, 32–33
National Geographic, 209–10, 215, 218, 223
National Public Radio, 229
National Woman's party, 97
Nazi propaganda, 149
NBC-TV, 151
"Nearer, My God, to Thee," 63, 78, 81, 82, 111, 120, 121, 144, 145, 162, 165, 198
Negulesco, Jean, 149
Nemerov, Howard, 231–32
New Deal, 145
New Orleans Times-Picayune, 29
New South, 52
Newsweek, 156
New York, N.Y., 104, 153
New York Herald, 32
New York Press, 47
New York Times, 12, 26, 31, 37–38, 46, 47, 53, 91–92, 156
New York World, 69
Night Lives On, The (Lord), 227
Night to Remember, A (Lord), 6, 149–63, 168, 171, 187, 202, 203
  as best seller, 149, 150, 158
  class differences in, 165–66
  condensed versions of, 150
  film version of, 28–29, 161–62, 165–66, 175, 208
  influence of, 173, 175, 178, 179, 182, 183–84, 185, 196, 197, 227
  marketing of, 150, 151
  modernist narrative of, 149, 151–55, 157

nostalgia in, 155–56, 157, 158, 160, 162, 167, 173
TV version of, 151, 160–61, 162
No Greater Love (Steel), 203–5
"No Man Shall Wrest Her Free" (Cronican), 195
nuclear family, 157, 164

oceanography, 213, 216
O'Connor, Richard, 166–67, 168
Odell, Jack, 200
O'Gorman, James A., 20
Old Testament, 65, 197
Olvera, Ruben and Jo Ann, 196
Olympic, 4, 6, 7, 120, 150, 202
O'May, James, 64
Orlando Sentinel Tribune, 233
"O Sea! A Dirge; the Tragedy of the Titanic, Memorable of 1912" (Watkins), 110
Outlook, 45, 56

Parkhurst, Charles H., 59–63, 64, 75
Parks, Leighton, 31–32
paternalism, 29, 45–46, 53, 71, 106
patriarchy, 78, 89
Paul, Alice, 97
Pellegrino, Charles, 7, 8, 223
personality, 80
Peterson, David, 185
Philadelphia Maritime Museum, 200
Philadelphia North American, 40
Philadelphia Tribune, 113
Phillips, Jack, 50–51
Phillips, Wendell, 12
Pillar of Fire sect, 97

Pittsburgh Courier, 112, 114
Poetry, 54
Polar the Titanic Bear (Spedden), 228, 229
Post, Louis F., 74
Postman, Neil, 225
Pravo, 129
Prechtl, Robert, 149
Progressive Era, 7, 64, 66, 70, 71
Progressive party, 118
Progressive Patriotic Protestantism, 70, 71, 82
Progressive Woman, 104, 106, 125–26
proletariat, 126, 127, 129
Protestantism, 59–84, 109
Proxmire, William, 214
Publishers Weekly, 150
Puritans, 65

Quayle, Dan, 232

racism, 10, 12, 50–51, 52, 106, 112–13, 115, 132
Railroad Trainman's Journal, 119
Rainey, Ma, 229
Rains, Claude, 151, 160, 161
Raise the Titanic! (Cussler), 206–8, 211, 213–14, 221
Rambo films, 211–12
Rauscher, William, 147
Rayner, Isidor, 70, 82
"Reaching Out for His Prey," 69
Reader's Digest, 150, 158, 214
Reagan, Ronald, 208, 213, 214, 216, 218, 219, 220, 221–22, 232, 233
Reaves, Edward S., 77
"Redeemed!" (Bentztown Bard), 82

redemption, 78–79, 80, 81–83, 104–5, 110–11, 128–29, 145
reform, 61, 62, 70, 71, 81, 103, 118
reincarnation, 184
Reitman, Ben, 17, 18
Religious Telescope, 80
"Rendezvous with Yesterday," 220–21
Republican party, 3, 4
"Requiem, A" (Monroe), 54–55
Reynolds, Debbie, 170
Reynolds Aluminum Company, 217
Rhode Island Historical Society, 143
Richmond, George Chalmers, 68–69, 73
Richmond Planet, 110
Riefenstahl, Leni, 149
Rivera, Geraldo, 218
Rizzetto, Darwin, 188–89
RMS Titanic, Inc., 230–31
Robertson, Morgan, 186
Rockefeller, Jay, 233
Roebling, Washington, 39, 46
Roosevelt, Theodore, 3, 4, 35, 49–50, 56, 118, 180
Root, Elihu, 20
Rosenfeld, Morris, 122
Rostron, Arthur, 143, 144
Rothstein, Arnold, 146
Rotundo, E. Anthony, 27
Rudd, Michael, 201
rural values, 59–61
Russell, Charles Edward, 127, 128, 131
Ryan, Agnes, 105
Ryan, Joseph, 182

Sachs, Charles, 185–86

St. Louis Post-Dispatch, 30
St. Paul Appeal, 113
Samuels, Jacob, 10
San Diego, 15–18
San Diego Union, 16
San Francisco Examiner, 38–39, 53
Sargent, John Singer, 87
Sartre, Jean-Paul, 156–57
Savalas, Telly, 218
Saved from the Titanic, 148
Sawicki, Jozef, 131
Schillow, Dru, 178
Scopes trial, 146
Scott, P. A., 109
Seaman's Act, 119
Seaman's Church Institute, 144
Search for the Titanic, 227
Selpin, Herbert, 149
Selznick, David O., 148
Seneca Falls Convention, 100
Serling, Robert, 227
7C's Press, 176, 180
Shaw, Anna Howard, 14
Shaw, George Bernard, 48
Sheen, Martin, 211, 223
Shine, 108, 115–17, 147
shipping regulations, 7, 71–72,
    105, 118–20
"Ship Titanic, The" (Anderson),
    171
Sinking of the Titanic, The
    (Bryars), 229–30, 231
Slater, Hilda, 46
Slotkin, Richard, 24, 216, 221–22
Smith, Edward, 47, 73, 188, 189, 227
Smith, Mr. and Mrs. Lucien,
    162–63
Smith, William Alden, 28
Social Darwinism, 49, 77, 116, 131
Social Gospel, 66, 74–75, 81, 118

Socialist party, 118
socialists, 118, 121, 125, 126–32
Something's Alive on the Titanic
    (Serling), 227
"Songe d'Automne," 63, 153, 161,
    229–30
Soror, 26
S.O.S. Eisberg, 149
space program, 179
Spencer, Anna Garlin, 14
Stallone, Sylvester, 211
Stanton, Elizabeth Cady, 14
Stanwood, Donald A., 205–6
Stanwyck, Barbara, 149, 150, 163,
    164, 166, 171, 174
Stead, W. T., 25, 39, 46, 47, 187
Steamship Historical Society of
    America, 193
Steel, Danielle, 203–5
Stephanos, Tarn, 191
Stewart, Marie, 13
Stimson, Henry, 78
Stires, Ernest M., 64–65
Stone, Lucy, 13
Strategic Defense Initiative
    (SDI), 214, 222, 224
Straus, Ida, 33–34, 39, 57, 106–7,
    124, 153, 194, 204
Straus, Isidor, 25, 34, 39, 41, 46,
    47, 48, 124, 153, 194, 204
suffrage movement, 10, 12–15,
    29–33, 52, 100–107, 125,
    132, 231
Summerlin, H. Wayne, 187
Sumner, William Graham, 26
Suroit, Le, 208
survivors:
    as celebrities, 199, 200
    interviews with, 21, 47
    list of, 23

survivors (continued)
   men, 27–29, 49, 164
   rescue of, 6, 9, 21, 23, 47, 50,
      86, 143, 146, 153, 154, 161,
      166, 185, 191, 193, 195, 227
   women, 31–32, 34, 45, 53–54
Susman, Warren, 75
synchronicity, 9

Taft, Helen H., 35, 36, 144
Taft, William Howard, 3, 4, 21,
   35, 36, 51, 52, 98, 118, 180
Tammany machine, 61
Tampa Tribune, 32
Tantum, William, 176, 179–80,
   217
William Harris Tantum IV
   Writing Competition, 193
Taylor, E. I., 37–38
telegraphy, wireless, 7, 9, 24, 50–
   51, 65, 154, 175
Thayer, John B., 25, 39, 40, 41,
   144
Theory of the Leisure Class, The
   (Veblen), 64, 84, 91, 92, 93
Thompson, Frank, 148
Thompson, Titanic (Alvin
   Clarence Thomas), 146
Timberline (Fowler), 168, 169
Time, 158, 229, 230
Time and Again (Finney), 180
Time Tunnel, The, 220–21
Titanensturz: Roman eines
   Zeitalters (Prechtl), 149
Titanic:
   building of, 148, 193, 201
   coal from, 230
   depictions of, 148, 178, 179,
      185, 215
   design of, 193–94

First Class passengers of, 38,
   44, 46, 57, 68, 71, 73–74, 75,
   82, 116, 122–26, 153
lifeboats of, 21, 37–38, 39, 45,
   46, 65, 121, 153, 166, 168,
   169, 170, 186, 189
maiden voyage of, 3, 203–5,
   209, 211, 212
menu from, 174, 185
models of, 175, 176, 177, 179
officers and crew of, 27, 28,
   46, 50–51, 55, 56, 123, 124,
   184
salvage operations for, 185,
   202, 206–25, 227, 229, 230–
   31
Second Class passengers of 38,
   46, 55, 125, 153
sinking of, see Titanic sinking
steerage passengers of, 38–39,
   45–47, 49–51, 57, 121–27,
   130, 153, 165
as symbol of progress, 5, 64,
   66, 67, 167, 212, 219, 222–
   23
technological achievement of,
   5, 66–68, 158, 167, 179, 197,
   220, 222–25, 232
as "$10,000,000 casket," 61, 71
as "unsinkable," 21, 37, 66,
   115–16
wreck of, 61, 71, 144, 185, 192,
   195, 202, 205, 206–25, 227,
   229, 230–31
"Titanic" (Leadbelly), 114–15,
   171
Titanic: An Illustrated History
   (Lynch and Marschall), 6,
   185
"Titanic, De," 111

Titanic: Psychic Forewarnings of a Tragedy (Behe), 186–87
"Titanic, The" (Anderson), 109–10
Titanic, the Psychic and the Sea, The (Brown), 187
Titanic: Triumph and Tragedy (Haas and Eaton), 192
Titanica, 228
Titanic Commutator, 175, 176, 179, 181, 182, 192, 193, 200
"Titanic Days" (McColl), 229
Titanic Disaster, The (Chapin), 143
Titanic Enthusiasts of America (TEA), 175–76, 190–91, 196
"Titanic!" exhibition, 227–28
Titanic Expedition Cruise, 230–31
Titanic (film), 149, 150, 161, 163–65, 166, 171, 174, 203, 229
"Titanic Funeral Ship," 10
Titanic Heritage Tours, 201–2
Titanic Historical Society (THS), 174–202, 217, 219
Titanic International, 181, 189, 191, 230
"Titanic Is Doomed and Sinking, The" (Lynch and Farrell), 42
"Titanic Man Blues" (Rainey), 229
Titanic Memorial Museum, 199
Titanic Memorial Service, 197–98
Titanic Museum, 174–75, 199–200
"Titanic Report" (Rizzetto), 188–89

Titanic sinking:
accounts of, 6, 28–29, 143–73
anecdotes about, 25, 41, 50–51, 53–54, 112, 116, 123
band's last tune in, 63, 120, 153, 191, 227
black response to, 107–18, 147
black stoker in, 50–51, 113
British inquiry into, 6–7, 73
British reaction to, 48–49
cartoons on, 69, 219–20
class issues in, 38–46, 50–51, 52, 64, 69, 73–75, 81, 83, 84, 91, 92, 93, 120–31, 154, 165–66, 178
as cliché, 224, 232–34
commemorations of, 35–37, 54, 56, 85–95, 103, 125–26, 132, 144–45, 183, 210–11, 217–18, 219
commercial exploitation of, 147–48, 162, 200–201, 215–20, 227, 230–31
confusion in, 37–38, 46–47
conventional narrative of, 7, 23–24, 52–53, 55–58, 71, 73, 75, 83–84, 107, 115, 118, 121, 125, 132, 209, 210, 225, 234
documentaries on, 188, 209, 211, 223, 228
editorial comment on, 24, 30, 32, 43, 46, 47, 56–57, 69, 73, 81, 82, 108–9, 112–14, 119–20, 121, 126–27, 217
as end of era, 3–4, 7, 8, 57–58, 67, 154–56, 161–62, 166–67, 178, 179, 180–81, 196–97, 203, 232
enthusiasts for, 6, 143–44, 173, 174–202, 203

ethnic issues in, 123–25, 154, 155

female heroism and, 53–55

films based on, 28–29, 148–49, 150, 161–62, 165–66, 175, 203, 208, 231

first anniversary of, 64–65

folk songs about, 98–100, 110–12, 114–15, 117–18, 147, 171

as God's punishment, 64–71, 73, 97–100, 112, 114, 127

high society in, 8, 39–40, 57–58, 80

historical interpretations of, 6–8, 181–83, 185–86, 188–89, 191–92, 202, 211–12, 226, 234

"honor roll" of, 40–41

hubris in, 66–69, 110, 127, 132, 167, 223–24

human nature and, 131–32, 156–58, 161, 166

humor about, 115–17, 190–91

iceberg in, 21, 37, 65, 67, 69, 129, 143, 152, 175, 186, 188, 194, 209, 227, 232

irony of, 155

jeremiads on, 65–68, 70, 72, 224

labor movement's response to, 118–32

literature on, 6, 97–98, 100, 149–63, 186–87, 192–93, 203–8, 224, 227

male heroism and, 23–58, 75–84, 103–7, 109, 112–13, 121, 122–26, 128–29, 130, 132, 144–47, 156, 178, 181, 210–14, 229

memorabilia from, 143–44, 150, 174–75, 184, 199–201, 217–20, 228–29

monument to, 35–37, 54, 56, 125–26, 144–45, 183

as myth, 8, 24–25, 71, 80, 149, 178, 183

Nature's supremacy in, 5, 35, 66–67, 69–70

news of, 9, 17, 23, 25, 117, 122, 153

noblesse oblige in, 26, 42–44, 53, 131

nostalgia and, 155–56, 157, 158, 160, 162, 167, 173, 178, 179, 180–81, 194–95

paranormal experiences and, 184, 185, 186–88

pedagogical value of, 181–83

political aspects of, 3, 4, 105, 129–30, 156, 162, 167, 169, 170–71, 208, 211–12, 220–25, 232–34

press coverage of, 9, 23, 24, 25, 30–32, 37–38, 39, 43, 53, 57, 68–69, 70, 72, 73–74, 97, 108–14, 117, 121, 123–24, 125, 147, 148, 230

racial issues in, 26, 47–52, 55, 56–57, 78

religious commentary on, 31–32, 42–43, 59–84, 97–100, 109–12, 127, 145–46, 197–98

rescue efforts in, 6, 9, 21, 23, 47, 50, 86, 143, 146, 153, 154, 161, 166, 185, 191, 193, 195, 227

responsibility for, 71–74

romance of, 57

safety precautions in, 72–74
shipping reforms as result of,
    7, 71–72, 105, 118–20
social context of, 9–21, 57–58,
    97–132
songs about, 40, 41–42, 46, 63,
    76, 81, 98–100, 110–12,
    114–15, 117–18, 147, 170,
    171, 229
suffragist response to, 100–
    107, 125
survivors of, *see* survivors
U.S. inquiry into, 6–7, 18, 21,
    27–28, 73, 118
verse on, 25, 30–31, 34, 41, 45,
    47–48, 54–55, 63, 65, 73,
    79–80, 82–83, 107, 109–10,
    120–21, 126, 127, 146
violence in, 46–47, 49, 57, 123–
    24
wireless messages in, 7, 9, 24,
    50–51, 65, 154, 175
"women and children first"
    rule in, 23–42, 44–45, 51–
    52, 102–7, 113, 121, 130,
    147–48, 163, 178
Titanic's Knell: A Satire on Speed
    (Brenner), 146
Titanic Suite (Cameron), 227
Titanic Tower, 144
*Titanic Tragedy—God Speaking to
    the Nations, The* (White),
    97–98, 100
"toasts," 107–8, 114, 115–17
Top Gun, 222
Towne, Charles Hanson, 25
Tragic Story of the Titanic, The
    (Frederick), 144
Travelers Insurance Company,
    147–48

Travel Marketing Associates, 201
Trinque, Bruce, 181–82
Trumbauer, Horace, 89, 90, 92
Turner, Ted, 215, 233–34
"Tuskegee machine," 110
Twain, Mark, 168

Underwood & Underwood, 148
United Mine Workers, 120
"Unsinkable Mrs. Brown, The"
    (Fowler), 168, 169
Unsinkable Molly Brown, The,
    170–71, 172, 173
USA Today, 230
U.S. Savings bonds, 168–69

Variety, 161
Vaughan, Alan, 187
Veblen, Thorstein, 64, 84, 91, 92,
    93
Vietnam Veteran's Memorial, 183
Vietnam War, 179, 183, 205, 212
vigilantes, 16–18
Voyage, 193

Wade, Wyn Craig, 7, 8
Wagner, Robert, 165
Wall Street Journal, 205
Warchol, Clara, 193
Warren, Robert, 202
Washington, Booker T., 12, 108,
    110, 112
Washington Post, 39, 56, 68–69, 80
Watkins, Lucian B., 110
Webb, Clifton, 149, 150, 163, 164,
    166, 171, 174
Weekly World News, 228
Weeks, Jack, 166
Wehrlin, Robin, 184
Weicker, Lowell, 218

Welles, Orson, 209

Western Christian Advocate, 79

Western Federation of Miners, 123

Westover, Kenneth, 191–92

Wheeler, Edward J., 69

White, Alma, 97–98, 100

White, William Allen, 70

White Star Line, 71, 72–74, 127–28, 175, 192

Whitlock, Brand, 47–48

Whitman, John, 199

Whitney, Gertrude Vanderbilt, 36–37

"Who Was to Blame?" (Baldwin), 65

Widener, Eleanor Elkins, 86–91

Widener, George, 25, 39, 40, 41, 89, 90

Widener, Harry Elkins, 39, 40, 85–95

Widener, P. A. B., 90

Harry Elkins Widener Library, 85–95

Willson, Meredith, 170

Wilson, Woodrow, 35, 118

Wise, Stephen, 13–14

Woman's Journal, 103

women:
  equality of, 29, 32, 97, 102, 106–7
  role of, 23–42, 101, 102, 107, 157, 162–63, 178, 183, 205, 207–8, 209
  as survivors, 31–32, 34, 45, 53–54

voting rights for, 10, 12–15, 29–33, 52, 100–107, 125, 132, 231

"Women and Children First" (Dorr), 103

"women and children first" rule, 23–42, 44–45, 51–52, 102–7, 113, 121, 130, 147–48, 163, 178

Women's Political Union, 13

Women's Titanic Memorial, 35–37, 54, 56, 125–26, 144–45, 183

Women's Trade Union League (WTUL), 105

Wood, Mrs. Leonard, 36

Woodman, H. Rea, 79–80

Woods Hole Oceanographic Institute, 208, 213, 215

Work, John M., 127

World War I, 7, 95, 144, 156, 180

World Wide Web, 231

Wreck and Sinking of the Titanic (Everett), 70

Wylie, Philip, 159, 160

xenophobia, 119

Yeager, Chuck, 210, 213

Yeltsin, Boris, 233

You Are There, 151

"You Don't Have to Be Jewish," 190

"You're Dead!" (Mizner), 146–47

Zarephath community, 97